Reading and Wisdom

NOTRE DAME CONFERENCES IN MEDIEVAL STUDIES

Number VI
Institute of Medieval Studies
University of Notre Dame
John Van Engen, Director

Reading and Wisdom

THE *DE DOCTRINA CHRISTIANA* OF AUGUSTINE IN THE MIDDLE AGES

Edited by

EDWARD D. ENGLISH

UNIVERSITY OF NOTRE DAME PRESS

Notre Dame and London

Library of Congress Cataloging-in-Publication Data

Reading and wisdom : the De doctrina Christiana of Augustine in the
Middle Ages / edited by Edward D. English.
  p.   cm. — (Notre Dame conferences in medieval studies :
no. 6)
  Papers originally presented at a conference held at the University
of Notre Dame, Apr. 4–7, 1991.
  Includes bibliographical references.
  ISBN 0-268-01650-X (alk. paper)
  1. Augustine, Saint, Bishop of Hippo. De doctrina
Christiana—Congresses. 2. Augustine, Saint, Bishop of Hippo—
Influences—Congresses. 3. Theology—History—Middle Ages,
600–1500—Congresses. I. English, Edward D.   II. Series: Notre
Dame conferences in medieval studies ; 6.
BR65.A6552R42   1995
230′.14—dc20   94-15467
                                                                CIP

∞ *The paper used in this publication meets the minimum requirements*
of the American National Standard for Information Sciences—Permanence of Paper
for Printed Library Material, ANSI Z39.48–1984.

Contents

Preface

From 4 to 7 April 1991, scholars from a wide range of interests met at the University of Notre Dame to attend a conference entitled "*De doctrina christiana:* A Classic of Western Culture" that Charles Kannengiesser and I had organized. The key question of the conference— Is the *De doctrina christiana* indeed a classic of western culture?— is taken up in the essays of this volume in the context of medieval and Renaissance culture. The papers treating the patristic and modern contexts of this important work have been edited by Duane W. H. Arnold and Pamela Bright and appear in a book that carries the title of the conference and has also been published by the University of Notre Dame Press.

The essays in the present volume make an excellent case for a positive answer to the basic question. The *De doctrina christiana* has long been recognized as fundamental in the Middle Ages for the understanding of the balanced interaction between classical learning and Christianity, of conscious personal study for spiritual development, and of the fundamentals of the homiletic and exegetical principles of preaching and of interpreting Sacred Scripture. The work has more recently come to be interpreted as also essential to a theory of signs, or semiotics, and hermeneutics beyond the study of Sacred Scripture in medieval culture.

The following essays show well the work's importance for the learned intellectuals of the Middle Ages, especially for the School of St. Victor, in pointing the way to combining a love of learning and a desire for God—that is, to achieve elegant and true wisdom. Approaching Augustine's seminal work from various points of view and over the course of several centuries and taking advantage in particular of the text's new appreciation as a starting point for modern semiotics, these essays lucidly demonstrate the role of this work in many facets of medieval culture: the spiritual interpretation or exegesis of both Scripture and pagan texts, concepts of allegory and aesthetics in literature and art, Christian humanism, the wise employment of classical texts and rhetorical principles in pastoral communication and for personal spiritual growth and wisdom, and lastly, the roles of reading, language, and writing within, and for, a Christian community, both clerical and lay.

I would like to thank all the speakers at the conference for their essays, the authors of the essays included in this volume, and the various chairs of the sessions at the meeting. I am sure that we would all like to express our appreciation to the Medieval Institute, the Department of Theology, and the Institute for Scholarship in the Liberal Arts of the University of Notre Dame for their sponsorship of the meeting. It was also a pleasure to work with the Center for Continuing Education and especially with Charles Kannengiesser and John Van Engen in putting the conference together.

Abbreviations

CCCM	Corpus Christianorum, Continuatio Mediaevalis. Turnhout, 1966–.
CCSL	Corpus Christianorum, Series Latina. Turnhout, 1953–.
CSEL	Corpus Scriptorum Ecclesiasticorum Latinorum. Vienna, 1866–.
DDC	Joseph Martin, ed. *De doctrina christiana, De vera religione*. Corpus Christianorum, Series Latina vol. 32. Turnhout, 1962. [Cited by book, chapter, and paragraph.]
PG	Patrologiae Cursus Completus, Series Graeca. 161 vols. Ed. J. P. Migne. Paris, 1857–1866.
PL	Patrologiae Cursus Completus, Series Latina. 221 vols. Ed. J. P. Migne. Paris, 1841–1864.
Robertson	*On Christian Doctrine*. Trans., with introduction, D. W. Robertson, Jr. New York, 1958. [The English translation used unless stated otherwise.]

Contributors

THOMAS L. AMOS, Lilly Library, Indiana University

CELIA CHAZELLE, Department of History, Trenton State College

EDWARD D. ENGLISH, Medieval Institute, University of Notre Dame

MARGARET T. GIBSON (deceased), Department of History, University of Liverpool

THOMAS S. MALONEY, Department of Philosophy, University of Louisville

JOHN MONFASANI, Department of History, State University of New York at Albany

CAROL E. QUILLEN, Department of History, Rice University

MICHAEL A. SIGNER, Department of Theology, University of Notre Dame

KAY BRAINERD SLOCUM, Department of History, Capital University

EILEEN C. SWEENEY, Department of Philosophy, Boston College

JOSEPH WAWRYKOW, Department of Theology, University of Notre Dame

GROVER A. ZINN, JR., Department of Religion, Oberlin College

"Not in Painting but in Writing": Augustine and the Supremacy of the Word in the *Libri Carolini*

CELIA CHAZELLE

In 1957 Ann Freeman justly wrote that the *Libri Carolini*[1] constitute "the most ambitious [treatise] of its age, in both theological importance and political implication. Charlemagne appears in his full stature as spokesman for the West, defender of its faith, and protector of its orthodoxy."[2] More recent scholarship has confirmed her judgment of the important place of the *Libri Carolini* (henceforth abbreviated as *LC*) among Carolingian writings.[3] Written in 790–793 by Theodulf of Orléans and revised by him with the help of Alcuin and other, unidentified colleagues, the *LC* provide the official response of Charlemagne and his court to the iconodulist decrees of the Second Council of Nicea, held in 787.[4] In denouncing those decrees Charlemagne's theologians not only sought to refute the belief that artistic images deserved the same worship—adoration—owed to God alone, which was how the Carolingians understood the iconodulism promulgated at Nicea II.[5] They also wanted to show that the Greek churchmen responsible for this one crime, in the Carolingians' view a fundamental and decisive deviation from orthodoxy, had fallen into other errors that the Carolingians thought were discernible in the Second Nicene acts and that they believed to be linked with the Greeks' misunderstanding of artistic images.[6] One set of these failings can be grouped together in that they all have to do with the desirability of possessing a sound command of vocabulary and knowing the rules that govern written language, in particular the rules learned through the study of grammar, rhetoric, and logic. A striking amount of attention is given to such issues in the *LC*. This has been remarked in earlier scholarship on the Carolingian treatise, some of which suggests that the concern with writing and language is significant

1

to identification of the treatise's principal author.[7] Although within this framework there has been some analysis of the relationship of the same features of the Carolingian treatise to the effort to oppose the Greek council's iconodulism,[8] their full role in this regard and the underlying intellectual motivations to pursue the line of attack on Nicea II that the attentiveness to words and language represents have yet to be thoroughly explored.

As scholars have often observed, the Carolingians' interest in refuting Byzantine iconodulism can be linked to the tensions that existed between East and West in the late eighth century, fueled by the Carolingians' view of Byzantium as a political and military rival as well as a model of imperial grandeur. These tensions came to a head with the arrival at Charlemagne's court of a fault-ridden Latin translation of the acts of Nicea II, which Carolingian churchmen mistakenly understood to have been produced at Constantinople but which was in fact made in Rome.[9] They were stung that a council proclaiming itself to be universal, and therefore presumably binding on all Christians, had been held in Byzantium without Frankish participation and had issued decrees that the Carolingians considered to be heretical. Moreover, the supposed heresies expressed in the acts of Nicea II as well as the tone of the writing there—in the Latin version—seemed to Charlemagne's churchmen to epitomize the lack of decorum of the empire to the east.[10] An important incentive to the *LC*'s attacks on the language of Nicea II and to the numerous other criticisms which the Carolingian treatise aims at the Greek council, then, was simply the desire to oppose every individual error that could be found in the Byzantine acts, in order to provide a suitable response to the eastern council's arrogance.

At the same time, Theodulf and his colleagues were convinced that many if not all of the errors they discovered in the acts of Nicea II grew out of a single problem: the failure of iconoclasts and iconodules in Byzantium to understand correctly the relationship of the material realm to the spiritual. For Theodulf and his asssociates, the Greeks had ignored the truth that, on the one hand, the material world is good and should not be destroyed; this is the realm to which the *LC* assign artistic imagery, and consequently, as the *LC* teach, the Greek iconoclasts were wrong to destroy images. Yet on the other hand, matter exists completely separated from the spiritual, so that any mortal who seeks to approach the spiritual must turn away from the material sphere. As I discuss more fully elsewhere, the concept that I have just outlined was one which Theodulf, a Visigoth, may have derived from a reading of Augustinian thought similar to that suggested in the work of some other theologians who came to the Carolingian realm from Spain or Septimania. In the *LC*, this notion of matter's relation to spirit provides a basic framework for the treatise's attack on both iconoclasm and iconodulism in Byzantium, and for the role the *LC* assign to written language.[11]

The precise manner in which questions of vocabulary, the principles of grammar, rhetoric, and logic, and other issues relating to written language are handled in the *LC* was likely influenced not simply by this broad, possibly "Augustinian" conception of the relationship of the material to the spiritual realm, however, but also, more narrowly, by the Carolingians' knowledge of *De doctrina christiana* (henceforth *DDC*). The several surviving early Carolingian manuscripts of *DDC* are one indication of the attention that Augustine's treatise attracted during this period,[12] while its impact on the *LC* is evident simply from the occasions that the Carolingian treatise quotes from or cites Augustine's work.[13] My main concern here is not to survey the *LC*'s borrowings of specific passages from *DDC*, though, but rather to explore a further connection between the *LC* and that work; for even where the *LC* do not directly refer to *DDC*, Augustine's treatise provided Theodulf and his colleagues with a broad model for the varied aspects of their attack on Nicea II that direct attention to the rules governing the written word. With *DDC* in mind, one of their aims in writing the *LC*, I will argue, was to offer proof that the Carolingians had far better knowledge than did the Greek iconodules of written language and its rules, because the Carolingians did not devote themselves to artistic images. This helped Charlemagne's theologians acquire a better comprehension of Holy Scripture than was demonstrated in the acts of Nicea II, since knowledge of these rules was essential to any correct understanding of the Bible's contents.

Let me begin by identifying the main features of the *LC* that indicate most clearly the preoccupation of Theodulf and his associates with the principles of written language. None of these features is necessarily unique to the *LC* or even to early Carolingian literature; what is significant about their presence in the *LC* is the manner in which they are brought together there, with the conscious purpose of forwarding the argument against Byzantine iconodulism.

The most pervasive indication in the *LC* of a concern with the principles governing written language is simply the document's prose style, striking from its opening pages.[14] As other scholars have remarked, the Latin of the *LC* displays a remarkable command of classical constructions. It is also ornate, frequently convoluted, long-winded, and exuberant, filled with seemingly endless sentences layered with subordinate clauses that are the despair of efforts to render them into English. Single chapters, some of which take up less than a page of Bastgen's edition, can move rapidly from restrained, precise argumentation to passionate explosions punctuated by florid turns of phrase.[15] Despite the assertions in the LC that they aim mainly for purity and simplicity,[16] Theodulf must have worked hard with his associates to produce the complex, widely varied sentence structures and flowery, often poetic, emotionally charged language that in fact characterize their treatise.[17]

The attention paid to the quality of the prose in the LC is further evident from many of the revisions done to the treatise's autograph manuscript, Vatican Latinus 7207. The surviving portions of the Vatican codex, which has lost the preface, part of book 1, and book 4, the final book of the treatise, contain the traces of over thirty-four hundred alterations made by Theodulf and his colleagues.[18] A number of different reasons for the changes can be discerned. Some, for example, were evidently provoked by disagreements among Theodulf and his associates over what to include in the LC text or over the substance of statements in Theodulf's original draft; others represent emendations to patristic and scriptural passages, and others reflect the contemporary development at Charlemagne's court of counterarguments to Spanish adoptionism.[19] In numerous cases, though, as Ann Freeman has most recently demonstrated, the purpose was to alter the character of the writing in the treatise: orthography was changed to remove spelling peculiarities that reflected Theodulf's Visigothic background, whole words were substituted, in some cases apparently because Theodulf's original choices were too Spanish in tone for his colleagues, and still further revisions can be found to wording and syntax.[20] To some extent such changes should be expected in a work of this magnitude and obvious importance, produced within Charlemagne's court circle and intended to oppose an eastern council that claimed to be ecumenical. Yet even so the sheer amplitude of the alterations, to spelling and choice of words as well as on a more substantive level, attests again the seriousness of the aim in the LC to write "correct" Latin.

The efforts put into the style and structure of the LC should be seen alongside the treatise's contentions that Nicea II was frequently guilty of misunderstanding and misusing the written word. According to the LC, the Greek council regularly mishandled the passages that it claimed to draw from the Bible and Church Fathers. Sometimes, Theodulf and his colleagues maintain, the iconodules referred to sources that were unknown to the Carolingians or that Rome did not accept as authoritative,[21] while the iconodules' references could be faulty even where they actually borrowed from older authorities or the Bible.[22] The Carolingians express particular concern with the Greeks' approach to Scripture. The iconodules at Nicea II failed to use patristic commentaries properly as aids in understanding Scripture,[23] neglected to take into account the figural as well as literal meaning of biblical texts,[24] and tried to read Scripture without attention to those areas of learning that, in addition to patristic writings, illumine its true meaning, such as vocabulary, the requirements of translations, the rules of grammar, and dialectic.[25] It is suggested that the iconodules' careless interpretations of individual words in Scripture and their ignorance of principles of dialectic were important factors motivating their erroneous ideas about images. One of the essential mistakes of both iconoclasts and iconodules in Byzantium, the preface to the *LC* argues, was to twist the words of Holy Scripture to new meanings. The iconoclasts had misinterpreted the second commandment by confusing the species, *idolum*, with the genus, *imago*, apparently without realizing that "while almost every idol is an image, not all images are idols."[26] But now the iconodules turned every place in Scripture and patristic commentaries that mentions images into a demand for their adoration. Whereas the iconoclasts confused "idol" with "image," the iconodules confused "to have" (*habere*) and "to adore" (*adorare*). In doing so they committed the greater of the two errors, the *LC* assert, since whereas "idol" and "image" are linked in that one is a species and the other a genus, no such connection can be made between the adoration of images, which the Carolingians reject, and the mere possession of them, which they allow.[27]

In addition to the charges that Nicea II could not interpret biblical and patristic texts correctly, the iconodulist council is accused of an inability to set forth its own beliefs clearly in writing. Along these lines the *LC* attack the iconodules, for one, for errors of "order," including a failure to organize the text of their acts properly[28] and to adhere to the methods of logical discourse.[29] The disorganization of the Second Nicene acts is highlighted by references to the contrasting "order" of the *LC*, such as the arrangement, in the first two books, of biblical and patristic texts mentioned by Nicea II in something close to their chronological sequence.[30] It is also underscored by the careful organization of the *LC* as a whole into four books of virtually equal length and by the rigidly structured argumentation in much of the treatise, an argumentation marked by syllogisms which, with their insistent repetition of terms, seem meant literally to pound the Greeks' opposition into submission.[31]

The most energetic attacks on the use of language in the Second Nicene decrees, however, are directed against the quality of their prose. Over and over again the Byzantine iconodules are criticized for the ungrammatical nature and lack of eloquence of passages in their acts, for their *infausta locutio* and *ridiculosissimum dictum*,[32] for writing like a drunk who, "with reeling steps, stripped of his senses, uses sometimes barbaric and sometimes Latin words."[33] Neither Nicea II nor the iconoclastic council held at Heireia in 754 had that "speech, with which the Apostle calls himself 'unskilled in speech, but not in knowledge,' nor [did they have] the light of his eloquence, shining with spiritual insight,"[34] the *LC* declare. The barbarity of Nicea II's prose is chiefly stressed; according to the Carolingian treatise the writing in the icon-odulist acts regularly strays so far from the rules of written language that it is next to impossible to understand what is being said.[35]

Given the poverty of the Latin translation of the Nicene *acta* available to the Carolingians and their belief that the document was the work of the Byzantine council, the dismay they voice at its lack of eloquence, its confusion, its errors in vocabulary, grammar, and syntax partly reflect the honest impression of Charlemagne's court that it had to deal here with people amazingly incompetent in their use of the written word. As Ann Freeman has observed, the sincerity of this conviction is es-pecially noticeable from the criticisms that the *LC* direct against what was thought to be the iconodules' own garbled translation, from Greek into Latin, of a text by Cyril of Alexandria.[36] In the end, though, the criticisms of Nicea II for its inability to use or understand (Latin) prose correctly must be seen as intended to do more than merely register the Carolingians' shock at the poor writing of the Greek acts, since these criticisms set off so clearly the prowess of the Carolingians' own writing, their ability to argue in an ordered manner, and their own grasp of vocabulary and the rules of grammar, rhetoric, and dialectic.

That one goal in the *LC* was to outwrite Nicea II is made even more apparent by remarks in the *LC*'s preface. Among the themes sounded there is the power of written language as a weapon for Charlemagne, in whose name the *LC* are written. The prose of the *LC* contains a strength that the Byzantine iconodules will not be able to withstand; for Charlemagne feels "compelled to write against the errors [of the Greek synod], in order that perhaps wherever [the synod] perhaps tried to befoul the hands of those holding or the ears of those hearing [its errors], it may be repulsed by the invective of our pen." That pen is "armed with the authority of divine scriptures," the preface goes on to assert.[37] Through it the Carolingian king rejects "the text of that most inept synod, which not only lacks that locution by which poor things are offered softly, moderate things temperately, great things grandly, but even neglects the mode of ordinary speech."[38] With God favoring, the ruler's pen will leave "nothing undiscussed, nothing untouched, nothing concealed in caverns of silence, unless perhaps some difficult or disorganized speech [in the acts] defies our understanding."[39]

The role that this focus on written language and its rules is meant to play in the *LC* can only be understood if two other features of the treatise are kept in mind. The first is the encomium of Scripture in *LC* 2.30, the culmination in a series of chapters explaining the differences between artistic images and objects mentioned in the acts of Nicea II which, the *LC* claim, are *res sacratae*, things God has specially blessed and which therefore, unlike artistic images, possess spiritual as well as material qualities.[40] The discussion of Scripture's status as a *res sacrata* in *LC* 2.30, the longest chapter in the *LC*, occurs virtually at the close of book 2 and thus near the treatise's symbolic midpoint. Artistic imagery bears some similarity to Scripture, it is suggested, because images are in a sense "read" by their viewers,[41] but the chapter's primary message is the sharp contrast between the Bible and artistic depictions. The Bible is affirmed to be unique among writings in that it is the divinely granted source of Christian erudition. It is a material object to which the Christian can in fact turn to gain knowledge of the spiritual realm, because it was granted by God for this purpose,[42] and anyone who has taken advantage of the vast learning that it contains, the *LC* pointedly declare, should have no trouble recognizing the error of attributing comparable sanctity to purely material artistic representations.[43] The wealth of knowledge to be discovered in the Bible, available to those who read it on both a figural and a literal level of understanding, includes everything necessary to uphold virtue and combat vice together with all the treasures of secular learning. In Scripture, therefore, "the instrument of heavenly instruction and the eternal preaching shining with purest eloquence,"[44] are found the laws of numbers, the rules of dialectic, grammar, and rhetoric, as well as the principles of every other liberal art.[45] The Greeks are unaware that any knowledge they might need as Christians is contained in Scripture, not in the artistic representations to which they are devoted, while their concern with artistic imagery is also directly linked with their ignorance of the beauty, richness, and complexity of scriptural language.[46]

While Scripture is distinguished from other texts because it is the word of God, though, the praise the Bible receives in the *LC* is tied up with the concept that writing in general has greater merit as an instrument of communication than does artistic depiction.[47] For Theodulf and his associates, the superiority of written words to artistic images as means of conveying information is proven by God's decision to preserve divine wisdom in writing rather than paintings. The Bible's very existence as a written text, *LC* 2.30 indicates, is a sign of divine approval of the written word *per se* for recording knowledge, over something depicted.[48] Writing surpasses artistic imagery in this respect, the *LC* show, because the artistic image is a likeness that only brings to mind things to which it possesses a resemblance. Since the image is a material object, as such existing entirely separate from the spiritual sphere, what it resembles, and consequently what it recalls, is also necessarily material. Artistic images cannot inform their viewers about the imperceptible world of the spirit.[49] But the written word constitutes the exception that proves the rule of the separation of the material from the spiritual realms. While it, too, is a thing of matter and has no inherent sanctity, it is a sign that does not have to resemble its subject.[50] As a result its material characteristics can designate things that are purely immaterial or spiritual, such as the virtues and the speech of holy persons, and it therefore far surpasses artistic imagery in its ability to express the precepts of the Christian faith.[51] Indeed, although the LC are emphatic concerning the difficulties encountered in efforts to understand written words and especially those of the Bible,[52] Theodulf and his associates thought that words present fewer such problems than do artistic images—even when it came to relaying information about the material world. One passage in the LC drives home the superior reliability of writing for this purpose with the observation that it can be impossible to tell whether a statue of a mother and child depicts Mary with Jesus or another mother with her baby, unless the statue is accompanied by an inscription.[53]

The LC's insistence on the Carolingians' ability to write well, their repeated references to the principles of written language, to the poverty of the writing and organization of the Second Nicene acts, and to the Greek iconodules' inability to read Scripture and the Church Fathers properly work together in several ways to forward the denunciation of Nicea II.[54] First, as I have already suggested, the LC demonstrate the Carolingians' superior mastery of the rules governing the written word and their greater ability, as a consequence, to argue clearly, precisely, logically, and eloquently—to express the truth in a prose that can be understood and that will convince the reader of its veracity. Second, it is implied particularly through the criticisms of Nicea II's handling of scriptural and patristic sources that the Carolingians' awareness of the rules of written language is a central reason why they can interpret more accurately what they read in other texts, including the Church Fathers but above all Scripture; for grammar, vocabulary, and dialectic are among the areas of learning that the LC make clear are fundamental to any attempt to understand these writings.

Third, the Carolingians' expertise in the skills relating to the use and understanding of written language is presented as itself testimony to their familiarity with Scripture, while the Greek iconodules' ignorance in the same areas demonstrates their neglect of the Bible. As Theodulf and his colleagues saw it, one cause of the iconodules' failure to possess the necessary skills to write correct prose and to interpret written texts, especially Scripture, was their focus on artistic images, objects confined to the material world, rather than on the Bible, something blessed by God. Their insufficient attention to Scripture, evident from their careless reading of biblical texts, had prevented them from discovering the secular and spiritual knowledge which Charlemagne's theologians knew the Bible to hold. The iconodules did not realize, then, that this was a source that could reveal to them the significance of grammatical constructions, the principles of logical argument and well-organized, eloquent writing, the mysteries of numbers, of musical harmony, and still other lore. Despite the circularity of this thinking, for Theodulf and his associates the Bible is the source the iconodules most need to study in order to gain the intellectual tools that will help them write well and that will assist them to avoid the mistakes they make in interpretation of the Church Fathers and Scripture.

Finally, the evidence the *LC* offer that the Carolingians write better than the iconodules, that they know how to argue more clearly, exactly, and persuasively, and that their knowledge of the principles of written language allows them to read the Bible and Church Fathers more accurately shows that in contrast to the Greeks they understand the superiority of written words *per se* to artistic representations, despite the place both occupy in the material sphere. Recognition of the centrality of Scripture to Christian salvation, the *LC* imply, goes hand in hand with awareness of the unique qualities of written language as a means of communication. While the iconodules concentrate on artistic depictions, the *LC* reveal that the Carolingians have turned to Scripture and therefore to words and written language, the tools that God chose for recording and teaching sacred wisdom. God's sanctioning of the written word and the proof this offers of the greater value of writing over artistic imagery for proclaiming Christian doctrine are yet further reasons why Charlemagne's churchmen have labored so hard to develop the skills that enable them to compose proper written prose—skills that, again, are also essential to interpretation of the Bible and the Church Fathers.

The *LC* draw on a wide array of authorities for the different prongs of their attack on Nicea II. Borrowings are frequent from other Church Fathers besides Augustine[55] and from other Augustinian works besides *DDC*.[56] Thus where the *LC* criticize the Byzantine iconodules for their ignorance of grammar, rhetoric, and logic, and for their neglect in other ways of the rules of written language, the influence is apparent not only of *DDC* and other writings by Augustine but of such diverse sources as Boethius's commentary on Aristotle's *Peri hermeneias*, the Pseudo-Augustinian *Categoriae decem*, Bede's *De schematis et tropis*, Isidor's *Etymologiae*, and Julian of Toledo's *Ars grammatica*.[57] In addition to the support that such texts and those of still other writers provide for particular claims made in the *LC* regarding the written word and its principles, the same writings affirm, more broadly, that the concern which the Carolingian treatise displays with the rules of written language was solidly grounded in the work of earlier theologians.

The *LC*'s emphasis on the principles governing the written word also links the Carolingian treatise with the program of educational reform under Charlemagne, as outlined for instance in the *Admonitio generalis* and more extensively in *De litteris colendis*.[58] Both texts call for the establishment of schools in the Frankish realm, where boys will be trained in letters as a basis for the study of Scripture and the spread of orthodoxy. *De litteris colendis* is especially noteworthy, since the document stresses the need to assure that clergy and monks will be able to please God by "right speaking" as much as by "right living." The study of letters is declared to be central to exploration of "the mysteries of divine Scripture," for "since figures of speech, tropes, and suchlike are to be found embedded in the sacred pages, there is no doubt but that the more fully anyone reading these is instructed beforehand in the mastery of letters, the more quickly he will gain spiritual understanding."[59] The importance of these educational aims in the Carolingian realm during Charlemagne's reign may have been another motivation for the *LC*'s attentiveness to issues of written language. In a certain sense, the *LC* proclaim that Charlemagne's theologians stand apart from the Greek iconodules because they have acquired the intellectual skills which all Christian clergy should possess.

Yet although a number of early sources play a part in the *LC*'s approach to issues concerning written language, and although the importance which the Carolingian treatise attaches to these issues brings to mind other early Carolingian documents, the closest parallels known to me for the entire core of ideas that Theodulf and his colleagues express regarding the written word are found in *DDC*. The degree to which the approach taken to written language in the *LC* recalls *DDC* is most easily shown if I briefly review certain themes in Augustine's treatise. Some of these are set forth primarily in *DDC* 4, where Augustine discusses the role of rhetorical skills in the teaching of Christian doctrine; but more significant are books 2 and 3, where he examines the nature of scriptural language and the appropriate methods of inquiry into the riches of biblical texts—riches, Augustine notes, that encompass every form of knowledge useful to the Christian.[60]

While the range of information that words can convey makes them the preeminent signs used by mortals,[61] Augustine acknowledges here, the enormous complexity of written language, above all of the writing in sacred texts, means that passages of Scripture are frequently subject to misunderstanding.[62] The Christian who does not pay close attention to the meanings of individual words, who cannot decipher phrases rendered difficult by problems of translation, grammar, pronunciation, or punctuation,[63] who fails to distinguish Scripture's figurative from literal language,[64] and who otherwise approaches the Bible improperly or carelessly[65] will not arrive at a true comprehension of its teachings. A variety of different areas of human knowledge are admitted in *DDC* to be useful to this quest, among them the rules of Latin grammar and logic, the sciences of numbers and music;[66] even more basically the reader of Scripture must know which texts in fact constitute sacred writings, and he is helped by a familiarity with the languages in which Scripture was originally written—Greek and Hebrew.[67]

Still other areas of human knowledge and endeavor are identified by Augustine as "useless institutions" that the student of Sacred Scripture should avoid, and of the several denounced in *DDC* one is artistic representation. The Christian must turn from such concerns in order to concentrate his attention on "nobler things."[68] Only the person who devotes himself to study of Scripture rather than to artistic imagery and similarly useless areas of learning, and who seeks the kind of knowledge that will help him understand Scripture's obscure passages, will reach an understanding of its mysteries.[69]

That person can then go on to instruct others in what he has learned, Augustine asserts in book 4 of *DDC*, and to do so he should receive training in the modes of eloquent, yet clear, oratory,[70] for which no better model can be found than the classical constructions, the eloquence, of Scripture itself.[71] With Scripture as his model, the instructor of Christian doctrine can seek "to teach, please, and persuade," and his speech will be eloquent because it is intelligible, pleasing, and convincing. Or as Augustine further explains, drawing on Cicero, "He will be eloquent, then, who, in order to teach, can speak about trivial subjects in a subdued style; in order to please, can discuss ordinary subjects in a moderate style; and in order to persuade, can treat of noble subjects in a grand style."[72]

In some respects the role that the *LC* give to issues relating to the principles of written language diverges from Augustine's teachings in *DDC*. Augustine's emphasis on the importance of establishing which texts count as sacred writings has no place in the Carolingian treatise, for one, while, second, unlike Augustine, Theodulf and his colleagues include the writings of Church Fathers such as Augustine himself among the texts that can help the Christian discover sacred truth and that are in need of study.

But these and other differences between the LC and DDC are ultimately minor ones that should not obscure the more fundamental points on which the two works agree. Thus both treatises insist on the supremacy of words as signs over all other forms of communication accessible to humans; both stress the difficulty, subtlety, and richness of written language, especially Scripture, and both maintain that the Christian who does not investigate the Bible's language carefully or with sufficient grasp of the rules governing written language runs the danger of misinterpreting Scripture's message. Both treatises make it clear that interest in artistic representations is incompatible with study of the Bible, and that the Christian who seeks the kind of knowledge that helps in the exploration of Scripture, including knowledge of vocabulary and the rules of grammar and dialectic, or of the differences between figural and literal locution, must turn away from such useless institutions as artistic imagery. Both works suggest that if the faithful do focus on the Bible rather than on useless things like artistic depictions, and if they therefore acquire the skills that aid in reading Scripture, they will gain access to the vast treasure of wisdom that is stored in the Bible, a treasure that encompasses the very skills they need in order to explore the Bible's contents.[73] Finally, both treatises agree that it is from Scripture that the Christian best learns, too, the techniques of eloquent oratory, or as the preface to the LC puts it, echoing either DDC or Cicero, the technique of setting forth "poor things softly, moderate things temperately, [and] great things grandly"; and both treatises make it clear that these rhetorical skills are crucial for the person who seeks to instruct others in the truth that Scripture teaches.[74]

To what extent Theodulf and his associates turned directly to a copy of DDC as they developed these lines of thought in the LC is unknown. In light of the familiarity that we know Charlemagne's theologians to have had with Augustine's treatise and the role that a range of Augustinian writings, including DDC, play in the LC, however,[75] the wide-reaching parallels between the two works are striking. They make it seem almost certain, first, that even when the LC do not quote or cite DDC directly Augustine's treatise was a major inspiration for the LC's approach towards words and written language and, second, that the Carolingians saw the parallels between their approach and Augustine's teachings as at least partial confirmation of their approach's validity. From the Carolingians' perspective, one further reason for their superiority to the Byzantine iconodules must have been loyalty to the precepts expressed in DDC.

The basic refrain to emerge from the characteristics of the LC on which I have just focused—that in contrast to the Greek iconodules the

Carolingians have turned not to artistic images but to Scripture as the source of Christian erudition, and therefore to mastery of the rules governing the written word—accords with the drive at Charlemagne's court to make writing a major tool of Carolingian government as well as a primary weapon in the spread and strengthening of the Christian faith.[76] This is one of many reasons that Theodulf's treatise can be regarded as a manifesto of the new direction in which western society was heading. Indeed, although the movement that would turn the Carolingian realm into an increasingly literate society was well underway by the 790s, the impetus Nicea II provided Charlemagne's theologians to produce so carefully elaborated, ambitious an attack on the Greeks, one which so forcefully affirmed the centrality to the Christian faith of Scripture and more generally of the written word, perhaps served as a catalyst to the continuation and broadening of that trend.[77] Through the *LC* we are allowed, too, a glimpse into the Augustinian base of the movement as a whole.[78]

Notes

1. See *Libri Carolini* (henceforth *LC*) 2.30 (Bastgen 93 [V, fol. 102r]). The *LC* edition currently used by scholars is that of Hubert Bastgen: *Libri Carolini sive Carolini Magni capitulare de imaginibus, MGH Legum sectio 3, Concilia 2, supplementum* (Hannover, 1924). My references to the *LC* give page numbers according to this text, though it will soon be superseded by the edition under preparation by Ann Freeman: *Opus Caroli regis contra synodum (Libri Carolini), MGH Legum sectio 3, Concilia 2, Neubearbeitung.* Alongside Bastgen's page numbers I therefore also indicate the relevant folios from the extant Carolingian manuscripts of the *LC*, Paris, Arsenal 663 (= A) and the autograph copy, Vatican Latinus 7207 (= V), since these folio numbers are indicated in both Bastgen's and Freeman's editions. This will permit the reader of this article to refer to either edition or to the manuscripts themselves.

I wish to express my gratitude to Ann Freeman, John Cavadini, David Ganz, and Thomas Noble for their perceptive comments on, and criticisms of, earlier drafts of this article, which have helped me enormously in its revision. I am also grateful to Ann Freeman for her generosity in showing me her unpublished commentary on the Latinity of the *LC* and her translation of the preface, part of her ongoing work on a translation of the whole.

2. Ann Freeman, "Theodulf of Orléans and the *Libri Carolini,*" *Speculum* 32 (1957): 663–705, at 665. Other articles by Freeman on the *LC* include: "Further Studies in the *Libri Carolini,* I and II," *Speculum* 40 (1965): 203–89; "Further Studies in the *Libri Carolini,* III," *Speculum* 46 (1971): 597–612; "Carolingian Orthodoxy and the Fate of the *Libri Carolini,*" *Viator* 16 (1985): 65–108; "Theodulf of Orléans and the Psalm Citations of the *Libri Carolini,*" *Revue bénédictine* 97 (1987): 195–224; "Additions and Corrections to the *Libri*

Carolini: Links with Alcuin and the Adoptionist Controversy," in Sigrid Krämer and Michael Bernhard, eds., *Scire litteras: Forschungen zum mittelalterlichen Geistesleben* (Munich, 1988), 159–69.

3. The scholarship on the *LC* is vast, stretching back to the sixteenth century. Particularly worth noting are: Hubert Bastgen, "Das Capitulare Karls des Grossen über die Bilder oder die sogenannten *Libri Carolini*, I," *Neues Archiv* 36 (1911): 631–66; "II," *Neues Archiv* 37 (1912): 15–51; "III," *Neues Archiv* 37 (1912): 455–533; Arthur Kleinclausz, *Alcuin* (Paris, 1948), appendix, "Alcuin et la question des images," 300–305; Wolfram von den Steinen, "Entstehungsgeschichte der *Libri Carolini*," *Quellen und Forschungen aus italienischen Archiven und Bibliotheken* 21 (1929–1930): 1–93. Of the later work, see especially studies by Luitpold Wallach: "The Unknown Author of the *Libri Carolini*: Patristic Exegesis, Mozarabic Antiphons and the *Vetus Latina*," in Sesto Prete, ed., *Didascaliae: Studies in Honor of A. M. Albereda* (New York, 1961), 471–515; "The *Libri Carolini* and Patristics, Latin and Greek: Prolegomena to a Critical Edition," in Luitpold Wallach, ed., *The Classical Tradition: Literary and Historical Studies in Honor of Harry Caplan* (Ithaca, 1966), 451–98; and *Diplomatic Studies in Latin and Greek from the Carolingian Age* (Ithaca, 1977). Wallach argued vigorously, but unconvincingly, that Alcuin was the *LC*'s author. Freeman has shown that Theodulf of Orléans actually wrote the treatise's initial draft; evidence is given in all her articles listed above in note 2, particularly those appearing in *Speculum*. See also (generally on the *LC*) Gert Haendler, *Epochen karolingischer Theologie: Eine Untersuchung über die karolingischen Gutachten zum byzantinischen Bilderstreit* (Berlin, 1958); Stephen Gero, "The *Libri Carolini* and the Image Controversy," *Greek Orthodox Theological Review* 18 (1973): 7–34; Paul Meyvaert, "The Authorship of the *Libri Carolini*: Observations Prompted by a Recent Book," *Revue bénédictine* 89 (1979): 29–57; Celia Chazelle, "Matter, Spirit, and Image in the *Libri Carolini*," *Recherches augustiniennes* 21 (1986): 163–84.

4. On Theodulf's authorship of the *LC*, see previous note. On the date and circumstances of the *LC*'s composition, see Freeman, "Carolingian Orthodoxy"; and on Alcuin's probable role in the revisions of the *LC*, her "Additions and Corrections," especially 163–69.

5. This is generally noted in the scholarly literature cited in notes 2 and 3. On the doctrine of the *LC*: Haendler, *Epochen*, 11–101; Gero, "*Libri Carolini*," 14–22; Chazelle, "Matter, Spirit, and Image."

6. The *LC*'s concern with other issues besides image worship has been given particular emphasis in Thomas Noble, "From Brigandage to Justice: Charlemagne, 785–794," in Celia Chazelle, ed., *Literacy, Politics, and Artistic Innovation in the Early Medieval West* (Lanham, Md., 1992), 49–75.

7. Cf. Bastgen, "Capitulare, III," 493–533 (who wrongly sees these aspects of the *LC* as evidence of Alcuin's authorship); Gero, "*Libri Carolini*," 10–14; Freeman, "Carolingian Orthodoxy," 78 f., and her "Additions and Corrections."

8. See Bastgen, "Capitulare, III," 521.

9. The mistake is evident, for one, from the *LC*'s comments on Nicea II's supposed translations of Greek patristic material into Latin: e.g., *LC* 2.20 (Bastgen

79 [V, fol. 85v–86r]). See Gero, "*Libri Carolini*," 10; Freeman, "Carolingian Orthodoxy," 69, 78–80. The political background to the *LC*, including relations of the west with Byzantium, is well covered in Judith Herrin, *The Formation of Christendom* (Princeton, 1987), 344–466. On Frankish-papal relations at the time, see Thomas F. X. Noble, *The Republic of St. Peter: The Birth of the Papal State, 680–825* (Philadelphia, 1984), 256–324.

10. E.g., *LC* 1.1–4 (Bastgen, 8–18 [A, fols. 8v–9; V, fols. 3–13v]); Freeman, "Theodulf of Orleans and the *Libri Carolini*," 663–66; idem, "Carolingian Orthodoxy," 80 f.

11. I deal with these issues in "Images, Scripture, the Church, and the *Libri Carolini*," *Proceedings of the PMR Conference* 16/17 (1992–1993): 53–76. A similar usage of Augustine seems apparent in Agobard *Liber contra eorum superstitionem* (*PL* 104:199–228, at 200 f., 202, 209, 211 f.). See also John Cavadini's comments on the Augustinianism of Claudius of Turin: "Claudius of Turin and the Augustinian Tradition," *Proceedings of the PMR Conference* 11 (1986): 43–50.

12. The manuscript evidence for the transmission of *De doctrina Christiana* (henceforth *DDC*) in the early Middle Ages is outlined in Michael Gorman, "The Diffusion of the Manuscripts of Saint Augustine's *De doctrina Christiana* in the Early Middle Ages," *Revue bénédictine* 95 (1985): 11–24. Gorman notes (14–18) the existence of eleven partial and complete Carolingian manuscripts of *DDC* dating to the late eighth and early ninth centuries. Augustine's treatise is edited by Joseph Martin, *Sancti Aurelii Augustini De Doctrina Christiana Libri IV*, CCSL 32 (Turnhout, 1962).

13. E.g., *DDC* 2.8.12 at *LC* 1.6 (Bastgen 20 [V, fol. 16]); *DDC* 3.7.11 at *LC* 2.24 (Bastgen 83 [V, fols. 90r–90v]); *DDC* 3.29.40 at *LC* 2.30 (Bastgen 96 [V, fol. 106]). Cf. *DDC* 4.17.34 for *LC*.praef. (Bastgen 6 [A, fol. 6]); *DDC* 2.41.62 for *LC* 2.28 (Bastgen 90 [V, fols. 98v–99]); *DDC* 2.42.63, 3.29.40, 4.17.34 (for example) for *LC* 2.30 (Bastgen 96 f. [V, fols. 106v–107]).

14. See above, note 1.

15. Note, e.g., the close of *LC* 4.9 (Bastgen 189 [A, fols. 200v–201r]):

Numquidnam omnes libri, in quibus auro argentove vel etiam quibuslibet coloribus historiae inter scripturas pictoria arte insertae sunt, quia imagines habent, aut ab illis sunt conburendi sive praecidendi aut ab istis colendi sive adorandi? Numquidnam sericae sive quarumlibet materiarum vestes sive pallia humanis usibus apta aut divinis cultibus mancipata, figuris quibusdam decorata variisque coloribus fucata eo, quod imagines habent, aut ab illis sunt concremanda aut ab istis adoranda? Numquidnam metalla sive ligna quibuslibet utilitatibus formata eo, quod sculptorio vel etiam caelatorio opere quibusdam imaginibus decorantur, ideo aut ab illis conburenda aut frangenda aut ab istis sunt adoranda?

Infelix mens, quae semper aut in exsecrandis aut e contrario in adorandis imaginibus aestuat! Infelix sensus, qui semper in abdicandis rebus, quae sine offensione haberi queunt et sine offensione adorari nequeunt, anhelat!

Infelix consuetudo, quae mediocritatis recto tramite aspernato fixam tenere regulam nesciens huc illucque semper nutabunda deflectitur, modo inordinate abdicans quod nequaquam est abdicandum, modo infauste adorans quod non est penitus adorandum, modo ultra quam ordo exigit rem minime deiciendam deicit, modo ultra quam ordo exposcit rem non nimium extollendam extollit et, rebus necessariis omissis, rebus non necessariis instans aut ob imaginum abolitionem aut ob earum adorationem, quod utrumque non convenit, synodos adgregat, quasi christianae religioni aut in habendo aut in non adorando quoddam possint afferre praeiudicium, cum videlicet imagines nihil, si non habentur, derogant, nihil, si habentur, prorogant, cum tamen abdicatae quandam incautam levitatem afferant, adoratae vero culpam inurant!

Cf. Freeman, "Additions and Corrections," 160, 162. Freeman notes ("Theodulf of Orléans and the *Libri Carolini*," 671, 672) that the tone of the *LC* is very different from what is found in Alcuin's treatises, and she cites comments by earlier scholars such as C. J. B. Gaskoin, who remarked on the *LC*'s "self-confident tones" (*Alcuin: His Life and Work* [London, 1904], 74, note 4).

16. Cf. *LC* 3.praef. (Bastgen 103 [V, fols. 114r–114v]); 4.praef. (Bastgen 169 [A, fol. 180r]).

17. See Bastgen, "Capitulare, III," 504–7, e.g., concerning the usage of rhymed prose in the *LC*, a technique also found, however, in other Carolingian writings by authors other than Theodulf. Cf. Freeman "Theodulf of Orléans and the *Libri Carolini*," 665 and note 5 (citing earlier literature).

18. Walther Schmandt, *Studien zu den Libri Carolini* (Mainz, 1966), 6. See also Freeman, "Additions and Corrections," 159 and note 2. Paris Arsenal 663, also a Carolingian manuscript, contains the complete *LC* (see above, note 1).

19. Freeman, "Further Studies, I and II," 205–22, 233 f.; and her "Additions and Corrections," 163–69.

20. Freeman, "Additions and Corrections," 160, 163; and her "Theodulf of Orléans and the *Libri Carolini*," 690–92.

21. *LC* 2.17 (Bastgen 76 f. [V, fol. 83r]); 3.21 (Bastgen 145–48 [V, fols. 164r–167r]); 3.30 (Bastgen 167 [V, fols. 189r–189v]); 4.5 (Bastgen 179–84 [A, fols. 190v–195v]); 4.10–11 (Bastgen 189–92 [A, fols. 201r–204r]).

22. E.g., *LC* 2.15 (Bastgen 74 f. [V, fol. 81r]; see Wallach, *Diplomatic Studies*, 123–39); 2.19 (Bastgen 77–79 [V, fols. 83v–85v]); 2.20 (Bastgen 79 f. [V, fols. 85v–86r]). Cf. *LC* 1.17 (Bastgen 40 [V, fols. 40v–41r]).

23. See, e.g., the first critiques of Nicea II's handling of scriptural passages: *LC* 1.9 (Bastgen 27 [V, fol. 25]); 1.11 (Bastgen 31 [V, fol. 29v]); 1.13 (Bastgen 32 f. [V, fols. 31v–32]).

24. E.g., *LC* 1.21 (Bastgen 48 f. [V, fols. 51r–52r]); 1.29 (Bastgen 57–59 [V, fols. 61v–65r]); cf. 1.17 (Bastgen 41 [V, fol. 42v]); 1.30 (Bastgen 60 [V, fols. 65r–65v]).

25. See, e.g., *LC* 1.1 (Bastgen 9 [V, fols. 3–3v]); 1.4 (Bastgen 16–18 [V, fols. 11v–13v]); 1.9 (Bastgen 27 f. [V, fols. 25v–26r]); 1.12 (Bastgen 31 [V, fol. 30r]);

1.14 (Bastgen 33 f. [V, fols. 32v–33v]); 1.17 (Bastgen 40 f. [V, fols. 40v–42v]); 1.20 (Bastgen 46 [V, fols. 48r–48v]); 1.23 (Bastgen 52 [V, fols. 55r–55v]); 1.24 (Bastgen 52 [V, fol. 56r]); 1.26 (Bastgen 55 [V, fols. 59r–59v]); 1.28 (Bastgen 56 [V, fol. 61r]); 2.4 (Bastgen 66 [V, fols. 71v–72r]); 2.15 (Bastgen 74 [V, fols. 80v–81r]); 3.3 (Bastgen 110 f. [V, fols. 122v–123r]). In *LC* 3.20 (Bastgen 144 [V, fols. 161v–163r]) Nicea II is accused of using ungrammatical prose in quoting from John Chrysostom. The concern with Nicea II's apparently careless approach to Scripture is in keeping with the identification of the *LC* author as Theodulf, a theologian who devoted enormous care outside writing the *LC* to research on the Bible's text (see Freeman, "Theodulf of Orléans and the *Libri Carolini*," 692 f.; Meyvaert, "Authorship," 51).

26. *LC*.praef. (Bastgen 3 [A, fol. 3r]). Cf. Wallach, *Diplomatic Studies*, 65. On logical studies at Charlemagne's court, see John Marenbom, *From the Circle of Alcuin to the School of Auxerre* (Cambridge, 1981), 30–66.

27. *LC*.praef. (Bastgen 3 f. [A, fols. 3v–4r]). Cf. *LC* 1.9 (Bastgen 27 f. [V, fols. 25v–26r]).

28. *LC* 1.5 (Bastgen 19 [V, fols. 15r–15v]). Cf. also *LC* 1.14 (Bastgen 33 f. [V, fol. 33r]); 3.12 (Bastgen 125–27 [V, fols. 139r–142r]); 4.16 (Bastgen 202 f. [A, fols. 215r–215v]).

29. E.g., *LC* 1.1 (Bastgen 9 f. [V, fols. 3v–4r]); 1. 2 (Bastgen 13 [V, especially fol. 8r]); 3.27 (Bastgen 162 [V, fol. 184r]); 4.23 (Bastgen 217–21 [A, fols. 232v–237v]). See Wallach, *Diplomatic Studies*, 63–79; Meyvaert, "Authorship," 51 (citing Wallach).

30. See *LC* 1.5 (Bastgen 19 [V, fols. 15r–15v]); 1.7–2.23 (Bastgen 22–82 [V, fols. 18v–89v]); Bastgen, "Capitulare, I," 635, 638–42.

31. E.g., *LC* 1.7 (Bastgen 24 f. [V, fol. 22]); 1.11 (Bastgen 30 [V, fols. 29–29v]); 1.24 (Bastgen 52 [V, fol. 56]); *LC* 2.21 (Bastgen 80 [V, fol. 86v]); cf. 3.9 (Bastgen 121 f. [V, fols. 135v–136]). I am grateful to Ann Freeman for reminding me in her unpublished commentary on the Latinity of the *LC* of the importance there of syllogisms. On the overall organization of the *LC*, cf. Bastgen, "Capitulare, I," 634–48.

32. E.g., *LC* 1.4 (Bastgen 18 [V, fol. 13v]): "O infausta locutio! O exsecrabilis error!" 3.19 (Bastgen 142 [V, fol. 160r]): "per hoc ridiculosissimum dictum Agapii." Cf. Gero, "*Libri Carolini*," 10; and *LC* 4.26 (Bastgen 225 [A, fol. 242r]), concerning the rules of eloquence.

33. *LC* 3.15 (Bastgen 133 [V, fols. 149r–149v]): "et in modum temulenti, qui nimio madefactus mero trementibus membris, titubantibus gressibus, nudatis sensibus, modo barbaris, modo Latinis utitur verbis." See also, e.g., *LC* 3.5 (Bastgen 115 [V, fol. 128v]); 4.5 (Bastgen 180 [A, fols. 191r–191v]); 4.16 (Bastgen 202 f. [A, fols. 215r–215v]); cf. praef. (Bastgen 5 f. [A, fols. 5v–6r]).

34. *LC*.praef. (Bastgen 5 [A, fol. 5v]).

35. E.g., *LC* 3.9 (Bastgen 122 [V, fols. 136r–136v]); 4.15 (Bastgen 201 [A, fols. 213v–214r]); cf. 4.2 (Bastgen 175 f. [A, fol. 186v]).

36. *LC* 2.20 (Bastgen 79 [V, fols. 85v–86r]); Freeman, "Carolingian Orthodoxy," 79 and n. 52.

37. *LC*.praef. (Bastgen 5 [A, fol. 5r]).

38. *LC*.praef. (Bastgen 6 [A, fol. 6r]). Cf. (drawing on Cicero) Augustine *DDC* 4.17.34–4.28.61.

39. *LC*.praef. (Bastgen 6 [A, fol. 6r]). See also, e.g., *LC* 3.praef. (Bastgen 103 [V, fols. 114r–114v]).

40. *LC* 2.30 (Bastgen 92–100 [V, fols. 101r–110v]). On the discussion here, see Bastgen, "Capitulare, III," 495–500. Other *res sacratae*—the Ark of the Covenant, the eucharist, the cross, and holy vessels—are identified in *LC* 2.26–29 (Bastgen 85–92 [V, fols. 92v–100v]). On the comparable status of these objects, see *LC* 2.29 (Bastgen 91 [V, fol. 100r]; 2.30 (Bastgen 92 [V, fol. 101r]). The term, *res sacrata*, is defined in *LC* 3.24 (Bastgen 153 [V, fol. 173v]), where it is implied that relics of the saints possess equivalent sacrality:

> Sicut igitur sacratis rebus—sive quae per legislatorem sive quae per Dei et hominum Mediatorem sacratae sunt, sive etiam quae quotidie a sacerdotibus divini nominis invocatione sacrantur et in mysterium nostrae redemptionis sumuntur—imagines nequaquam coaequandae sunt, ita etiam nec sanctorum martyrum seu confessorum reliquiis, quae apud fideles ipsorum amore venerationi habentur, coaequandae creduntur.

These references to the *res sacratae* indicate that they differ from artistic images because, as is not true with images, the spiritual merit granted to their material forms makes them things to which the faithful can and should turn to draw closer to heaven. They are mediating links that God has provided between the worlds of matter and spirit, things that participate in both realms, but which for this reason must be distinguished from artistic representations.

41. *LC* 2.30 (Bastgen 92 [V, fol. 101r]): artistic images favor only the eyes, "per quos quasi per quosdam legatos gestarum rerum memoriam cordibus mandent." The notion of reading images probably comes from Gregory the Great's correspondence with Serenus of Marseilles, where comments are made on the same theme. Passages from Gregory's second letter to Serenus are quoted in *LC* 2.23 (Bastgen 82 [V, fols. 88v–89v]): Gregory I *Registrum epistularum* (ed. Dag Norberg, *CCSL* 140–140A [Turnhout, 1982]), 140A:*ep.* 11 (10).873–876; cf. *ep.* 9 (209).768.

42. This is a theme running throughout the chapter and even the *LC* as a whole; see especially *LC* 2.30 (Bastgen 93–95 [V, fols. 102–104v]).

43. See *LC* 2.30 (Bastgen 95 [V, fol. 105r]).

44. *LC* 2.30 (Bastgen 98 [V, fol. 107v]).

45. *LC* 2.30 (Bastgen 96 f. [V, fols. 106r–107r]). Scripture helps Christians avoid vice and embrace virtue: *LC* 2.30 (Bastgen 95 f. [V, fols. 105r–105v]). Cf. *LC* 2.30 (Bastgen 97 f. [V, fols. 107v–108]).

46. Especially *LC* 2.30 (Bastgen 98 [V, fol. 108r]):

> Nihil igitur horum, quae perstrinximus, sive his similium, quae brevitatis studio praetermisimus, in imaginibus, o imaginum adorator, o rerum insensatarum cultor, invenire posse te constat. Quae dum his omnibus

meritorum praerogativis careant, dolendus potius quam mirandus es, quur eas divinae Scripturae libris, in quibus tot bona reperiuntur, aequiperare affectes? Tu, qui fidei tuae puritatem in imaginibus conservare te dicis, supplex eis adstare memento cum timiamatibus; nos praecepta Domini solerti indagatione perquiramus in divinae legis codicibus! Tu luminaribus perlustra picturas; nos frequentemus divinas Scripturas! Tu fucatorum venerator esto colorum; nos veneratores et capaces simus sensuum archanorum! Tu depictis demulcere tabulis; nos divinis mulceamur alloquiis! Tu figuris rerum insta, in quibus nec visus nec auditus nec gustus nec odoratus nec tactus est; nos instemus divinae legi, quae est inrepraehensibilis, in qua testimonium Domini iustitiae sive praecepta, timor sive iudicia eius inveniuntur!

Also *LC* 2.30 (Bastgen 100 [V, fol. 110v]).

47. Cf. Gerhart Ladner, "Die Bilderstreit und die Kunstlehren der byzantinischen und abendländischen Theologie," *Zeitschrift für Kirchengeschichte* 33 (1931): 1–23, at 15, 17.

48. *LC* 2.30 (especially Bastgen 93–95 [V, fols. 101v–105r]).

49. For the importance of likeness in an artistic image, cf. especially *LC* 1.8 (Bastgen 25 f. [V, fols. 22–23v]). Artistic images do not depict imperceptible, immaterial things, such as the virtues: cf., e.g., *LC* 1.17 (Bastgen 41 [V, fol. 42r]); 3.23 (Bastgen 153 [V, fols. 172v–173r]); 3.16 (Bastgen 137 [V, fols. 154r–154v]). According to the *LC*, artistic images are useful only because they decorate the places in which they appear and aid recollection, above all the recollection of past events: e.g., *LC*.praef. (Bastgen 3, 4, 5 f. [A, fols. 3r, 4v, 5v]); 2.9 (Bastgen 70 [V, fol. 76v]); 2.13 (Bastgen 73 [V, fol. 79r]); 2.21 (Bastgen 80 [V, fol. 87r]); 2.31 (Bastgen 102 [V, fol. 113r]); 4.18 (Bastgen 206, 207 [A, fols. 220r, 220v]); 4.19 (Bastgen 209 [A, fols. 223r–223v]). Cf. 3.23 (Bastgen 150 f. [V, fol. 170r]); and (concerning images recalling the saints or Christ) 2.13 (Bastgen 73 [V, fols. 79v–80r]); 4.2 (Bastgen 176 [A, fols. 187r–187v]); 4.15 (Bastgen 201 [A, fols. 214r–214v]). For Theodulf and his colleagues, both roles accorded with the notion that the artistic image was a material object unconnected with the sacred. See my "Matter, Spirit, and Image," especially 178 f.

50. *LC* 2.30 (Bastgen 92 f. [V, fols. 101–102r]): written letters are "indices rerum sive signa verborum." See Isidor *Etymologiae* 1.3 (*PL* 82:74. 62).

51. E.g., *LC* 1.17 (Bastgen 41 f. [V, fols. 42r–43v]). *LC* 3.23 (Bastgen 153 [V, fols. 172v–173r]):

Numquidnam verba ipsius Domini et apostolorum singula a pictoribus possunt demonstrari? Pictores igitur rerum gestarum historias ad memoriam reducere quodammodo valent, res autem, quae sensibus tantummodo percipiuntur et verbis proferuntur, non a pictoribus, sed ab scriptoribus conprehendi et aliorum relatibus demonstrari valent.

Cf. 3.16 (Bastgen 137 [V, fols. 154r–154v]).

52. In particular, this is a constant theme as the Carolingians rebuke Nicea II for its faulty usage of scriptural and patristic sources, in LC 1.7–2.17 (Bastgen 22–77 [V, fols. 18v–83r]).

53. LC 4.21 (Bastgen 213 [A, fols. 228v–229r]); cf. 3.16 (Bastgen 137 f. [V, fols. 154v–155r]); 4.16 (Bastgen 204 [A, fols. 216v–217v]). Cf. Rosamond McKitterick, ed., *The Uses of Literacy in Early Mediaeval Europe* (Cambridge, 1990), 309.

54. Cf. Bastgen, "Capitulare, III," 495–500, 521.

55. E.g., Ambrose, Isidore, Bede, Jerome; and see below, at note 57. Cf. Wallach, "Unknown Author," and *Diplomatic Studies*, 59–122, which should be read with caution alongside Freeman, "Further Studies, II," 223–86, and Meyvaert, "Authorship."

56. E.g., *De diversis quaestionibus liber unus* at LC 1.7 (Bastgen 23 f. [V, fols. 19v–21v]); *Quaestiones in Heptateuchum* at LC 1.9 (Bastgen 27 [V, fol. 25]); *De trinitate* at LC 3.4 (Bastgen 114 f. [V, fols. 127v–128v]); *Enarrationes in Psalmos* at LC 3.18 (Bastgen 141 [V, fol. 159]); *De diversis quaestionibus* at LC 3.27 (Bastgen 162 [V, fol. 184]); *De haeresibus* at LC 4.25 (Bastgen 224 [A, fols. 240v–241]). The general Augustinianism of the LC is often noted in earlier scholarship: e.g., Adolf von Harnack, *Lehrbuch der Dogmengeschichte*, vol. 3, 5th ed. (Tübingen, 1932), 303 f.; Walter Delius, *Die Bilderstreit im Karolingerreich* (Diss. Halle, 1928), especially 29–31; Hans Liebeschütz, "Wesen und Grenzen des karolingischen Rationalismus," *Archiv für Kulturgeschichte* 33 (1950): 17–44, especially 27; Herbert Schade, "Die *Libri Carolini* und ihre Stellung zum Bild," *Zeitschrift für katholische Theologie* 79 (1957): 69–78, at 71.

57. Boethius *Commentarii in librum Aristotelis Peri hermeneias, prima editio* (ed. Carl Meiser [Leipzig, 1877]) at LC 4.23 (Bastgen 217 f. [A, fols. 233–234v]); Pseudo-Augustine *Categoriae decem (anonymi paraphrasis themistiana* (ed. L. Minio-Paluello, *Aristoteles Latinus 1.1–5: Categoriae vel praedicamenta* [Bruges, 1961] 128–88) at, e.g., LC 1.1 (Bastgen 9 f. [V, fols. 3v–4]; cf. Wallach, *Diplomatic Studies*, 63 f.); Bede *De schematis et tropis sacrae scripturae liber* (*PL* 90:175–86) at, e.g., LC 2.30 (Bastgen 94 [V, fol. 103v]); Isidor *Etymologiae* (*PL* 82:73–728) at, e.g., LC 3.24 (Bastgen 130 [V, fols. 145v–146]); Julian of Toledo *Ars grammatica* (ed. Mariá A. H. Maestre Yenes [Toledo, 1973]) at LC 2.1 (Bastgen 63 f. [V, fol. 69v]). Ann Freeman informed me in a personal communication (22 August 1991) of the use of Julian at this point in the LC, which is overlooked in Bastgen's edition of the Carolingian treatise. More broadly on Isidore's influence on the LC, see Elizabeth Dahlhaus-Berg, *Nova Antiquitas et Antiqua Novitas: Typologische Exegese und isidorianisches Geschichtsbild bei Theodulf von Orléans* (Cologne, 1975), 190–201.

58. *Admonitio generalis* (ed. A. Boretius, *MGH Capitularia regum Francorum* 1 [Hannover, 1883], 52–62, at 59 f.); *De litteris colendis* (ed. A. Boretius, *MGH Capitularia regum Francorum* 1 [Hannover, 1883], 78 f.). Both documents are translated into English in P. D. King, *Charlemagne: Translated Sources* (Lancaster, 1987), 209–20, 232–33. Cf. Noble, "From Brigandage to Justice," 57–65.

59. "Cum autem in sacris paginis schemata, tropi et caetera his similia inserta inveniantur, nulli dubium est, quod ea unusquisque legens tanto citius spiritualiter intelligit, quanto prius in litterarum magisterio plenius instructus fuerit." *De litteris colendis* (Boretius, *MGH Capitularia* 1:79 [trans. King, *Charlemagne,* 232 f.]). Cf. *Admonitio generalis* (Boretius, *MGH Capitularia* 1:72.59 f.).

60. *DDC* 2.42.63. While many of the early manuscripts of *DDC* only contain portions of the treatise, complete copies are found from Charlemagne's reign (Gorman, "Diffusion," 14–18, and above, note 12).

61. E.g., *DDC* 1.2.2, 2.3.4.

62. Cf. *DDC* 2.5.6–2.6.7, 2.9.14–2.11.16.

63. *DDC* 2.11.16–2.16.23, 3.2.2–3.4.8, 3.29.40.

64. *DDC* 2.10.15, 2.16.23, 3.5.9–3.28.39.

65. Cf., e.g., the discussion of Tyconius's rules, *DDC* 3.30.42–3.37.56.

66. E.g., *DDC* 2.16.25–2.18.28, 2.28.42–2.40.61; cf. 3.30.42–3.37.56.

67. *DDC* 2.8.12–2.11.16.

68. *DDC* 2.25.38–2.26.40; cf. 2.17.27–2.24.37.

69. Cf., e.g., *DDC* 3.1.1:

Homo timens deum uoluntatem eius in scripturis sanctis diligenter inquirit. Et ne amet certamina pietate mansuetus; praemunitus etiam scientia linguarum, ne in uerbis locutionibusque ignotis haereat, praemunitus etiam cognitione quarundam rerum necessariarum, ne uim naturamue earum, quae propter similitudinem adhibentur, ignoret, adiuuante etiam codicum ueritate, quam sollers emendationis diligentia procurauit, ueniat ita instructus ad ambigua scripturarum discutienda atque soluenda.

70. On the value of clarity, cf. *DDC* 4.9.23–2.11.26.

71. *DDC* 4, especially 1.1–7.21. In *DDC* 4.7.21 Augustine states,

Et plura quidem, quae pertineant ad praecepta eloquentiae, in hoc ipso loco [i.e., in Scripture], quem pro exemplo posuimus, possunt reperiri. Sed bonum auditorem non tam, si diligenter discutiatur, instruit, quam si ardenter pronuntietur, accendit. Neque enim haec humana industria composita, sed diuina mente sunt fusa et sapienter et eloquenter non intenta in eloquentiam sapientia, sed a sapientia non recedente eloquentia. Si enim, sicut quidam disertissimi atque acutissimi uiri uidere ac dicere potuerunt, ea quae oratoria uelut arte discuntur, non obseruarentur et notarentur et in hanc doctrinam redigerentur, nisi prius in oratorum inuenirentur ingeniis. Quid mirum si et in istis inueniuntur, quos ille misit, qui fecit ingenia? Quapropter et eloquentes quidem, non solum sapientes, canonicos nostros auctores doctoresque fateamur tali eloquentia, qualis personis eiusmodi congruebat.

72. *DDC* 4.17.34, quoting Cicero *Orator* 29.101.

73. Here see especially *DDC* 2.42.63.

74. See *LC*.praef. (Bastgen 6 [A, fol. 6r]), and above, at note 38. The "eloquence" of the *LC* therefore demonstrates that the Carolingians are capable of instructing others about Scripture's truth, because they possess the proper rhetorical skills, while the Greek iconodules have shown their inability to do the same.

75. See above, at notes 12, 13, 56.

76. See Rosamond McKitterick, *The Carolingians and the Written Word* (Cambridge, 1989); and her *Uses of Literacy*, especially on the relation between artistic imagery and the written word for the Carolingians (297–318).

77. See McKitterick, *Uses of Literacy*, especially 298–300.

78. I am grateful to John Cavadini for making this last point clear to me.

Augustine and the Education
of the Early Medieval Preacher

THOMAS L. AMOS

A work can only become a classic of western culture through engaging the attention of subsequent generations as fully as it engaged the attention of the period which produced it. It becomes important, therefore, to understand how succeeding ages understood such a work and how they employed it within the terms of their own culture. In our own time, for example, there has been much debate concerning the nature of Augustine's *De doctrina christiana*. Henri Marrou considered the work a charter for Christian culture. E. Hill regarded it as a handbook on the teaching of Christianity, while many others, including Christine Mohrmann and James J. Murphy, saw it as the first Christian guide to rhetoric.[1]

During the early Middle Ages, long before our great debate over the nature and meaning of the work would rage in this century, people's attention was fully engaged by the content of the work itself. They took an altogether more practical view of the *DDC*. The work won its place in Carolingian culture because it was regarded as the preeminent guide for exegetes, the cornerstone of that immense edifice that was Augustine's *opera exegetica*. This understanding of the work provided much of its importance for Carolingian masters who taught from it and for sermon authors who drew upon Augustine's approach to Scripture and his rules for interpreting it to shape their own scriptural expositions.

To the Carolingians, the *DDC* presented a book of rules for the education of the Christian preacher and exegete. In the work, however, Augustine assumed access to a level of prior education that few of the societies which immediately followed his were able to provide easily or uniformly. By the time of the Carolingian ecclesiastical reforms, when clerical education and preaching once more became major concerns, Augustine's work had acquired several competitors in these areas. Some of the competitors, themselves influenced by the *DDC*, replaced parts of Augustine's program. Despite the attention paid in capitularies and canons to this other literature, however, it was the *DDC* and especially the work's approach to exegesis that formed much of the basis of Carolingian attempts to educate clerics so they could preach.

I shall examine the use of the *DDC* as an educational tool primarily in this period, when emphasis was placed on the exegetical guide contained in the first three books. Through looking at the manuscript evidence, *collectanea* and *florilegia* used in schools and the Carolingian adaptations and educational handbooks, we can examine the role of this work in clerical education and its influence on the sermons and the program of Carolingian religious reforms (see the table below, a timeline of the various early medieval forms of transmission of the *DDC* and extracts from it).

Although much has been written about early medieval schools, we know little about the actual teaching process within them. Even the most prolific Carolingian masters—Alcuin, Lupus of Ferrieres, Rabanus Maurus—have left many works but little to satisfy our curiosity on the methods of their teaching. Recent studies of Carolingian education have turned to the manuscripts used by masters in the schools in order to reconstruct types of interchanges between masters and students.[2] We must therefore examine the manuscript evidence in order to draw some preliminary conclusions about the nature of clerical education and the *DDC*'s role in it.

The Carolingian manuscript evidence for the work itself points immediately to the popularity it enjoyed in eighth- and ninth-century schools. Joseph Martin, William Green, and Michael Gorman have described twenty-four complete manuscripts dating from the period 750–950.[3] This figure comes from a total of thirty-one manuscripts or fragments from before the year 1000. Most of the major schools and scriptoria— Tours, Fulda, St. Gall, and Reims, among others—are represented by these manuscripts. Two of them, from unidentified centers in northern France, contain marginal glosses, apparently by masters, which offer further testimony to their use in schools.[4] The *DDC* was so connected to Carolingian schools that both John Contreni and Gorman both expressed surprise that Laon did not produce or own a copy. Instead, the school at Laon had a copy of Eugippius,[5] which reminds us that we also need to consider other types of evidence, such as *florilegia* and other types of collections, to understand how the work was used.

Diffusion of the *De doctrina christiana*
in the Early Middle Ages

Year	Number of Mss. Produced (complete and fragments)	Borrowings [Replacements] and Excerpts from *DDC* in Other Works
400		
	1	
		[Pomerius, *De vita contemplativa*]
500		
		Eugippius, Excerpta
		[Cassiodorus, *Institutes*]
600	1	
		[Isidore, *Etymologiae*]
700	1	Bede, *Explanatio Apocalypsis*
		Florilegia
	2	
	2	
800	3	
	5	Rabanus Maurus, *De Institutione clericorum*
	5	Salzburg Handbook
	4	Florus of Lyons, *Collectanea in Epistolae*
	3	*Florilegia*
900	1	
	1	
		Florilegia
	3	
1000		

Other vehicles for the transmission of parts of the *DDC* were equally as important as manuscripts of the full work itself. One form of transmission came through other works which dealt with aspects of Augustine's educational program. Pomerius's *De vita contemplativa* could be regarded as a set of extended variations on the theme developed in book 4 that the preacher's life should exemplify the doctrine he preached.[6] Cassiodorus's *Institutes* set out an educational program for copyists and interpreters of Scripture that was more extensive than book 2.[7] The popular and encyclopedic *Etymologies* of Isidore of Seville contained numerous borrowings from the *DDC*.[8] These other works, however, tended to replace, rather than supplement, the relevant parts of the *DDC* with an alternative vision of clerical education under the Carolingians.

Yet another form of transmission came from excerpts of the work used in commentaries and collections written for educational and exegetical purposes. Bede's popular *Expositio in Apocalypsis* contained in its prologue the section of *DDC* 3 with the rules of Tyconius.[9] In addition, purely Augustinian *collectanea* and *florilegia* were particularly common in this period. Using only the printed catalogues of the Bibliothèque Nationale,[10] Henri Rochais has identified fourteen such collections which date from the eighth and ninth centuries.

Despite recent claims for fairly widespread literacy in the Carolingian world, teaching remained an oral process. The *florilegia, collectanea,* and handbooks were not read by students in the schools but served as the basis for the master's discourse.[11] This type of manuscript provides our best evidence for the use of the *DDC* in Carolingian schools. This manner of using the text of the work through excerpts was first established by Eugippius in the *Excerpta ex operibus sancti Augustini*.[12] The *Excerpta* contained seven long passages from *DDC* book 1, thirteen from book 2, and all but nine chapters of book 3, including the rules of Tyconius. Eugippius either completely ignored book 4 or did not have access to it. Passages from the *DDC* are most commonly found in the large collections on the Epistles. Bede, for example, used six excerpts in his *florilegium* and Florus of Lyons, over a century later, used seventeen in his collection.[13] These *florilegia* served a number of purposes, since they could be used as sources for commentaries or as teaching texts. The number of eighth- and ninth-century manuscripts of such works associated with educational centers helps indicate the importance that the first three books of the *DDC* had for them.

Carolingian school texts ignored or heavily adapted Augustine's idea of a Christian rhetoric, developed at length in book 4. Since the entire work could obviously be read by Carolingian masters and exegetes, we can conclude that this neglect was purposeful. Rabanus Maurus employed heavily adapted excerpts from book 4 in the third book of his *De clericorum institutione*, composed in 819.[14] He abandoned Augustine's defense of biblical Latinity and the use of pagan literature in education. The former cannot have made much sense to a people who themselves had to learn Latin as a foreign language, while the latter defense was no longer necessary.[15] The process of amalgamating Greco-Roman and Christian cultures into something new was, if not virtually complete, at least something no longer requiring justification. There were, for example, no Carolingian analogues to Gregory the Great's letter to Bishop Desiderius of Vienne which pointed out that bishops could not teach grammar or the pagan classics.[16] The cultural and religious institutions which had sustained classical literature were now at a far enough remove for the Carolingians not to feel the tensions involved in "despoiling the Egyptians" which had bothered their predecessors.

In the excerpts from book 4 that Rabanus used, Augustine is called upon to state the three purposes of speaking and the three types of orations, both of which are given a strongly moralistic bent.[17] Rabanus's editor noted the borrowings, which he regarded as plagiarism, and ignored the adaptations which help to explain them.[18] The adaptations were necessary to fit the *DDC* into the changed pattern of needs felt by Carolingian clerics, similar to the usage in the Salzburg compilation described below. The remainder of Rabanus's homiletic program drew heavily upon Cassiodorus's *Institutes*, especially for the explanations of the liberal arts, including rhetoric.[19] Despite the Carolingian interest in Cicero, even his presence in book 4 of the *DDC* did not give it interest for them.

Sections of book 4, also adapted, appeared in a manual for bishops written at Salzburg under Bishop Angilramn (821–853). The collection consisted of sixteen chapters, written in sermon form, drawn from Jerome's commentaries on the Pauline Epistles, Pomerius's *De vita contemplativa*, and other works.[20] Each chapter sandwiched its long, adapted excerpts between an original introduction and conclusion. The form is similar to *collectanea* or handbooks put together in other Carolingian centers.

The adaptations of the material from *DDC* 4, which appear in chapter 14 of the manual, make it clear that the purpose of Carolingian preaching was teaching. Persuasion and pleasure, the two other purposes of the orator which Augustine borrowed from Cicero, did not even appear in the discussion. Augustine's borrowed formula *grande dicendi genus* became in these excerpts *sermo terribilior et disciplinatior*.[21] The compiler combined the other two *genera dicendi* to derive a *lenis et blanda oratio*. Its use was also didactic, since it was intended to praise the virtues and to inculcate good in the hearer.[22] In other words, bishops preached to teach and they were to make their sermons as exhortatory and admonitory as possible. Other than the occasional excerpts from book 4 found in the *florilegia* on the Epistles, Rabanus and the Salzburg Handbook make the only recorded instances of Carolingian use of this part of the *DDC*.

What is the connection between Augustine's work and the type of education which the Carolingians directed toward the preacher? Rabanus provides one direct model, but there is also an indirect influence of Augustine that should be considered. Paris, Bibliothèque Nationale, Ms. lat. 10612 (described in the appendix below), offers the example of a ninth-century preacher's handbook constructed on the model of the exegetical education set out in the *DDC*.[23] Despite the fact that there are no actual Augustinian texts in the manuscript, it contains the types of material he recommended for the preacher's education. The *Expositio quattuor evangeliorum* of Pseudo-Gregory treated the explication of figurative signs. The works on the *quaestiones*, along with the other short exegetical texts, provided materials for the preacher which emphasized the explanation of literal signs, although they also contain some treatment of figurative signs as well. The fifteen sermons— attributed in the manuscripts to Augustine, but actually the work of Caesarius of Arles and others—contain both types of interpretation and serve as models for the preacher's own works. The manuscript concludes with a short treatise on orthography, returning us to literal signs. This handbook was a popular collection; five other manuscripts connected with important schools contain its major elements.[24]

The *DDC* played an important, if somewhat restricted, role in Carolingian clerical education. The reasons for the restrictions and adaptations of Augustinian material tell us something important about the nature of that education. The Carolingians took their Latin from the grammarians Donatus and Priscian and the commentaries on them.[25] Their interest in language was in words and their meaning, Augustine's *res* and *signa*. But his initial career as a rhetor would have been far beyond the comprehension of most ninth-century clerics.[26] They therefore used in their educational texts those portions of his work that spoke directly to their needs and interests, or used earlier adaptations of it.

When we examine the influence of the *DDC* on the texts of Carolingian sermons, we should remember an important fact about its composition. Sometime around 396 or 397, Augustine completed books 1 and 2 and much of book 3.[27] He set out at the beginning of his episcopate a body of ideas about interpreting and expounding Scripture that would inform his own writings. In addition to having Augustine's finished thoughts on Christian doctrine upon the completion of the work in 427, the reader of Augustine also has a large body of treatises, commentaries, and sermons which embody the *DDC*'s ideas about scriptural exegesis and exposition.[28] For a variety of reasons, the practical examples taken from these other works proved more influential than the *DDC* as sources for early medieval sermon texts.

We do not find, for example, sections of the *DDC* excerpted in sermons as in the sort of relationship that exists between Alcuin's *Liber de virtutibus et de vitiis* and the sermons of Rabanus Maurus.[29] Augustine used the Apostle Paul as his example of the Christian orator and treated many passages of the Epistles in his work.[30] Since the Carolingian sermons most often explicated Gospel passages, it is difficult to compare passages of individual sermons with the Scripture used as examples in the *DDC*. As is well known, Augustine provided few concrete examples of his exegetical methods in the *DDC* itself. The discussion of methodology is confined to his discussion of the rules of Tyconius.[31] Yet the influence from the *DDC* is at work in the sermons, and it runs at a level far deeper than borrowings revealed by *Quellenkritik*.

In book 3, in particular, Augustine sought to establish a set of rules for the application of allegorical interpretation to Scripture.[32] In establishing these rules, he also displays an exegetical pattern that he established throughout much of his other work. After selecting a scriptural passage, from the Gospels, for example, he would make a first approach at its explication by drawing out its meaning through the use of another scriptural passage. Quite often this analogous or drawing-out passage came from one of his favorite Old Testament books—Genesis, Psalms, or Isaiah.[33] Equally often, multiple passages were applied to the text to be explicated, and Old and New Testament passages were used in combination. The explication concluded with the interpretation, often allegorical in nature, which this process permitted one to arrive at as the meaning of the original passage.[34] Augustine did not invent the use of Scripture to explain Scripture, but he does apply the method in a systematic way. It certainly became one practical use of his belief that scriptural passages must agree with other scriptural passages.[35]

This type of pattern may, perhaps, be too common to attribute to any one person, or it is even too commonly found to be considered a distinctive pattern. But I would point out that what made this exegetical pattern so common was its widespread transmission through the works of Augustine and the sermons of Caesarius of Arles. The fact that this style of exegesis could be used in a sophisticated manner by a master such as Augustine and still be used effectively by a less well-educated sermon author in the ninth century, offers eloquent testimony to the Carolingian perception of Augustine as a teacher, as does the rapidity with which the pattern spread.[36] Further, most of Caesarius's sermons circulated in the Middle Ages under Augustine's name, further reinforcing the authoritative weight of the pattern and its use.

Not surprisingly, this same exegetical pattern became a fairly common feature of Carolingian sermons. It is found obviously in those sermons which borrow heavily from or adapt excerpts of sermons by Augustine or Caesarius of Arles. It is also present in sermons which use other sources. The sermons of Pseudo-Eligius (edited in *PL* 87), written sometime between 810 and 860, provide good examples.[37] Sermon 4 is based on John's account of Christ washing the feet of the disciples at the Last Supper. The pericope is presented, and drawn out with texts from Hebrews and the Psalms to help reach the interpretation that the washing represents the cleansing of the soul through penitence.[38] The sermon goes on to develop the types and aspects of penance through a further application of the same methods. We can see other examples of this style of exegesis in sermons of Pseudo-Boniface and in the Bavarian and Italian homiliaries.[39] The conclusion I would draw here is that the *DDC*, in conjunction with Augustine's other works, created an exegetical environment which in turn shaped many eighth- and ninth-century sermon texts.

A larger pattern of the *DDC*'s pervasive background influence can be seen in the unfolding of the Carolingian reforms. First, let us briefly reexamine what Augustine sought to accomplish in the first three books. In book 1 he described the message of Scripture as the faith necessary to read Scripture properly and stated that the proper end of this faith was love of God and neighbor. Book 2 dealt with the means required to interpret the unknown literal and figurative signs of Scripture, textual criticism, and the education needed to read and understand the text. Book 3 set out rules for interpreting ambiguous figurative and literal signs and established a pattern for allegorical exegesis. All of this, of course, was intended for the training of those who would teach the Scriptures to others.

This summary also describes the programmatic reforms by which Charlemagne and his advisers sought to renew the Frankish Church. For example, individual chapters of the capitulary *Admonitio generalis* of 789 called for the emendation of corrupt scriptural and liturgical texts and the establishment of schools to train boys in subjects that would allow them to copy texts correctly and read them properly.[40] These matters were pursued in the *Epistola de litteris colendis*, sent to Abbot Baugulf of Fulda in 795, and other legislation.[41] Among the results produced by the legislation were the recensions of the Bible by

Àlcuin and Theodulf of Orléans, and the provision of schools and school texts such as Rabanus's *De institutione clericorum* and the *florilegia* and handbooks previously described.

Above all, the *Admonitio generalis* called upon the clergy to preach on a regular basis. The suggested topics for their sermons listed in chapter 82 included such items as the nature of the Trinity, faith and hope in God, human sins to be avoided, and love of God and neighbor.[42] The topics and their arrangement remind us of Augustine's discussion of faith in book 1.[43] These chapters of the *Admonitio generalis* might not have been taken directly from the *DDC*. They were, however, written by clerics who knew the work well, and they certainly show the influence of Augustine's program.

We may dispute the matter of what "political Augustinianism" really meant, if indeed such a concept existed, and we may also debate precisely what ideas Charlemagne took away from those evening readings from the *City of God* that Einhard described.[44] But I think we risk missing a fundamental understanding of Carolingian religious culture if we fail to perceive the essentially Augustinian atmosphere which shaped and nurtured it. Given the background and training of Alcuin and the other reformers and Charlemagne's own tastes and inclinations, it is not greatly surprising to see the course of scripturally based programmatic reform in the Frankish Church following the scripturally based educational program in Augustine's *DDC*.[45]

Previous interpreters of this work have told us that it had a formative influence on medieval culture. I think we can add some precision to this interpretation by seeing the *DDC*'s influence in the early Middle Ages as normative. The Carolingians ransacked the works of their predecessors to find rules for grammar, the other liberal arts, and exegesis. In terms of how it was read and used, especially by the Carolingians, Augustine's work served as a guide, program, and source of rules for explicating Scripture.

This view does not minimize the importance of the *DDC*. As we have seen, the Carolingians received Augustine's program from a variety of sources, including the work itself. Despite the various means of transmission, the program it contained became, to paraphrase Marrou, a sort of charter for the Carolingian reforms and for the intellectual and educational activities that sought to implement the reform program. It shaped the education and approach to Scripture of compilers of sermon collections and authors of sermons. Augustine's more direct influence on sermon texts came from his own sermons and works such as the *De catechizandis rudibus*, which in turn were formed in the pattern and style of exegesis that he first articulated in the *DDC*. The Carolingians more than amply repaid their borrowings by virtually recreating the manuscript transmission of this text, yet another sign of their intense and active interest in it.[46] In its early steps toward becoming a classic of western culture, the *DDC* literally earned its way as a working tool which Carolingian reformers, masters, preachers, and exegetes used to help shape their own religious culture. In so doing, they also helped to shape the type of influence which the *DDC* would have on succeeding generations.

Appendix:

An "Augustinian" Handbook for Preachers
Paris, BN lat. 10612

1. fol. 2r–4v	*Hi IIII sinodi venerabili id sunt nicena tre centorum XVIII episcoporum habet capet XXIII . . . // . . . et stephano vel sequaces eorum seigium paulum honorium polliciosum.* (Nine lines of prayers follow this work.)
2. fol. 5r–15r	*Incipit Doctrina Dogma Ecclesiastica Secundum Nicenam Concilium. Credimus unam esse deum patrem et filium . . . // . . . libere confitemur imaginem in aeternitate similitudinem in moribus inveniri.* = Gennadius (Ps.-Isidore) *De ecclesiasticis dogmatibus* (PL 83:1227D–1244B).
3. fol. 15–81r	*In Christi Nomine Incipit Expositio Sancti Evangeli Edita Gregorii Papa Urbis Romae. Matheus sicut in ordine primus ponitur . . . // . . . nam homines secundam mensuram accipiunt gratiam spiritui sancti. Explicit Evangelium.* = Ps.-Gregory the Great *Expositio IV evangeliorum*. See Bruno Greisser, "Die handschriftliche Überlieferung der *Expositio IV Evangeliorum* des Ps.-Hieronymus," *Revue Bénédictine* 49 (1937): 278–80 and 314–15.
4. fol. 81r–96r	*Incipit Liber De Interpraetatione Quorundam Nominum Veteris Noviquae Testamenti. Dominio meo et dei servo orosio episcopo*

hysidorus . . . // . . . et interpraetatione aliqua egent breviter.
= Ps.-Isidore *Liber de Ortu et Obitu Patrum* (PL 83:1275B–1294C).

5. fol. 96r–106r   *De Septe Formis Spiritus Sancti. Egrediatur Vir Gadera dic eo esse et flos de radice eius . . . // . . .*

6. fol. 106r–108r   *Incipiunt Questiones de Litteris Vel Singulis Causis. Quia video te de scriptura velle contendere . . . // . . . pars minima est littera pars maxima est deus in aeternum.*

7. fol. 108r–112r   *Incipiamus De Sanctum Scriptuarum. Et a sacrorum numero librorum quanti libri canonici in sancta ecclesia recipiuntur septuagint et duo . . . // . . . Apocrifa autem dicta, id est secreta, quia eorum est origonasta.*

8. fol. 112r–117r   *Incipit Questio De Libri Genesis. Ubi primum in sacris sancta trinitas discribitur? In exordio libri genesis . . . // . . . Idem petit fratres suos ut eius ossa expostarent.*

9. fol. 117r–120r   *Item De Exodo. Quare moyses non alium signum coram pharonem ostendit nisi serpentem . . . // . . . apud se semel locutus est deus quia unum verbum genuit deus.*

10. fol. 120r–121r   *Hii Sunt Grados Septem In Quibus Christos Advenit. Primus lector fuit quando apervit librum isaiae . . . // . . . primum deum plus quam nostras animas diligamur.*
Ed. André Wilmart, *PL Supplementum* 4:943–44.

11. fol. 121r–122v   *De Decimis Offerendis In Genesi. Et dedit decimas ab omnibus suis item illic et vovit iacob . . . // . . . et votum eius super illum et immolat in qui nata domino.*

12. fol. 122v–123v   *Dicta Leonis Episcopi. "Credo in deum patrem . . . filioque precendentem." His tribus sententiis omnium fere hereticorum machine destruuntur . . . // . . . et sactramentum divinum per quod salvati sumus. Explicit Dicta Sancti Gregorii Papae.*

13. fol. 123v–124r   *In expositione origenes super levitico homelia VIII. Christus ergo unum est verbum animo*

caro . . . // . . . et in quo est ipse est et tamen ipsud est.
Not from Origen's *Homily 8 in Leviticus* in the *PG* ed.

14. fol. 124r–128r   *In Christi Nomine Incipit Homelia De Nativitate Domini. Dominus Noster Iesus Christus, Fratres Karissimi, qui in aeternum est . . . // . . . non formationis sed reformationis Ipso adiuvante qui vivit et regnat in s. s. amen.*
= Ps.-Augustine *Sermo* 128 (PL 39:1997–2001).

15. fol. 128r–130v   *Sermo De Epiphania Domini Nostri Iesu Christi. Epiphania Fratres Karissimi Grecum vocabulum est . . . // . . . ad ecclesiam veniat. Praestante domino qui cum patre et spiritu sancto vivit et regnat in s. s. Explicit.*
= Caesarius, *Sermo* 195 (ed. G. Morin, CCSL 104:789–91).

16. fol. 130v–134r   *Admonitio Sancti Agustini Episcopi De Initio Quadregesimi. Rogo Et Admoneo Fratres Karissimi . . . // . . . et hominem que mereavat liberavit. Cui est honor et gloria in s. s. amen.*
= Caesarius *Sermo* 199 (CCSL 104:803–7).

17. fol. 134r–135r   *Sententia De Amore Dei. Qua mensura amandus est christus qui anima nostra post innumera mala . . . // . . . conlaudant creatorem inconspectu domini nostri iesu christu. Ipse nobis hoc praestat qui vivit.*

18. fol. 135r–137r   *Excarpsum De Libro Sancti Effrem Diaconi De Beatudine Anima. Beatus Qui Hodio Habuerit hunc mundum . . . // . . . initium bone vias suscipere quae perducit ad vitam aeternam.*
= Latin version of Ephraim's *De beatudine anima* (see ed. E. Dekkers *Clavis Patrum Latinorum*, rev. ed., [Steenbrugge, 1961], 1143).

19. fol. 137r–140v   *Homelia Sancti Agustini Episcopi. Rogamus vos fratres karissimi ut attentius cogite . . . // . . . et vos feliciter venietis ad regnum. Praestante domino nostro iesu christi qui cum patre et spiritu sancto vivit.*
= Caesarius, *Sermo* 13 (CCSL 103:64–68).

20. fol. 140v–141v *Scarpsum De Libro Sancti Hysidori. Scito Homo Te Met Ipsum Scito quid sis quare sis natus . . . // . . . in omnibus operibus tuis adiutorem et retributionem postula.*
= Isidore *Synonymorum* 2.2–13 (PL 83:845B–848B).

21. fol. 141v–143r *Homelia Sancti Agustini Ad Monachos. Qui inter multos vitam agere constituerunt aut cum grande fructi . . . // . . . dum in saeculo viverimus et aut fiant extrema nostra peiora prioribus.*
= Eusebius "Gallicanus" *Homilia* 42 (ed. F. Glorie, *CCSL* 101A:497–505).

22. fol. 143r–144v *Item Homelia Legenda. Fratres mei dilectissimi necesse est ut aspera sint tempora quare nec ametur terrena felicitus . . . // . . . domino nostro orationem de omnibus reddituri sumus. Ipso praestante.*

23. fol. 144v–146v *Homelia De Duabus Viis. Audistis fratres dilectissimi cum evangelium legeretur . . . // . . . et ad aeternam beatitudinem feliciter. Praestante domino.*
= Caesarius *Sermo* 144 (CCSL 104:609–12).

24. fol. 146v–150r *Homelia Sancti Agustini Episcopi. Fratres karissimi ad memoriam reducimus . . . // . . . Quanta praeparavit dominus diligentibus se. Praestante domino.*
= A Caesarian *centon*, according to G. Morin (see *CCSL* 104:966).

25. fol. 150r–151r *Homelia Legenda. Rogo vos fratres considerate si hodie conventu ecclesias huius aliquis . . . // . . . vel cuius iustitiae gemmis ornati esse mereamur quod ipse prestare dignetur qui vivit et regnat.*
= Ps.-Augustine *Sermo* 229.4–6 (PL 39:2167–2168).

26. fol. 151r–154r *Admonitio Sancti Faustini Ut Semper De Peccatis Nostris Et de Diem Iudicii Vel De Aeterna Beatudine. Modo Fratres Karissimi Cum Divina lectione . . . // . . . in gaudium domini tui. Praestante domino nostro iesu christo.*
= Caesarius *Sermo* 58 (CCSL 103:254–58).

27. fol. 154r–155r   *Homelia Sancti Agustini Episcopi De Contempto Saeculi. "Cum Enim Dormierint homines venit inimicus super seminavit zizania." Inimicus in figura homo dicitur . . . // . . . si quis moritur non habens filium accipiat frater eius uxorem illius et suscitet semen fratris sui.*

28. fol. 155r–157v   *Incipit Ordographia. Ordographia Grecae Latinae recte scriptura interpraetur ordo enim recte graphia . . . // . . . Nam cum iustitia sonum Z littera.*
Ed. J. Thurot, *Extraits de divers manuscrits latins des doctrines grammaticales* (Paris, 1869), 11–15.

Notes

1. H. I. Marrou, *Saint Augustin et la fin de la culture antique* (Paris, 1938), 343–45; E. Hill "*De doctrina christiana:* A Suggestion," *Studia Patristica* 6:446; C. Mohrmann, "St. Augustine and the *Eloquentia,*" in *Etudes sur le latin des chrétiens,* 2 vols. (Rome 1961), 1:351–70; and J. J. Murphy, "St. Augustine and the Debate about a Christian Rhetoric," *Quarterly Journal of Speech* 46 (1960): 400–410. This is, of course, only a very small sample.

2. One of the best surveys of education in the Carolingian period is P. Riché, *Ecoles et enseignement dans le haut moyen âge* (Paris, 1979), pp. 214–66. M. L. W. Laistner, *Thought and Letters in Western Europe, A. D. 500 to 900,* rev. ed. (Ithaca, N.Y., 1957), 189–224, is also useful, although both authors, along with most other writers on the subject, concentrate on similarities with classical education.

3. See the introductions to the editions of *DDC* by J. Martin (*CCSL* 32:xix–xxvii), and W. M. Green (*Sancti Aureli Augustini Opera,* section 6, part 6, *CSEL* 80 [Vienna, 1963], xiii–xxiii); and M. Gorman, "The Diffusion of the Manuscripts of Saint Augustine's *De doctrina christiana* in the Early Middle Ages," *Revue bénédictine* 95 (1985): 11–24. My own citations of the text come from Green's edition.

4. The manuscripts are Paris, Bibliothèque Nationale, MS lat. 2704, written in the last third of the ninth century; and Chartres, Bibliothèque Municipale 118(96), written at the end of the ninth or the beginning of the tenth century.

5. J. J. Contreni, *The Cathedral School of Laon from 850 to 930: Its Masters and Manuscripts,* Münchener Beiträge zur Mediävistik und Renaissance-Forschung 29 (Munich, 1978), 75 and 175; and Gorman, "Diffusion," 20.

6. Pomerius of Arles *De vita contemplativa* 1.21–25 (*PL* 59:435C–440D), which should be compared with *DDC* 3.4–7. For a study of Pomerius's sources

and other analogies, see the notes to M. J. Suelzer's translation of Pomerius in Ancient Christian Writers 4 (Westminster, Md., 1947).

7. Cassiodorus *Institutiones* (ed. R. Mynors [Oxford, 1937]), e.g., praef.7, 1.12.1–2, 1.14.4, and 1.16.4. See also I. Opelt, "Materialien zur Nachwirkung von Augustins Schrift *De doctrina christiana*," *Jahrbuch für Antike und Christentum* 17 (1974): 66–67.

8. Analysis of sources for Isidore's *Etymologiae* by J. Fontaine, *Isidore de Séville et la culture classique dans l'Espagne wisigothique*, 3 vols. (Paris 1959–1983), 1:281–86, shows heavy use of book 4 of *DDC* for its rhetorical and educational materials. See also Opelt, "Materialien," 67–68.

9. Bede *Explanatio Apocalypsis* (PL 93:129D–206A). The citations from Tyconius appear in the prefatory letter to Eusebius (131B–132D), and Bede makes it clear (134A) that he is taking this material directly from Augustine. On the diffusion of this work, see M. L. W. Laister and H. H. King, *A Hand-List of Bede Manuscripts* (Ithaca, N.Y., 1943), 25–30.

10. H. Rochais, "Contribution à l'histoire des florilèges ascétiques du haut moyen age," *Revue bénédictine* 63 (1953): 250–57.

11. See note 2, above; and Contreni, *Cathedral School*, 114–34.

12. Eugippius *Excerpta ex operibus sancti Augustini* (ed. P. Knöll, CSEL 9.1 [Vienna, 1885]). See also the remarks by M. Gorman, "The Manuscript Tradition of Eugippius's *Excerpta ex operibus sancti Augustini*," *Revue bénédictine* 92 (1982): 15–20, on its uses for the text of *DDC*.

13. I. Fransen, "Les commentaires de Bède et de Florus sur l'Apôtre et saint Césaire d'Arles," *Revue bénédictine* 65 (1955): 262–66; and see also her "Description de la collection de Bède le vénerable sur l'Apôtre," *Revue bénédictine* 71 (1961): 22–70.

14. *Rabani Mauri De institutione clericorum libri tres*, ed. A Knöpfler, Veröffentlichungen aus dem Kirchenhistorisches Seminar München 5 (Munich, 1901), is the critical edition. As it is relatively hard to find, I shall also cite from the older edition in *PL* 107.

15. For the change in Latin during the Carolingian period, see R. Wright, *Late Latin and Early Romance*, ARCA Papers and Monographs 8 (Liverpool, 1982), especially 112–19; and for the difference between learning "proper" Latin as opposed to "vulgar" Latin, see P. Riché, *Education and Culture in the Barbarian West Sixth through Eighth Centuries*, trans. J. J. Contreni (Columbia, S.C., 1976), 468–73.

16. Gregory the Great *Registrum Epistolarum* 11.34 (ed. P. Ewald and L. Hartmann, *MGH Epistolae* 1–2, 2 vols. [Berlin, 1887–1899], 2:303); and see Riché, *Education and Culture*, 154–55.

17. Compare Rabanus Maurus *De institutione clericorum* 3.18 and 29 (PL 107:395A–396C and 407C–408C; ed. Knöpfler, 224 and 248) with *DDC* 3.87–89 and 4.25–30.

18. On this point, see also B. Blumenkranz, "Raban Maur et saint Augustin: Compilation ou adaptation?" *Revue du moyen âge latin* 7 (1951): 106–10.

19. Rabanus Maurus *De institutione clericorum* 3.16–31 (PL 107:392B–409B).

20. The work, cited here as Salzburg Handbook, is found in Salzburg, Stifts-bibliothek St. Peter, MS a VIII 32, and the relevant portion is on fols. 113r–122r, which has been edited by K. Forstner, "Eine frühmittelalterliche Interpretation der augustinischen Stillehre," *Mittellateinisches Jahrbuch* 4 (1967): 61–71. I would like to thank Julian G. Plante of the Hill Monastic Manuscript Library for furnishing me a microfilm copy of this manuscript.

21. Compare *DDC* 4.133–38 with the passages in the Salzburg Handbook on fols. 114v–117v (ed. Forstner, "Frühmittelalterliche Interpretation," 63–66).

22. As the compiler makes clear: "Trea igitur dictionum esse genera quemque doctorem ecclesiasticum in sua oportet tenere doctrina. Sumisse id est suaviter quosque ad omne bonum studium incitare. Temperanter [these two correspond to the *lenis et blanda oratio*] id est obsecrando et diligenti studio ammonendo quae bona sunt facienda vel etiam imitanda. Granditer [i.e., *sermo terribilior et disciplinatior*] autem dicendi genus est errantes, ut ad viam veritatis redeant, castigare" (Salzburg Handbook, fol. 117v [ed. Forstner, "Frühmittelalterliche Interpretation," 66]). Note that in describing the *genera dicendi*, the compiler employs only two types, but in summarizing the discussion he returns to the three *Genera* of his original.

23. The series of catalogues for the Bibliothèque Nationale do not yet include this manuscript. For a description of it, see my dissertation, *The Origin and Nature of the Carolingian Sermon* (Michigan State University, 1983), 394–97.

24. This collection is also found in Cologne, Dombibliothek 85; Orléans, Bibliothèque Municipale 313(266); Paris, Bibliothèque Nationale MSS. lat. 614A and 2175; and Zurich, Zentralbibliothek Rh. 99.

25. Riché, *Enseignement,* 246–52; Laistner, *Thought and Letters,* 215–17; and Wright, *Late Latin,* 113–15.

26. I do not mean to argue that the Carolingians did not study rhetoric as part of the trivium, but rather that the idea of a professional teacher of rhetoric as a subject outside of the context of ecclesiastical education would have been incomprehensible to them. For the Carolingian idea of rhetoric, see the introduction to W. S. Howell's *The Rhetoric of Alcuin and Charlemagne* (New York, 1965), which makes the point clearly.

27. On the composition of *DDC*, see P. Brown, *Augustine of Hippo: A Biography* (Berkeley, 1975), 363–66.

28. I concentrate here on sermons. See F. Van Der Meer, *Augustine the Bishop,* trans. B. Battershot and G. Lamb (London, 1961), 405–32, for a good introduction to Augustine as preacher; and M. Avilis, "Predicación de san Agustín: La teoría de la retórica agustinian y la práctica de sus sermones," *Augustiniana* 38 (1983): 401–7.

29. R. Etaix, "Le recueil de sermons composé par Raban Maur pour Haistulfe de Mayence," *Revue des études augustiniennes* 32 (1986): 132–33. Alcuin's *Liber de virtutibus et de vitiis* was also extracted for use in the sermon collection described by J. P. Bouhot, "Un sermonnaire carolingienne," *Revue d'histoire des textes* 4 (1974): 195–96.

30. *DDC* 3.3–24. See also the *collectanea* on the Epistles, referred to above in note 13, which used some of these passages as sources.

31. *DDC* 3.98–134.

32. *DDC* 3.1–9.

33. *DDC* 2.30 and 3.1–2 for what seems to be the first formal setting out of a theory of using Scripture to explain Scripture. For an example of this theory in practice, consider *Tractatus* 12 from Augustine's *In Iohannis evangelium tractatus* (ed. R. Willems, *CCSL* 36 [Turnhout, 1954]), 120–29. In this sermon, preached in 413, Augustine develops the theme from the pericope John 3:6–21 by using six citations from Genesis, three from the Psalms, five from other chapters of John, five from the Pauline Epistles, and four from other books. This is fairly typical of the pattern found in Augustine's other sermons.

34. Augustine *In Ioannis evangelium tractatus* 12 (*CCSL* 36:128–29).

35. *DDC* 3.45.

36. On the structure and spread of this early medieval sermon type, see J. Longère, *La prédication médiévale* (Paris, 1983), 42–46; and see my chapter on early medieval sermons in the forthcoming *Medieval Sermons,* Typologie des sources du moyen age, ed. B. M. Kienzle.

37. There are sixteen sermons attributed originally to Eligius of Noyon but now known to have been written between 800 and 900 by or for an unknown bishop in northern France (*PL* 87:593B–654A).

38. Pseudo-Eligius *Homiliae* 4 (*PL* 87:607A–608D). The sections in question begin with the pericope from John and contain, to develop the theme, citations from three of the Psalms, two earlier chapters from John, two of the Epistles, and Matthew.

39. The sermons of Pseudo-Boniface are found in *PL* 89:843C–872A; and see J. P. Bouhot, "Un sermonnaire carolingien," 187–202; and G. Folliet, "Deux nouveaux témoins du sermonnaire carolingien récemment reconstitué," *Revue des études augustiniennes* 23 (1977): 181–98, for analyses of the Bavarian Homiliary. See also H. Barré, *Les homéliaires carolingiens de l'école d'Auxerre: Authenticité, inventaire, tableaux comparatifs, initia,* Studi e testi 225 (Vatican City, 1962), 19–21.

40. *Admonitio generalis* c. 72 (ed. A. Boretius, *MGH Capitula Regum Francorum* 1 [Hannover, 1883], 60). See also E. P. Pride, "Ecclesiastical Legislation on Education, A.D. 300–1200," *Church History* 12 (1943): 240–42; and R. McKitterick, *The Frankish Church and the Carolingian Reforms 789–895* (London, 1977), 4–7.

41. *Epistola de litteris colendis* (*MGH Capitula Regum Francorum* 1:78–79). See also Riché, *Ecoles et enseignement,* 70–72; and L. Wallach, "Charlemagne's *De litteris colendis* and Alcuin," in *Alcuin and Charlemagne: Studies in Carolingian History and Literature,* Cornell Studies in Classical Philology 32 (Ithaca, N.Y., 1959), 209–11.

42. The chapter contained Charlemagne's program for preaching in which bishops and their priests were to preach belief in the triune God who created all things and to stress the orthodox view of the Trinity. Preachers should also describe the incarnation of Christ and his death and resurrection and tell their people that Christ would sit in majesty to judge each person according to his merits, sending the wicked to eternal flames with the devil and the just to eternal

life. They were also to preach the resurrection of the dead. The capitulary also listed the capital sins, taken from Galatians 5:19–21, and told the bishops to warn their people that those guilty of such crimes could not gain the kingdom of heaven. A list of virtues which were necessary for salvation followed. The list included such things as love of God and neighbors, and charity and confession of sins (*Admonitio generali* c. 82 [*MGH Capitula Regum Francorum* 1:61–62]).

43. *DDC* 1.89–95.

44. For political Augustinianism as applied to the Carolingian period, see H. X. Arquillière, *L'augustinisme politique*, 2nd ed., L'église et l'état au moyen âge 2 (Paris, 1955), 163–64. Einhard *Vita Caroli Magni* 24 (ed. G. Pertz, *MGH Scriptores* 2 [Hannover, 1826], 456) contains the account of Charlemagne listening to *De civitate dei*. For views on what the readings meant to Charlemagne, compare G. B. Ladner, "Die mittelalterliche Reform-Idee und ihr Verhältnis zur Idee der Renaissance," *Mitteilungen des Instituts für Österreichische Geschichtsforschung* 60 (1952): 54 and note 109, with J. Nelson, "On the Limits of the Carolingian Renaissance," in *Renaissance and Renewal in Christian History*, ed. Derek Baker, Studies in Church History 14 (Oxford, 1977), 68–69.

45. On the various motives of Carolingian religious reform, see W. Ullmann, *The Carolingian Renaissance and the Idea of Kingship*, Birbeck Lectures for 1968–1969 (London, 1969), 9–10; E. Delaruelle, "Charlemagne et l'église," *Revue d'histoire de l'église de France* 39 (1953): 181–84; and McKitterick, *Frankish Church*, 2–3.

46. Only the Leningrad Codex, Publichnaya Biblioteka Q.v.I.3, containing books 1–3 of the *DDC*, and some papyrus fragments in Geneva are earlier than 750. Ironically, our earliest witnesses for book 4 are Carolingian. See the works cited in note 3, above.

The *De doctrina christiana* in the School of St. Victor

MARGARET T. GIBSON

"Are there not four labyrinths in France: Peter Abelard, Peter Lombard, Peter of Poitiers, and Gilbert de la Porrée?"[1] The monster that dwells within each labyrinth is an erroneous articulation of the two natures of Christ—as blasphemous and unnatural as the Minotaur himself, half man, half bull.[2] Walter of St. Victor, who thus employs one of the old nightmares of the classical world as an image of christological heresy, is writing in 1177/1178,[3] at the end of half a century of Victorine scholarship. Hugh was active from the 1120s until his death in 1141; Richard, Andrew, and Achard follow him *c.* 1145–1160; Godfrey's *Fons philosophiae* strikes me as juvenilia of the 1150s, while the verses of Adam of St. Victor enlighten the whole period.[4] Walter—well, Walter is something of an embarrassment. His treatise *Contra quattuor labyrinthos franciae* is a comprehensive and impassioned dismissal of the scholastic theology of *c.* 1140–*c.* 1170. Every family has a skeleton in its cupboard; and that is Walter's traditional place in the house of St. Victor. To Glorieux, who edited the *Four Labyrinths* without pausing to think through the metaphor, "on prend sur le vif l'animosité d'un esprit chagrin, aigri, malveillant."[5] Rarely has an author so got under his editor's skin. "Derivative, superficial and harshly expressed," writes Jean Châtillon; "worthless," says Michaud-Quantin.[6] Walter is unworthy of the school of St. Victor and atypical of its scholarly inheritance.

I wonder. Walter was fighting, at the critical point in twelfth-century theological debate, the relation of the two natures of Christ. Did Christ assume his human nature fully (and, if so, how?) or merely "as a garment"? The enquiry continued into the 1220s and 1230s in the work of William of Auxerre and his contemporaries on what came to be called

41

the *hypostatic union*.[7] Walter himself is responding to the pressures of organized secular learning, and specifically to the pressure of scholastic theology. He was unnerved by the showmanship of the nascent university of Paris: "Igitur isti *theatrales*, ut sint ecclesiastici doctores necesse est diuinas artes sequantur, non liberales; apostolos imitantur, non philosophos."[8] Walter hates the style of the secular masters, and he rejects their method of argument quite as forcefully as the content of their teaching. As prior, he spoke for his community, for what he understood to be Victorine orthodoxy: its common premises and its common goal. Walter lays the cards on the table, that the Victorine tradition as such is not compatible with the new scholasticism. Roads that had once seemed parallel (if distinct) were sharply divergent by the 1170s; and every man had to choose one or the other.

For us too it is a straight choice. Either Walter was a self-deluded stray from the Victorine fold (as Glorieux would have it), or his antithesis of Victorine tradition and the schools of the 1170s is essentially valid, even if it is harshly expressed.

The role model for a Victorine—as scholar, teacher, and man of prayer—was in principle Augustine himself, as patron of the canons regular and author of their rule.[9] I say "in principle," because I do not know to what degree there was a cult of Augustine within Augustinian houses. But the Victorines did undoubtedly read his books;[10] and the man who reads and accepts the *De doctrina christiana* cannot in the long run tolerate the method and direction of twelfth-century scholasticism. The *De doctrina christiana* is not the prime Augustinian source for Victorine authors. The *De trinitate*, the *Enarrationes in Psalmos*, and the sermons are far more widely cited. Nevertheless, the positions that Augustine develops in the *De doctrina christiana*—few but non-negotiable—are the basis for Hugh's curriculum, Richard's contemplative writings, and Andrew's exegesis.

"Res ergo aliae sunt quibus fruendum est, aliae quibus utendum, aliae quae fruuntur et utuntur."[11] Everything that we do should be geared to our more complete union with *res quibus fruendum est*, namely, the Holy Trinity. That union cannot be achieved at once or directly; there are many steps on the road. But we should never for ten seconds forget where we are going. The exile returning to his own country must go by chariot and by ship as the route demands.[12] The voyage may be a pleasant one, through fine scenery; let him beware of enjoying that voyage for its own sake—perhaps making a little detour to see the Falls of the Rhine. His job is to get home, and all distractions, however innocent *per se*, cease to be innocent if they hinder him, even momentarily, in that single purpose. The logic is simple and comprehensive, with no escape clauses.

When Hugh of St. Victor wrote the *Didascalicon* (or, when he finally drew it together), he used the same metaphor of exile:

> It greatly strengthens the spirit to learn to *exchange* some visible and transitory things for others, so that they may eventually be given up entirely. That man is weak who still loves his own country, strong if every country is his own, but perfect if the whole universe is but exile to him.[13]

"Mundus totus exilium est." The *Didascalicon* as a whole—*de studio legendi*—is a preparation for devotion, *studium meditandi*. Its wide-ranging contents, its list of Greek and Latin secular authors, its elaborate provision for the liberal and mechanical arts: all these are what Augustine would designate *res quibus utendum est*. Hence the pragmatism of the *Didascalicon*. It is not a complete survey of knowledge; it is what you need to know for a higher purpose. Hugh states his position more clearly and formally as he begins the *De sacramentis*:

> All the arts of the natural world subserve our knowledge of God, and the lower wisdom—rightly ordered—leads to the higher. The trivium serves the literal meaning, the quadrivium the figurative meaning. Above and before all these is that divine being to whom Scripture leads by faith and works; in the knowledge of whose truth and the love of whose excellence man is restored to his true [nature].[14]

Wherever Hugh started out on his educational pilgrimage, the main thrust of his teaching, and his legacy to his successors, was the orderly construction of a road to heaven, through the *artes*: a road on which the further you traveled the lighter your baggage became. Augustine's fundamental distinction of *frui* and *uti*, although it is not explicitly used as a motto, is in practice fully observed.

In the *De doctrina christiana* Augustine reviews the several ways in which we may perceive the truth. Often it is by way of a physical creature or a historical event; thus fully to understand what we are seeing we may need linguistic or technical help. The names in Scripture—Sion, Jericho, Jerusalem; the properties of stones and metals and herbs—how the hyssop clings to the rock, how the carbuncle gives off its own light:[15] any part of that specialized information may be essential for the full understanding of a given text. Indeed, how useful it would be if some public-spirited scholar were to construct a handbook of such data organized by categories and literally explained.[16] The Christian would be spared both tedious work and the dangers of exposure to classical fiction. Isidore of course took up that challenge, and Hugh of St. Victor makes extraordinarily good use of him.[17]

A knowledge of the liberal and mechanical arts, the customs and manners of different peoples, chronology, and foreign languages: all these were justified as *tools* with which to unlock the full meaning of Scripture. The point was fully taken at St. Victor. Hugh begins his exegesis of the Pentateuch with a trenchant criticism of those who in their heart of hearts believe that the Vulgate is more accurate than the Septuagint, and the Septuagint in turn to be preferred to the original Hebrew.[18]

Andrew's exegesis was more specialized in that he had some access to Hebrew, though not to Greek. Moreover he seems to have concentrated on providing scriptural apparatus to the exclusion of all else; he has left no treatises, no letters, no sermons. Commenting, for example, on the first verses of Genesis, he expands Hugh's brief allusion to the three uncreated first principles—God, the exemplar, and matter—into a plain account of the theory of God as craftsman rather than creator, Plato's authorship of this theory, and Aristotle's equally inadmissible alternative.[19] Given this basic information, the reader can understand these verses within the whole context of twelfth-century learning, without himself having to consult either the *Timaeus* itself or a radical contemporary such as Thierry of Chartres. As a scholar, Andrew was the servant of all.

The third great player on the Victorine stage is Richard, who is said to have come from Scotland,[20] to have studied with Robert of Melun at St. Geneviève in the later 1130s.[21] For myself, I see no difficulty in his entering St. Victor *c.* 1137, thus allowing him a few years' direct experience of Hugh and two decades of research before he turned to administration as subprior in 1159.[22] On this chronology, Richard's major works belong to the 1140s and 1150s. For him, above all secular learning had a subordinate role: in Hugh's words, "Omnes artes naturales diuinae scientiae *famulantur*."[23] They are the servants. To quote Richard himself at his most extreme, "Thought is disorganized, idly wandering about here and there: Cogitatio *semper uago motu* de uno ad aliud transit."[24] Note the echo of the inconstant monk in the *Rule of St. Benedict*.[25] *Meditatio* strides purposefully towards its goal; but *Contemplatio* is already there, instantly and effortlessly. The single eye of the contemplative sees clearly what *Meditatio* can grasp only in part, and *Cogitatio* not at all.[26] Richard is not always like this. But he is certainly less interested in *studium legendi* and even *studium meditandi* than in flying free on the wings of contemplation—"circling round and disporting itself at will on the mountain-tops."[27] In Augustine's language, Richard is concerned only with what can and should be enjoyed for itself; he has no spontaneous interest in secular learning, and little need for its service. The best guide here is the *Liber exceptionum*, in which the *artes* rate only a cursory and derivative review in the opening pages.[28]

Hugh, Andrew, and Richard are the backbone of Victorine scholarship. By 1160 they had established a tradition that was steadily in accord with the *De doctrina christiana*, widely though Richard and Andrew might differ in their cast of mind. By 1160 this Victorine tradition was perceptibly at odds with the times. Victorines were not much interested in the discovery of new texts, nor in the refinement of scholastic language and argument. They rarely participated in public debate. Achard's *De trinitate*, which is probably a work of the 1150s, holds a line that is very conservative by comparison with the teaching of Peter Lombard half a mile to the west.[29] By the 1170s the chasm between the Victorine tradition and the schools of Paris could no longer be ignored. It is vividly, if harshly, expressed in the *Four Labyrinths of France*. There Abelard and Gilbert de la Porrée were figures of history, but the Lombard's *Sentences* had textbook status in the nascent university, while the *Sentences* of Peter of Poitiers—the fourth "labyrinth"—were still wet from the press.[30] Walter of St. Victor is not merely giving vent to his own prejudices and emotions (as Glorieux would have it); he is speaking for all the Victorines in the face of the new scholasticism.

At this parting of the ways between monastic learning and the schools, the *De doctrina christiana* afforded a reasoned defense of the monastic tradition. How far it was so used is another question. In the cut and thrust of polemic the instant antitheses, the vivid epigrams, were better supplied by Jerome, in whose words Walter of St. Victor's Christian protagonist confounds his heretical opponent:

> What has light to do with darkness, Christ with Belial, Horace with the Psalter, Virgil with the Gospels, Cicero with Paul? Is not your brother offended if he should see you taking your ease in a temple of idols?[31]

Notes

1. Walter of St. Victor, *Contra quattuor labyrinthos franciae* (ed. P. Glorieux, "Le *Contra quattuor labyrinthos franciae* de Gauthier de Saint Victor," *Archives d'histoire doctrinale et littéraire du moyen âge* 27 [1952], 201).

2. For images of the labyrinth in the twelfth century, see: Haubrichs, *"Error inextricabilis:* Form and Function der Labyrinthabbildung im mittelalterlichen Handschriften," in *Text und Bild,* ed. C. Meier and U. Ruberg (Wiesbaden, 1980), 63–174. Note especially the manuscripts Munich, Staatsbibliothek, CLM 14731; and Paris, Bibliothèque Nationale lat. 12999 and 13013. There is a fine color reproduction of the first in *Regensburger Buchmalerei*—the published

catalogue (Munich, 1987) for an exhibition at Regensburg between 16 May and 9 August 1987—item no. 32.

3. The treatise is dated by Glorieux ("Le *Contra quattuor labyrinthos franciae*," 194–95). Walter, a subprior of St. Victor who became prior in 1173, has attracted little scholarly attention: see F. Bonnard, *Histoire de l'abbaye royale et de l'ordre des chanoines réguliers de St. Victor de Paris*, 2 vols. (Paris, 1907), 1:235, 1:249.

4. Hugh's chronology is well established: J. Taylor, *The "Didascalion" of Hugh of St. Victor: A Medieval Guide to the Arts* (New York, 1961), 36–39; see in detail J. Taylor, *The Origin and Early Life of Hugh of St. Victor: An Evaluation of the Tradition*, Texts and Studies in the History of Medieval Education 5 (Notre Dame, Ind., 1957). For Richard, see notes 20–22, below. Andrew had two periods of scholarly activity in St. Victor, before about 1147 and after about 1154/1155; see B. Smalley, *The Study of the Bible in the Middle Ages*, 3rd ed. (Oxford, 1983), 112–95. For Achard—teaching in the 1140s and 1150s, abbot in 1155—see J. Châtillon, *Théologie, spiritualité et métaphysique dans l'oeuvre oratoire d'Achard de St.-Victor: Etudes d'histoire doctrinale précédés d'un essai sur la vie et l'oeuvre d'Achard*, Etudes de philosophie médiévale 58 (Paris, 1969). For Godfrey, see P. Delhaye, *Microcosmos*, 2 vols., Mémoires et travaux publiés par les professeurs des facultés catholiques de Lille 56 (Lille, 1951)—a study that is open to serious question. For Adam, see F. J. E. Raby, *A History of Christian-Latin Poetry from the Beginnings to the Close of the Middle Ages*, 2nd ed. (Oxford, 1953), 348–55.

5. P. Glorieux, "Mauvais action et mauvais travail: *Contra quattuor labyrinthos franciae*," *Recherches de théologie ancienne et médiévale* 21 (1954): 179–93, at 193. Walter is quite specific that the minotaur is the monstrous *concept* in the tortuous mind of the heretical author: "Queris quid sit labyrinthus. Quo clausus fuit Minocentaurus. . . . Talis Christus istorum phantasticus; etiam deus ipsorum non homo, non deus est; deus est, homo est, neuterque" (Glorieux, "Le *Contra quattuor labyrinthos franciae*," 202). Bonnard took the point (*Histoire de l'abbaye royale*, 1:120–21).

6. J Châtillon, *Galteri a sancto Victore et quorumdam aliorum sermones inediti triginta sex*, CCCM 30 (Turnhout, 1975), 4. P. Michaud-Quantin, "Walter of St. Victor," in *New Catholic Encyclopedia* (New York, 1967), 14:791.

7. The *locus classicus* is Petrus Lombardus *Sententiae* 3.6–7 (ed. I. Brady, 2 vols., Spicilegium Bonaventurianum 4–5 [Grottaferrata, 1971–1981], 2:49–67); see W. H. Principe, *William of Auxerre's Theology of the Hypostatic Union*, Studies and Texts 7 (Toronto, 1963), 64–70; and L. O. Nielson, *Theology and Philosophy in the Twelfth Century* (Leiden, 1982), 246–55.

8. Walter of St. Victor, *Contra quattuor labyrinthos franciae* 4.1 (Glorieux, *Archives d'histoire doctrinale et littéraire du moyen âge* 27 [1952], 270).

9. The *Regula Augustini* itself is authentic but brief (*PL* 32:1377–84); see the critical edition in D. de Bruyne, "La première règle de Saint Benoit," *Revue bénédictine* 42 (1930): 318–26. For the rules of St. Victor in the mid-twelfth century, see the *Liber ordinis sancti Victoris parisiensis*, ed. L. Jocqué and L. Mills, CCCM 61 (Turnhout, 1984).

10. For our current knowledge of the St. Victor library in the twelfth century, see F. Gasparri, *"Scriptorium* et bureau d'écriture de l'Abbaye Saint Victor de Paris," in J. Longère, ed., *L'Abbaye parisienne de Saint-Victor au moyen âge* (Paris and Turnhout, 1991), 119–34, at 132–33, with further references. The fifteenth-century library is recorded in de Grandrue's catalogue (*Le catalogue de la bibliothèque de l'Abbaye de Saint Victor de Paris de Claude Grandrue,* ed. G. Ouy and V. Gerz-von Buren [Paris, 1983]).

11. *DDC* 1.7.9.

12. *DDC* 1.8.10.

13. Hugh of St. Victor *Didascalicon* 2.19: "De exsilio" (ed. C. H. Buttimer, *Hugonis de sancto Victore Didascalicon de studio legendi* [Washington, D.C., 1939], cap. 19, p. 69).

14. Hugh of St. Victor *De sacramentis* prol.6 (*PL* 176:185C–D).

15. *DDC* 2.59–61.50–51.

16. *DDC* 2.141.74. Carlotta Dionisotti drew my attention to this passage.

17. Isidore's *Etymologiae* are the most-quoted source in the *Didascalicon.*

18. Hugh of St. Victor *Adnotationes in Pentateuchon, in Genesim* cap. 1 (*PL* 175:32B).

19. Andrew of St. Victor *Expositio super Heptateuchum* (ed. C. Lohr and R. Berndt, *CCCM* 53 [Turnhout, 1986], 8–9, lines 92–99); cf. Hugh of St. Victor *Adnotationes in Pentateuchon* (*PL* 175:33B).

20. Bonnard, *L'histoire de l'abbaye royale,* 1:116, quoting John of Paris about 1300; and at 1:248, quoting an epitaph of the early sixteenth century ("Quem tellus genuit felici Scotica partu, / Tu fouet in gremio Gallica terra suo").

21. See the letter written jointly by Prior Richard and Abbot Ermiss in the spring of 1164 to Robert of Melun, their former teacher, now bishop at Hereford (*PL* 196:1225A–C).

22. Bonnard, *Histoire de l'abbaye royale,* 1:117. Richard became prior in 1162.

23. Hugh of St. Victor *De sacramentis* prol.6 (*PL* 176:185C–D).

24. Richard of St. Victor *Beniamin maior* 1.3 (*PL* 196:67B).

25. *Benedicti regula* 1.11 (ed. R. Hanslik, *CSEL* 75 [Vienna, 1960], 19): "semper uagi et numquam stabiles et propriis uoluntatibus et guilae inelecebris seruientes."

26. Richard of St. Victor *Beniamin maior* 1.3 (*PL* 196:66C–67B).

27. Richard of St. Victor *Beniamin maior* 1.3 (*PL* 196:66D).

28. Richard of St. Victor *Liber exceptionum* 1.1.7–12 and 1.1.22–24 (ed. J. Châtillon, Textes philosophiques de moyen âge 5 [Paris 1958], 106–9, 111–12).

29. Petrus Lombardus *Sententiarum libri IV* (ed. I. Brady).

30. Petrus Pictauiensis *Sententiarum libri V* lib. 1–2 (ed. P. S. Moore and M. Dulong, 2 vols., Publications in Medieval Studies 7, 11 [Notre Dame, Ind., 1943–1950]; *PL* 211:789–1280).

31. Walter of St. Victor *Contra quattuor labyrinthos franciae* 4.4 (Glorieux, *Archives d'histoire doctrinale et littéraire du moyen âge* 27 [1952], 273).

The Influence of Augustine's
De doctrina christiana upon the Writings
of Hugh of St. Victor

GROVER A. ZINN, JR.

When the canons of the Abbey of St. Victor, located on the left bank of the Seine just outside the twelfth-century walls of Paris, gathered for their main meal, they followed a practice long sanctioned in monastic rules and taken over into their own *Liber ordinis*.[1] As individuals, the canons kept silence during mealtime; as a community gathered in the refectory, they listened to the voice of the *lector* as he read from selected works deemed appropriate for such daily reading. We are fortunate in having for the Victorine community a list that identifies a substantial number of works assigned for reading during meals. Found in chapter 48 of the *Liber ordinis* under the title "De lectione mensae,"[2] the list shows that at mealtime, which was one of the few times outside of a chapter meeting or the daily round of liturgical celebrations when the canons gathered as a group, they listened to the *lector* reading from a prescribed sequence of works, mostly patristic, that tended to be homilies or biblical commentaries. Among the authors whose works are specifically mentioned in this list is Augustine of Hippo, whose homilies and biblical commentaries comprise a significant portion of the yearly cycle of readings. In this distinctive, communal reading and hearing, Augustine was present for the canons in a way set apart from the regular liturgy and periods of instruction or study, each of which also offered numerous opportunities to encounter Augustine's writings.[3]

The yearly plan of readings as given in the *Liber ordinis* begins in Advent and runs through the course of the liturgical year. For some periods of the year the "reading assignment" is stated in purely general terms. For example, from Christmas day to the octave of Epiphany, the *lector* is expected to read from "fitting expositions of the Gospels and sermons for the time."[4] In the event that the work or works assigned for a particular period in the liturgical year turn out to be too short for the time assigned, the *Liber ordinis* instructs the *armarius* to provide the *lector* with additional patristic treatises that are suitable for the period of the year.[5] On feast days of saints their *vitae* and *passiones* are to be read.[6]

There are, however, periods during the year for which the *Liber ordinis* names specific authors and works to be read. Three patristic authors are so named: Augustine of Hippo, Origen of Alexandria, and Gregory the Great. Augustine appears four times on the list, Origen three, and Gregory once by name and perhaps a second time, if the mention of an "exposition of Ezekiel" means Gregory's sermons on Ezekiel.[7]

From the octave of Epiphany until Septuagesima the readings are to be from "the exposition of Augustine on the Psalms."[8] In the two weeks preceding the celebration of Easter, the *lector* is to read from Augustine's "exposition of the passion of the Lord" in addition to reading from Jeremiah, from an unidentified exposition of Lamentations, and from unidentified sermons "on the passion of the Lord."[9] Augustine's exposition of the first letter of John is to be read during Easter week, along with unidentified "sermons and expositions of the Gospel and Epistle [readings] for this week."[10] From the octave of Easter until Ascension the lector reads Augustine's exposition of Paul's Epistles, along with readings from the Apocalypse, canonical Epistles, and Pauline Epistles.[11]

Origen's sermons on Isaiah, on the Old Testament, and on the books of Kings were assigned for reading during three separate periods of the year. The sermons on Isaiah were to be read in Advent, along with readings from Isaiah, the twelve prophets, and "sermons concerning Advent."[12] Origen's sermons on the Old Testament were read from Septuagesima until the second Sunday before Easter; also read during that time were "the five books of Moses and those following up to the books of Kings and expositions of the Gospel [readings] and sermons pertaining to Quadragesima."[13] His sermons on the books of Kings (along with the books of Kings themselves) were the set reading for the period from the octave of Pentecost through the first of July.[14] Along with Origen and the books of Kings, the *lector* also read from Chronicles.

The *Moralia in Iob* of Gregory the Great was prescribed reading for the entire month of August.[15] An exposition of Ezekiel, quite possibly the sermons on that book by Gregory the Great, was assigned from the beginning of November until the beginning of December, along with the books of Daniel and Ezekiel.[16]

The list shows that for approximately two-thirds of the year, the works designated for reading by the *lector* during specific periods of the year included specifically named exegetical works by three great biblical interpreters and preachers from the patristic period. Approximately one-fourth of the year was dedicated to Augustine, slightly less to Origen, and about one-sixth to Gregory, if one assumes the "expositio super Ezechielem" was his.

Augustine's words were heard on a regular yearly schedule by the canons of the Abbey of St. Victor in the context of communal, shared listening. Moreover, this listening was carried out in a setting outside the liturgy and apart from formal study or private reading. As a biblical interpreter and as a preacher, the bishop of Hippo was regularly experienced as a verbal presence integrated into the daily life at the abbey.

I am concerned here only tangentially with the actual commentaries and homiletical works that provided the verbal Augustinian presence in the refectory at St. Victor as the brothers ate in silence while engaged in communal listening. Nevertheless, the established annual cycle of readings in the refectory establishes an Augustinian presence that surrounds, as it were, the Augustinian and Victorine texts that we shall be considering in the analysis that follows.

I

My analysis suggests that, in addition to the more general Augustinian presence that obtained at the Abbey of St. Victor from the round of refectory readings, as well as, perhaps, from formal study and private reading, Augustine's *De doctrina christiana (DDC)* exerted a more specific influence that we can observe in Hugh of St. Victor's exegetical approach. In the *De doctrina christiana* Augustine set down "precepts" to guide readers and interpreters of Scripture in his day as they sought to work out an accurate (or, at the very least, not inaccurate) interpretation of the sacred texts, and he says plainly that the work is concerned with two topics, namely, how to discover what is to be understood when treating of Sacred Scripture and how to teach what one has understood;[17] it seems appropriate, therefore, to seek the influence of *DDC* on Hugh's writings by examining works that address the same concerns. To that end, this paper focuses primarily on the two of his works that have the most to do with the theory and rules of biblical interpretation: the *Didascalicon*[18] and *De scripturis et scriptoribus sacris*.[19] One other text, the preface to Hugh's *Chronicon*, which carries the title *De tribus maximis circumstantiis gestorum*,[20] will also come within our purview in this study.

As one seeks detailed evidence for the nature and extent of Augustine's influence on the *Didascalicon* and *De scripturis et scriptoribus sacris*, one thing becomes apparent very quickly. As a text, *DDC* is conspicuously absent from the group of sources that Hugh either cites directly or draws upon in some way in these two works most connected with exegesis. The author most frequently quoted or paraphrased in passages concerning Scripture in these works is Isidore of Seville, with an occasional passage drawn from Jerome. This is true especially in the chapters listing the canonical books of the Old and New Testaments, giving the authors of biblical books, and defining terms such as *bibliotheca*, *codex*, and the like.[21] Even the presentation of the seven rules of Tyconius in the *Didascalicon* is drawn not from Augustine but rather from Isidore's *Libri sententiarum*.[22]

The absence of any quotations from the text of *DDC* in the *Didascalicon* is set in relief by the attempt of one medieval scribe to add a glimmer of *DDC* to the *Didascalicon*. A manuscript now in the Bibliothèque Mazarine has a marginal gloss that indicates that Augustine also treats the seven rules of Tyconius in *DDC*.[23] The same manuscript also has inserted in book 4, chapter 8, a sentence from *DDC* (2.8.13) concerning the books of Wisdom and Ecclesiasticus.[24]

If there are no quotations from *DDC* in the *Didascalicon* and *De scripturis et scriptoribus sacris*, it seems appropriate to ask what Augustinian texts, if any, are quoted in these works. The only work by Augustine that has been identified as a source for direct citations is *De genesi ad litteram*. Three passages from that work appear, two in the *Didascalicon* and one in *De scripturis et scriptoribus sacris*. Interestingly enough, these three quotations appear in sections of the *Didascalicon* and *De scripturis* that deal directly with basic questions of exegetical method. In them, Hugh is addressing how the well-trained and perceptive exegete ought to seek out the deeper meaning of Scripture. In the *Didascalicon* this deeper meaning is called the *sententia*; in *De scripturis* the deeper meaning is associated with seeking out the meaning of things (*res*) as contrasted with the meaning of words (*verba*).[25]

Chapter 11 of book 6 of the *Didascalicon*, the penultimate chapter in the work, comprises primarily two quotations from *De genesi ad litteram*.[26] Both quotations address the question of adhering to the intended meaning of the author when one discovers that a Scripture passage has more than one deeper meaning, or, as Hugh phrases it here, more than one *sententia*. This is a particularly significant passage, for it turns out to be the only one in the work where Hugh discusses the very important topic of the deeper meaning (*sententia*) of Scripture. The consideration of *sententia* comes after he has devoted a single chapter to each of the other two levels of biblical exposition, "letter" (*littera*) and "sense" (*sensus*). This threefold division of letter, sense, and deeper meaning should be seen as a very particular formulation of levels, or perhaps aspects, of meaning in a text, and is especially to be distinguished from the three "disciplines" of history, allegory, and tropology that Hugh presents in the opening chapters of book 6 of the *Didascalicon*.[27]

In the *Didascalicon* Hugh gives very little attention to, and essentially no explicit guidance in, the actual way in which one should proceed in expounding the text of Scripture. He gives a series of examples of difficulties with passages that are oddly constructed, obscure in language, or (wrongly) judged to have no literal / historical sense.[28] When it comes to the deeper sense, however, Hugh gives, not any guidance (his own or from others) concerning the methods that can be used for allegorical or tropological exegesis (the *sententia*, generally speaking), but rather texts taken from Augustine that address a general question. In this regard *De scripturis et scriptoribus sacris* represents a more complete approach, for in that work methods and techniques for exegesis, especially allegorical exegesis, are more fully explored and explained.

The third quotation (actually a paraphrase) from *De genesi ad litteram* is found in *De scripturis et scriptoribus sacris*.[29] The passage is drawn from the conclusion of Augustine's discussion of the perfection of the number six, a discussion that Augustine carries out in the course of interpreting the six days of creation. In this instance we again discover that Hugh has introduced material drawn from (and attributed to) Augustine at an important juncture in a passage that is directly concerned with the method for eliciting the deeper sense of Scripture. Augustine has been summoned as an authority to introduce the discussion of number as one of the six categories that the well-trained exegete will use in seeking the deeper sense of a Scripture passage. Hugh presents the passage drawn from Augustine to support his assertion that numbers do, in fact, have a deeper signification and, in particular, that the number six signifies perfection.[30]

> Number signifies, as for example, six signifies perfection. Blessed Augustine says, "Six is not a perfect number because God carried out all His works in six days; rather, God chose that number for his working because it is perfect." But because number has a many-sided signification, it should be treated more broadly.[31]

The preceeding analysis has shown that direct citations drawn from the text of *DDC* are not present in Hugh's works that are concerned with biblical interpretation. The absence of direct citations does not mean, however, that the work exerted no influence on Hugh's exegetical theory and practice.

II

At least two instances indicate the probable influence of *DDC* upon Hugh's hermeneutical writings. The first instance is found in Hugh's use, twice, of 1 Peter 5:8, "Watch, because your adversary the devil goeth about as a roaring lion," as an example of how things (*res*), not merely words, have a meaning in Scripture. The second instance is Hugh's use of the categories of person, place, and time when discussing both the order that is to be found in history and the proper method for discerning the deeper, i.e., allegorical and/or tropological, meaning to be found through the close analysis of the significance of things (*res*) in Scripture.

In *DDC* (3.25) Augustine uses 1 Peter 5:8, along with several other passages of Scripture, to illustrate the point that what a thing signifies in one place in Scripture is not necessarily what it will signify in other passages. While *lion* (the thing, not the word) signifies the devil in the passage from 1 Peter, Augustine points out, in a passage like Revelation 5:5, "The lion of the tribe of Juda . . . has prevailed," the lion (again, the thing) has as its deeper signification Christ, not the devil. Other examples of things that have radically different, indeed opposed, significations in various verses of Scripture are leaven, serpent, and bread.

Twice in Hugh's writings (in *Didascalicon* and *De scripturis*) he uses the passage from 1 Peter as the primary illustration of the fact that things have a deeper significance in Scripture. In the *Didascalicon*, book 5, at the outset of the discussion of the properties of Scripture and how it should be read, Hugh presents the idea, derived from Augustine's distinction in *DDC*, that in Scripture not only words but also things have a further significance.[32] Indeed, as Hugh puts it, "the philosopher knows only the significance of words," while Scripture is such that not only do words signify things, but things themselves signify other things as a deeper meaning. Having said this, Hugh then laments that "less well-instructed persons" take no account of this deeper dimension of Scripture and suppose that the Bible has no subtle meaning concerning divine things but only a surface, literal sense. To counter such a deficient understanding of Scripture, Hugh quotes 1 Peter 5:8 and points out that in this verse it is the thing *lion*, not the word *lion*, that stands for the devil. As he summarizes, "It remains, therefore, that the word *lion* signifies the animal, but that the animal in turn designates the devil. And all other things are to be taken after this fashion, as when we say that worm, calf, stone, serpent, and other things of this sort signify Christ."[33]

Hugh's emphasis on the signification of things in Scripture, which follows so closely the Augustinian formulation of the distinction between words and things, works in two quite different ways in the course of the argument of the *Didascalicon*. On the one hand, it sets Scripture apart from other writings. Philosophy works only with the signification of words; the student of Scripture can find the deeper signification of things as an added dimension of knowledge. On the other hand, Hugh presents a point of view that sees the literal sense as a stumbling block for many, who might read it and find very little concerning "divine" or "subtle" matters and then turn instead to the philosophers. Hugh's call to these "less well-instructed persons" is that they pay attention to the deeper meaning of things in Scripture. In connection with this exploration of the deeper meaning of things they will find the discussion of divine things for which they long.

In later writings, for instance in *De scripturis*, Hugh presents the narration of sacred history as the characteristic that sets Scripture apart from other literature.[34] In the *Didascalicon* he says explicitly that the philosophers (who have only words) seem to discourse at length on topics related to God and spiritual goods (Hugh speaks of "the eternity of God and the immortality of souls," "eternal rewards," and "eternal punishments"), while the Scriptures seem to be concerned mostly with "the state of this life and . . . deeds done in time, while rarely is anything clearly to be drawn from them concerning the sweetness of eternal goods or the joys of the heavenly life."[35] This characterization of Scripture shows that when he wrote the *Didascalicon*, Hugh had not yet developed his mature appreciation of the historical narration of the works of redemption as the core meaning of Scripture and the basis of its presentation as a unique, sacred text. The *Didascalicon* insists upon the fundamental importance of reading the Bible in its historical meaning, and the place of that reading as the first way in which the Bible is to be read by the student. However, the theoretical place of history as a category in Hugh's thought and hermeneutic was yet to be worked out.

That the consideration of the signification of things, supported by the citation of 1 Peter 5:8, is followed immediately in the *Didascalicon* by a presentation of the seven rules of Tyconius lends some further support to the idea of an Augustinian influence of some sort. In *DDC*, Augustine follows the citation of 1 Peter 5:8 and several other examples of diverse, indeed opposed, deeper meanings for the same thing, with a few more remarks on ambiguous meanings of things and the usefulness of an understanding of tropes in biblical interpretation. Then, to close his discussion of the first topic of *DDC*, namely, "the way of discovering the things that are to be understood," Augustine presents an account of the rules of Tyconius.[36] In a similar way, immediately after the discussion of how things signify other things, Hugh introduces the seven rules of Tyconius in a summary fashion, but based on the version given by Isidore of Seville, not the version by Augustine.[37]

Following the rules of Tyconius, Hugh concludes book 5 of the *Didascalicon* with a series of instructions having to do not with techniques for reading texts but with students, their behavior, goals, etc.[38] In book 6 he devotes all but two brief chapters to the topic of the order in which one studies the disciplines of Scripture interpretation (history, allegory, tropology), the order in which one reads the biblical books in these disciplines, and, finally, the order in which one expounds the biblical text (i.e., letter, sense, deeper meaning [*sententia*]). The penultimate chapter of book 6 is a brief chapter devoted to the method (*modo*) of expounding a text. The final chapter considers the "second part" of learning, following upon reading, namely, meditation, which Hugh declares he will not treat in that work. Thus the closing portions of book 5 and almost all of book 6 reflect the concerns of a teacher either dealing with pupils or establishing a curriculum of readings (the order of readings, etc.) rather than of an exegete explicating a method of interpretation. Only in the final chapters of book 6, the chapters on letter, sense, and deeper meaning, and the chapter on method (*modo*), do we get a glimpse beyond the curriculum to how one reads a text—but it is only a glimpse.

If we turn now to the presentation of exegetical theory in *De scripturis et scriptoribus sacris*, we find that Hugh's point of view and concerns have undergone some change since the *Didascalicon*. First, Hugh argues at great length, and more forcefully than in the *Didascalicon*, about the centrality of a proper understanding of the signification of things in the interpretation of Scripture. Second, he proposes that Scripture's most important characteristic is the fact that through the narrative of deeds done in time it gives an account of the "works of redemption" which are presented in the history recounted in the biblical text; the writings of the philosophers (seen in the *Didascalicon* as so beguiling with their talk of divine things) are now viewed as giving only an account of the "works of creation," i.e., the world as created and known through ordinary experience.[39] Thirdly, person, time, and place become primary categories for understanding both the literal and the symbolic senses of the biblical text.

When considering the relation of word, thing, and deeper signification in *De scripturis*, Hugh enters into a highly charged and very polemical presentation. In chapter 5 he attacks persons whom he judges to be violating the rules of proper signification.[40] There are those, says Hugh, who want to go directly from the word *lion* to the allegorical meaning *Christ*. They argue that since a lion sleeps with its eyes open, the word *lion* signifies Christ. But, as Hugh points out, it is not the spoken expression *lion* that sleeps with its eyes open but the animal itself. Hugh is attempting to restore the middle term in a relationship which he sees as comprising a three-member set in which one thing (the word) signifies a second thing (the animal lion), by which the third thing (the person of Christ) is signified. This is, of course, precisely what Augustine was working with in book 3 of *DDC* and is the presupposition of his interpretation of the signification of 1 Peter 5:8. Only by first understanding fully what the word, as word, signifies (a person, place, deed, or the like) can a person then advance to the next stage to ascertain the deeper meaning which is signified by the thing that is signified by the word.

By means of the extended analysis and argumentation carried out in *De scripturis*, Hugh has done much more than take over Augustine's example of the deeper meaning of the thing *lion*. Hugh has used the Augustinian material to face a new problem and define its solution. Hugh wants to focus on the need to recover a sense of the reality of "deeds done in time" as the key foundation for all exegesis and, indeed, all theology. The fact that Scripture deals with the *materia* of history as its main topic, a topic that was perceived as something of a stumbling block in the *Didascalicon*, becomes a primary datum in Hugh's new view of the exegetical task. Closing his argument for recovering the missing middle term in the set of three elements of signification in exegesis, Hugh uses two biblical citations to drive his point home.[41] The first is from Paul's first letter to the Corinthians: "first comes the fleshly, then the spiritual" (1 Cor. 15:46); the second is a reference to the clay that Jesus used to cure a blind man, a miracle narrated in the Gospel of John, chapter 9. Only through the *materia* of the world (signified by the clay used by Jesus) can the invisible goods of God be grasped. And in order to grasp both the *materia* and the invisible goods, one needs a principle of order and method.

Hugh may well have found a significant clue for both order and method in book 3 of *DDC*, in the passage in which Augustine advises those who seek to understand the things (*res*) of Scripture to pay careful attention to "what is proper to times, places, and persons."[42] The immediate context of Augustine's observation is the problem of distinguishing deeds that may be permitted at one time and illicit at another, for instance the multiple wives of the patriarchs as recorded in the book of Genesis. But the point to be observed is that at a key juncture in analyzing the practice of biblical interpretation, Augustine used the specific characteristics of times, places, and persons to make fundamental distinctions that would guide exegesis. These characteristics of time, place, and person are, of course, part of the classical rhetorical tradition, for they are among the means to be used to amplify an argument. In addition, they form three components of one of the schemes for the genre of *accessus ad auctores*, or introductions to authors, that became so popular in the schools of the twelfth century to introduce both secular authors and commentaries on biblical books.[43] However, the application of the terms by Augustine in such an explicit manner to an exegetical problem would suggest an Augustinian background for Hugh's use.

In *De scripturis*, when Hugh affirms in chapter 14 that Scripture is set apart by the fact that in it things have a further signification, he immediately presses on to explain how that deeper sense is to be sought—without the rules of Tychonius that concluded the discussion of the significance of things in the *Didascalicon*. In *De scripturis* this search for the deeper sense is to be carried out by inquiring about the meaning of things under the categories of thing, person, number, place, time, and deed. The explication of these categories, with their significance and application to Scripture, includes a citation from Augustine's *De Genesi ad litteram liber imperfectus* (concerning the symbolism of *number*) in connection with Hugh's analysis of number as applied to exegesis.[44] Hugh explains each of the categories, or "circumstances," in some detail, offering his longest discussion of method in any of his hermeneutical works. Each category is accompanied with examples of characteristics or scriptural instances so that the student can draw conclusions concerning how to apply the category.

In another work written after the *Didascalicon* and connected with exegesis, *De tribus maximis circumstantiis gestorum, id est persona, locus, et tempus* (the preface to Hugh's *Chronicon*), we find the three categories of person, place, and time again prominently displayed and used by Hugh.[45] In this case, person, place, and time are the key circumstances that define history as the ordered sequence of "deeds done in time" that are the "foundation of the foundation," or the foundation for the discipline of reading Scripture according to the literal/historical sense. However, in the *Didascalicon*, the "facts" of history are likened to a jumbled and disordered set of stones placed underground to support the first carefully fitted and finished stones that make up the base of the wall of theology.[46] In the preface to the *Chronicon* the "facts" of history are seen (in contrast to the earlier view in the *Didascalicon*) as an ordered whole that provides the basic substructure for the unfolding of the divine work of salvation in time. Just as the *Didascalicon* fails, as we have seen, to find an intrinsic principle that defines Scripture as sacred whereas *De scripturis* finds that principle in the definition of the ordered *materia* of the "works of restoration" as unfolded in history, so in the *Didascalicon* the literal sense of the text as historical event has not yet taken on the full meaning and ordered structure it comes to have in *De tribus maximis*. The order in history (person, place, and time) enables it to serve as the foundation of the foundation in the conceptual scheme of *De tribus*.

Augustine had, in *DDC*, provided the clue for using person, place, and time as categories useful in defining "how to discover what is to be understood in Scripture." In *De scripturis*, especially, but also in *De tribus maximis*, we can see Hugh taking the clue and turning it into the key.

Notes

1. L. Jocqué and L. Milis, eds., *Liber ordinis sancti Victoris Parisiensis*, CCCM 61 (Turnhout, 1984).

2. *Liber ordinis* (CCCM 61:211–15); cited hereafter as *LO*.

3. For the early history of the abbey and school, see Jean Châtillon, *Théologie, spiritualité et métaphysique dan l'oeuvre oratoire d'Achard de Saint-Victor: Etudes d'histoire doctrinale précédés d'un essai sur la vie et l'oeuvre d'Achard*, Etudes de philosophie médiévale 58 (Paris, 1969), 53–85. Still useful is Fourier Bonnard, *Histoire de l'abbaye royale et de l'ordre des chanoines réguliers de Saint-Victor de Paris*, 2 vols. (Paris, 1904–1907). See also the essays in Jean Longère, ed., *L'abbaye parisienne de Saint-Victor au moyen âge*, Biblioteca Victorina 1 (Paris and Turnhout, 1991).

4. *LO* (CCCM 61:212, lines 17–19).

5. *LO* (CCCM 61:214, lines 49–52).

6. *LO* (CCCM 61:214, lines 52–53).

7. See below, at note 16.

8. *LO* (CCCM 61:212, lines 19–20). Cf. Augustine *Enarrationes in psalmos* (ed. E. Dekkers and J. Fraipont, CCSL 38, 39, 40 [Turnhout, 1956]).

9. *LO* (CCCM 61:212, lines 24–27).

10. *LO* (CCCM 61:212, lines 27–30).

11. *LO* (CCCM 61:212–13, lines 30–32).

12. *LO* (CCCM 61:212, lines 15–17). Among the manuscripts from Saint-Victor that are preserved in the Bibliothèque National, Paris, are several twelfth-century manuscripts that contain works of Origen (for example, Paris, BN lat. MS 14286).

13. *LO* (CCCM 61:212, lines 20–24).

14. *LO* (CCCM 61:213, lines 35–37).

15. *LO* (CCCM 61:213, lines 40–41).

16. *LO* (CCCM 61:214, lines 45–47). Jean Longère accepts the reference as being to Gregory's sermons on Ezekiel (see "La fonction pastorale de Saint-

Victor à la fin du XIIe et au début du XIIIe siècle," in *L'abbaye parisienne,* 295).

17. See *DDC* 1.1.1 (*CCSL* 32:6–7). Augustine repeats the two things needed for the interpretation of Scripture (4.1.1 [*CCSL* 32:116]).

18. Hugh of St. Victor *Didascalion* (*PL* 176:741–812). *Hugonis de Sancto Victore Didascalicon de studio legendi: A Critical Text,* ed. Charles Henry Buttimer (Washington, D.C., 1939). *The "Didascalicon" of Hugh of St. Victor: A Medieval Guide to the Arts,* trans. Jerome Taylor (New York, 1964).

19. Hugh of St. Victor *De scripturis et scriptoribus sacris* (*PL* 175:9–28); cited hereafter as *DSSS.*

20. Ed. W. M. Green, in "Hugo of St.-Victor: *De tribus maximis circumstantiis gestorum,*" *Speculum* 18 (1943): 488–92.

21. See Buttimer, 137–38 ("Index locorum: Auctores"). See the notes in Taylor, 216–19, for *Didascalicon,* book 4, which confirm and give more detail on the use of Isidore and Jerome. My examination of relevant chapters of *De scripturis et scriptoribus sacris* reveals the same basic dependence on Isidore.

22. The *Rules* of Tyconius are given by Augustine in *DDC* 3.30–37, where they compose the concluding chapters of book 3 and, indeed, the conclusion of the treatment of the first necessary matter, namely, the "way of discovering those things which are to be understood" in Scripture (trans. Robertson, 117). Book 4 treats the "way of teaching what we have learned" (trans. Robertson, 117).

23. See Buttimer, p. xxvii, with reference to Paris, Bibliothèque Mazarine, MS 732 (Buttimer's MS A), from the twelfth century.

24. Cf. Buttimer, 82, with the note in textual apparatus for line 23.

25. In the *Didascalicon,* Hugh's attention in 6.11 to the *sententia* of Scripture (Buttimer, 128–29; Taylor, 149–50) is paralleled in 3.8 by a consideration of the *sententia* of literary texts (Buttimer, 91–92; Taylor, 58).

26. The passages Hugh quotes are from *De genesi ad litteram* 1.21 (*PL* 34:262) and 1.18 (*PL* 34:260). Cf. Taylor (150, and notes 50 and 51 on 225). Buttimer (129) identifies only the first passage as a quotation.

27. For *littera,* cf. *Didascalicon* 6.9 (Buttimer, 126; Taylor, 147–48). For *sensus,* cf. *Didascalicon* 6.10 (Buttimer, 126–27; Taylor, 148–49). Hugh's distinction between the three divisions of exposition (letter, sense, and deeper meaning) and the three disciplines (history, allegory, and tropology) for the study of Scripture is crucial for grasping his concept of order in study and in interpretation. The distinction has been neither appreciated nor studied sufficiently. For disciplines, cf. *Didascalicon* 6.1–5 (Buttimer, 113–23; Taylor, 135–45). In addition, the topics of order in the disciplines and order in the exposition of a text are also considered in book 3 of the *Didascalicon,* in the concluding portion of Hugh's discussion of the study of philosophy (see *Didascalicon* 3.8–9 [Buttimer, 58–59; Taylor, 91–92]). There are important parallels, as well as distinctions, between the uses of these topics in books 3 and 6.

28. *Didascalicon* 6.10 (Buttimer, 126–28; Taylor, 148–49).

29. *DSSS* 14 (*PL* 175:21D).

30. Augustine addresses the figurative meaning of numbers in scripture in *DDC* 2.16.25 (*CCSL* 32:50–51).

31. *DSSS* 14 (*PL* 175:21D). The passage from Augustine is from *De Genesi ad litteram liber imperfectus* 4.7.13. A translation is found in John Hammond Taylor, trans., *St. Augustine: The Literal Meaning of Genesis,* 2 vols. (New York and Ramsey, N.J., 1982), 1:122.

32. Cf. *Didascalicon* 5.3 (Buttimer, 96–97; Taylor, 121–22). Books 2 and 3 of *DDC* are devoted to the analysis of words and things as signs.

33. *Didascalicon* 5.3 (Buttimer, 97; Taylor, 122).

34. For the dating of Hugh's writings, and specifically for the dating of the *Didascalicon* as earlier than *De scripturis,* see Damien van den Eynde, *Essai sur la succession et la date des écrits de Hugues de Saint-Victor* (Rome, 1960).

35. *Didascalicon* 4.1 (Buttimer, 70–71; Taylor, 102–3).

36. *DDC* 3.30–37 (*CCSL* 32:42–56).

37. See Isidore *Libri sententiarum* 1.19.1–19; see notes in Buttimer and Taylor, for *Didascalicon* 5.4. The use by Hugh of the version of the *Rules* in Isidore of Seville, rather than the version given in *DDC* renders the claim for the influence of *DDC* at this point weaker than it might be.

38. *Didascalicon* 5.5–10 (Buttimer, 102–12; Taylor, 126–34).

39. *DSSS* 1–2 (*PL* 175:9–11D).

40. *DSSS* 5 (*PL* 175:13A–15A).

41. *DSSS* 5 (*PL* 175:14D–15A).

42. *DDC* 3.12.18–20.

43. See A. J. Minnis, *Medieval Theory of Authorship: Scholastic Literary Attitudes in the Later Middle Ages,* 2nd ed. (Philadelphia, 1988). Minnis discusses a type of *accessus* or prologue used by Remigius of Auxerre that drew upon the seven rhetorical circumstances for its categories. The use of these seven categories, or a shortened series of three (person, place, and time) by Remigius is not at all the same as the use to which Augustine and Hugh put the categories of person, time, and place in their exegetical theory and practice. Moreover, Minnis (17, at note 60) has misunderstood Hugh's use of the categories of person, time, and place in his introduction to his *Notulae* on Leviticus (*PL* 175:74A–C). Minnis represents this use as a typical *accessus* use, i.e., concerned with the author, the place of writing, and the time of writing. For Hugh, these three categories serve, in that particular introduction, to furnish categories for organizing the material in the Book of Leviticus in a systematic fashion, in order to "reduce" the content to some sort of memorable order, one suspects.

44. See above, n. 31 and related text.

45. See above, note 20. Van den Eynde (*Essai*) dates *De tribus,* like *De scripturis et scriptoribus sacris,* after the *Didascalicon.*

46. *Didascalicon* 6.4 (Buttimer, 140–41; Taylor, 140–41).

Hugh of St. Victor:
The Augustinian Tradition of Sacred and Secular Reading Revised

EILEEN C. SWEENEY

In this essay I would like to speculate about the ties between Hugh of St. Victor's *Didascalicon* and Augustine's *De doctrina christiana*. I should rather say, in the tradition of both works, that I wish to offer a parallel reading of these two works that is guided more by the principle of charity than the letter, more by doctrinal, than historical, connections. I take the title of this paper and its reference to reading quite literally, for I want to argue (or rather, read) these two texts as offering an account of 'reading' both in the literal sense of advising the Christian on what and how to read, but as offering at the same time a reading and interpretation, not only of sacred and secular texts but of the text of the world and our lives. What I propose, in other words, is a reading of Augustine and Hugh which has both a literal and a figurative level. At the literal level, what we find in these two works are ways of integrating secular texts into Christian education, and of structuring that Christian education into a more formal program of study; what changes at the literal level from Augustine to Hugh is not the aim of integration between the two realms but the context and mode of such integration.

At a deeper level, however, what we find in both texts is that reading is the ruling metaphor or model for understanding and action. To paraphrase Wittgenstein, all problems of philosophy are for Hugh and Augustine problems of interpretation. Thus, the literal advice about reading and interpretation given by Augustine and Hugh has another meaning; it becomes a figure for morality and, reflexively, for their own work. In Augustine the errors of superstition, idolatry, fundamentalism, and materialism, the sins of pride and concupiscence are forms either of misinterpretation, the taking of signs for the wrong things, or of noninterpretation, of the taking of signs for things. The subtext of his text, its figurative meaning, seems to be to remind us of the constant temptation to take signs as things, to reify, and hence to deify, everything; this applies to our own interpretations and understandings and, Augustine reminds us, to his as well.

In Hugh these themes take a slightly different and more structured form; instead of turning morality into a problem of interpretation, Hugh translates reading into a moral project, the academic life into the Christian life. Hence, understanding, the soul, and the soul's path toward salvation itself are made symmetrical to the path of reading, mirroring the levels of meaning from literal to allegorical and tropological. Thus not only is Christian education described literally as a course of reading, but its stages also follow the stages of reading, from an inadequate grasp of things because of an ignorance of signs, to the understanding of things *via* signs, to the reinterpretation of things as signs pointing beyond themselves. However, because at best we only move beyond signs in a relative rather than absolute sense, we can never be certain of, nor reach a point of rest in, our interpretations. Thus progress on the path of interpretation/salvation is not continuous and unidirectional; it is always necessary to return to the beginning again to reground, expand, and multiply interpretations, a structure and restructuring that applies to Hugh's interpretations.

This way of interpreting both of these works gives them a kind of unity they seem to lack otherwise. The traditional formulations of the 'problem' of DDC focus on its genre and intended audience; the same questions could and perhaps should have been raised about the *Didascalicon*.[1] Both texts contain moral and exegetical principles, histories of the secular arts, basic descriptions of the content of faith and the workings of the mind—diverse material that has frustrated those looking for a handbook on exegesis, preaching (or in Hugh's case, prayer), or curricula. The logic of these texts and the topics they consider must be more than a loose connection of these matters to education; what unites them, I contend, are the notions of reading and interpretation. The diverse topics find their place in these texts as texts to be read, as principles to be used in interpretation, or, more often, as both. What Hugh and Augustine realize is that reading both secular and sacred texts requires exposure to more than the texts themselves, and more than literal texts can be 'read' and interpreted; hence 'signs' and 'things' must be linked. It is the way they become linked in both texts, united by the model of interpretation in which everything becomes a text to be read and a thing to be used in the interpretation of texts, that I wish to trace in this essay. But as both Augustine and Hugh would warn, such claims, claims about the more than literal meaning of their work, need to be grounded in the letter of the text, so I begin, as one must, with the letter before I proceed to the spirit.

The Literal Level:
The Role and Method of the Arts
and Scripture

If we start with a glance at the structure of the two texts, we immediately get a sense of what binds them together as well as separates them. The first three books of Augustine's *DDC* are concerned with the order of discovery, and the fourth with teaching. The first, then, has as its subject things (God); the second and third, signs. The problem of the text is the interpretation of the signs in Scripture; the second book describes the arts from secular culture which can help in this task. The third focuses on principles and examples for moving between the literal and figurative levels of meaning, offering a hermeneutic for Scripture. Of these first three books Hugh offers a rewriting, both literally and figuratively. The first effect of that rewriting is a splitting of Augustine's three books into six, three each dedicated to secular and sacred reading; within each half and for each realm, Hugh's text accomplishes the same three tasks: Just as Augustine opens with an account of 'things', some to be enjoyed (the Father, Son, and Holy Spirit), others to be used (all else, even ourselves and others), Hugh first discusses the 'things' that give learning its *telos* and context, describing God as the end and Christ as the means to that end.[2] Secular and sacred learning serve that end either in restoring what is divine in our nature or in relieving our all-too-human weakness.[3] Second, then, both place the arts within the context of Christian education, Augustine seeing them as things to be used, as instruments for the interpretation of Scripture, Hugh describing them as serving the ends of restoration and relief. Lastly, just as Augustine lays out guidelines for interpretation, so does Hugh.

What is already clear at the formal level, that the arts, to which Hugh gives both separate and equal treatment, have a greater role to play in Hugh than they do for Augustine, is borne out at a more substantive level. Augustine's intent in *DDC* is to set out the rules to guide the faithful in the reading and teaching of Scripture. In a general sense, the arts fit into his plan as signs rather than things. Like things to be used rather than enjoyed, signs are, for Augustine, simply vehicles to a goal; he warns his readers not to take too much delight in the mode of transportation lest they forget the destination.[4] For Augustine, the arts help us to reach the third step along the road to wisdom, knowledge. In order to understand revelation, we must be able to discern the meaning of unknown literal or figurative signs.[5] Languages are learned so that we may interpret unknown literal signs; to understand unknown figurative signs, we need a knowledge of languages and of things.[6] Thus, Augustine explains, we need a knowledge of physics because we need to know the natures of animals, plants, or stones that are mentioned in Scripture.[7] Knowledge of mathematics is necessary for the interpretation of numerical expressions used figuratively.[8] The arts of disputation (rhetoric and dialectic) are to be learned because rhetorical and dialectical arguments are used in Scripture (e.g., in the Epistles of St. Paul) and because knowledge of valid argument forms and rhetorical devices will teach one to distinguish good arguments from bad and will help us to avoid being duped by sophists.[9] The arts, then, are signs for the interpretation of further signs, either the words of Scripture or the things named by those words, which are in turn signs of the divine. Hence, unlike Hugh, Augustine's main concern cannot be to give a division of the arts intrinsic to their nature; they are signs used in the interpretation of Scripture and, as such, have their value and nature from Scripture's structure, not their own.

Augustine does offer a more systematic account of the arts, but it places them even more firmly in the realm of signs rather than things. The human arts are either established by God (and discovered by humankind) or instituted by humanity; some of them are superstitious, some useful, conventions.[10] Those instituted by God are subdivided into those that pertain to the senses and those that pertain to reason.[11] History, or the writing about past times, and the description of present time (writings about places, animals, plants, stones, stars, etc.) pertain to the senses, as do the mechanical arts.[12] The sciences of disputation and numbers pertain to reason.[13]

Though this division seems to be of the arts *per se*, it is nonetheless a division based on their status as signs and hence as related to and dependent on things. Their division fills out the division based on the distinction between *signa data* and *signa naturalia* which opens *DDC* book 2.[14] The arts instituted by human beings function as signs merely by agreement (*signa data*) and as representing an artificial order; those established by God are signs which represent the natural or created order. But both are signs. Moreover, more and more falls ultimately into the category of signs by agreement and convention since, Augustine notes, human discourse about the natural or created order, and Scripture itself, because transmitted through human language, are both *signa data* even though about *signa naturalia*.[15] And for Augustine more than language *per se* falls into the category of conventional signs; so do practices, clothing, money, and weights, for example.[16] The most important feature of all signs, but especially those of human invention, is the uncertainty of their relationship to their referents.[17]

Furthermore, even in the context of discussing the arts in their own terms, Augustine emphasizes that the arts have two legitimate purposes; either they help in the interpretation of Scripture, or the information they yield will be helpful in our familial, social, or political life.[18] He summarizes his account of the arts and their usefulness by likening them to the ornaments, food, and clothing taken from the Egyptians in the Exodus to be put to a better use by the chosen people. The student is reminded, however, that "although he comes forth rich from Egypt, unless he carries out the Pasch, he cannot be saved."[19] The riches of pagan culture do not, in other words, constitute the 'things' in and through which salvation comes about.

From the opening of the *Didascalicon*, it is clear that Hugh has a greater role in mind for philosophy and the arts than their being servants in the interpretation of Scripture. Hugh begins by defining philosophy as the love of wisdom and as "the discipline which investigates fully the ideas (*rationes*) of all things human and divine."[20] All human action is, for Hugh, correctly directed toward two ends: the restoration of our nature and the relieving of our weakness.[21] When we seek to restore what is divine in our nature, we attempt to discover truth and virtue; the speculative and practical arts are devoted to these; the mechanical arts are designed to minister to our finite human nature by helping us overcome the difficulties present in this life. Hugh then adds logic to this threefold division of philosophy because, he notes, true wisdom cannot be pursued unless we have learned to reason correctly.[22] His derivation of the four parts of philosophy (speculative, practical, mechanical, and logical) from an examination of human nature and its ends serves to place the arts and sciences as paths to the fulfillment of our nature. His account of the parts of knowledge or philosophy gives substance to the plan that the structure of the book suggests: that the reading of secular texts forms an integral and not merely instrumental part of Christian education.

Despite these differences, I want to maintain that Hugh has carried out, rather than contradicted, albeit in a new time and context, Augustine's exhortation that pagan knowledge should be converted to Christian uses and purposes. Hugh's outline of the conversion is different from and, on the surface at least, more complete than Augustine's perhaps only because Hugh is confronting an age where the arts are receiving an unparalleled amount of attention and concern, a context in which Augustine's answers must be rearticulated to form a credible alternative to the undisciplined invasion of the arts and their methods into the educational program.[23] The image of the arts as unruly maids converted into helpful and obedient handmaidens of theology is, of course, a stock metaphor. Hugh, however, converts the cliché into a reality by working out the mechanics of their conversion, or rather re-conversion, in a carefully thought-out fashion.

But if Hugh must reformulate the nature and role of the arts, he must also reformulate the structure and method of sacred study. Here the changes are perhaps less radical since Augustine has already taken up the task of offering a set of principles to guide others in the interpretation of Scripture rather than simply another interpretation of it. Having assimilated the ends of the arts to restoration and salvation, Hugh's most important addition is the division of sacred study into like 'disciplines' also aiming at this end. Like Augustine, for Scripture Hugh gives information and advice on such scholarly matters as translations, canonical books, etc.[24] Hugh, however, once again goes a step further than Augustine in attempting to develop a systematic division of Scripture to parallel that of the arts. Connecting Scripture as well as the arts with the pursuit of knowledge and virtue, Hugh divides both temporally and logically. It is divided in the first way into the Old and New Testaments which have as their subjects the works of creation and restoration, respectively.[25] It is divided in the second way according to the three levels of meaning of Scripture: history, allegory, and tropology. Hugh explains,

> The fruit of sacred reading is double, since it either educates the mind with knowledge or furnishes it with morals. For it teaches that which it delights us to know and is expedient for us to imitate. Of these, the first, knowledge, pertains more to history and allegory, the second, instruction of morals, to tropology.[26]

History and allegory are associated with pursuit of knowledge, as are the speculative arts; tropology, with virtue, as is the secular study of ethics. Thus the three levels comprise the different 'disciplines' of Scripture, just as logic, physics, ethics, and the mechanical arts are the subdivisions of philosophy. Just as with Hugh's expansion of the role of the secular arts, the change from Augustine seems designed as a systematization and reformulation suited to a new context in which Scripture study is being scrutinized in terms of the standards for scholarly rigor associated with the arts, standards it meets in being paralleled with the arts.

Exactly this kind of change takes place in the third topic, the development of a hermeneutic for Scripture, which Augustine describes in his third book, and which Hugh discusses in the third book on the arts and the third of his books on Scripture. Augustine begins his account by assuming that with the help of a knowledge of words and 'things', most unknown literal and figurative signs can be deciphered.[27] His hermeneutic is for the ambiguous signs which remain. For ambiguous literal signs our first recourse is, then, to the orthographic and grammatical construction of the text; however, when that fails, Augustine advises us to "consult the rule of faith as it is learned from the clearer places of the Scriptures and in the authority of the Church."[28] If the 'rule of faith' leaves several possible meanings, Augustine tells us to move to the context surrounding the problematic text. However, in the end, even at this very literal level, Augustine leaves open the possibility of, even recommends, the acceptance of a multiplicity of readings of a given passage, given their consistency with the context and the principles of faith.[29] Even at the lowest of literal levels, at the level of words and punctuation, Augustine advises, "where neither the rules of faith nor the context of the words themselves can explain the ambiguity, nothing prevents the punctuation of a sentence according to whichever of those which have been shown [to be consistent]."[30]

The same recommendation remains at the figurative level. Augustine recognizes that there are two possible problems with figurative meanings, either the taking of the literal for the figurative or the taking of the figurative for the literal. He is, however, more concerned with the literalization of Scripture than the contrary. Stating a principle almost the converse of Hugh's, Augustine recommends that we take as figurative "whatever in the divine Word that does not literally [*proprie*] refer to moral virtue or to the truth of faith."[31] In two ways, I think, such a principle takes us away from literalism. First, it recommends we take passages figuratively unless we have a reason to take them otherwise. Second, in order to apply such a principle, we must be equipped with an understanding of the faith and the possession of the virtues. For Scripture, Augustine says, "teaches nothing but charity, nor disapproves anything but cupidity"; if we are lacking in charity or overcome by cupidity, we will mistake the literal for the figurative and vice versa.[32]

Thus for Augustine a 'correct' interpretation is one "leading toward the reign of charity," so the ultimate guideline is not the letter of the text but the charity and faith which one brings to the text as a condition of the possibility of reading it fruitfully and which our reading should expand.[33] To be locked into a literal reading is, Augustine tells us, "a miserable servitude of the soul," a "subjection of the intellect to the flesh."[34] Just as divine charity overflows into the diversity of creation, so it has in Scripture multiple expressions. Hence, multiple interpretations not only are possible but also are an essential part of the text; and so

Augustine asks, "What could God have more liberally and bountifully provided in the divine writings than that the same words might be understood in a number of ways?"[35]

The cliché, of course, is that this very fluid hermeneutic with its emphasis on the figurative and multiple meanings of Scripture is replaced by a 'new' emphasis on the literal level at the school of St. Victor, and to some degree that cliché finds support in Hugh's text.[36] This change, to the degree that it takes place, however, I want to argue, is better understood as the result of a more fundamental change, of Hugh's attempt to construct parallels between sacred and secular study, here continued in the development of parallel orders and methods for their study. The parallel order given is an account of the order in which these disciplines should be studied. This order in the arts begins with the trivium, the study of words, and progresses to the study of things in the speculative disciplines and to virtue in the practical disciplines. Likewise in Scripture one proceeds from the literal level to the allegorical and tropological levels, which are concerned with doctrine and morality, respectively.

Logic, by which Hugh means the arts of language, must precede the other disciplines, Hugh explains, because without an understanding of words and concepts "no treatise of philosophy can rationally be explained."[37] So also in the study of Scripture, the student must be humble enough to begin with the literal level, with the meaning of the words, before proceeding to the spiritual level, that is, to an understanding of the *things* named in Scripture.[38] Just as in the arts we must begin with grammar and logic, we must, in Scripture, begin with the historical sense. Without it, Hugh says, we will be as lost as if we had never learned the alphabet.[39] Here we have the evidence for Hugh's emphasis on the literal level, but it is qualified in two ways: first, by the fact that it seems motivated by the attempt to make scriptural interpretation more systematic by making it formally parallel to secular study; second, this simple, linear ordering of disciplines is complicated at both the secular and sacred levels in a way that is clearly indebted to Augustine.

Logic must come first, Hugh writes, because without it we will assume that real things conform in a direct way to language and to our ways of reasoning. Hugh explains the errors of the Epicureans as a result of their "lack of discernment concerning words and concepts"; in reasoning, unlike math, Hugh notes (quoting Boethius), things do not conform to our conclusions, but "whatever [the Epicureans] understood by reasoning, this same thing they judged to result in things."[40] Hugh adds that studying Scripture without a foundation in the historical sense holds the same perils as the investigation of the natures of things without a knowledge of grammar and logic. One of the results of a careful study of the literal sense is a realization that not every line of Scripture can be read literally. These passages must be carefully construed so that nothing is overlooked and passages are not "violently contorted to [say] what they were not written to say either through negligence or importunate diligence."[41] Thus the same temptation that befell the ancients because of their lack of logic ("contorting" reality to conform to their language) can befall students of Scripture unless they attend to the literal meaning. But, of course, a knowledge of words alone will not allow us to discern the lack of conformity between words and things, any more than knowledge of the literal level alone will tell us when the literal meaning is insupportable.

The problem for both areas is solved with the help of Augustine, on the sacred level by his hermeneutical principles and on the secular level by his account of human understanding. In this context Hugh repeats Augustine's guidelines for scriptural interpretation in which the foundation and final arbiters of meaning are "the principles of faith."[42] This hermeneutic, of course, yields a circular structure of inquiry; in Scripture are found the things to be believed, yet they can only be extracted when guided by some previous knowledge of the content of that faith. Advising the student, Hugh confirms this hermeneutic for Scripture in which the foundation of the literal level is preceded by a foundation in faith:

> For in such a great sea of books and in the multiple intricacies of meanings (*sententiarum*) whose number and obscurity often confound the soul of the reader, the person who does not recognize briefly *in advance*, in every genus, so to speak, some definite principle which is supported by firm faith and to which all may be referred, will scarcely be able to bring together (*colligere*) any single thing.[43]

Thus the literal sense is not purely or absolutely first; it must be preceded by some knowledge of the content of faith and a level of moral formation which will allow it to be recognized. The relationship between the literal and figurative meanings, the meanings of parts of the text and that of the whole, is dialectical or circular rather than linear as the interpreter moves back and forth between part and whole, literal and figurative, each one confirming and adjusting the other.

The same structure is found in the relationship of the secular disciplines of the trivium (the study of words) and physics (the study of things). Just as one cannot without other criteria determine when the literal sense is false, so one cannot without some knowledge of things determine when the structure of language is not mirrored in reality. And just as faith and charity must to some degree precede and inform our reading of Scripture, so knowledge of words and things is preceded by a kind of foreknowledge of things in the "ideas of reason," the reflection in our mind of the divine ideas.[44] Thus the trivium must at least indirectly, through reason, rely on physics, the knowledge of things, things which are the divine ideas as made concrete in the world. The dialectic between figurative and literal meaning in Scripture, then, is mirrored in the relationship between physics and logic, and reason and experience.

This hermeneutic is truly different from Augustine's in its being more formally plotted, adapted to a different scholarly environment (the environment of the school and monastery which require more definite structures for teaching and learning) rather than in its substance. And if Hugh's admonitions not to forsake the literal level are missing from Augustine, it may not be because Hugh has a substantially different view of the literal level, but rather because he is more attuned to possible abuses of figurative meanings, by the twelfth century a more clear and present danger than the literalism Augustine combats.[45] Moreover, Hugh does not merely carry over a version of Augustine's interpretive model in his account of scriptural interpretation, he extends it into the world of secular learning, reminding the reader that all understanding, whether of secular or sacred matters, is marked by the structure of reading and interpretation; it begins not from a blank slate but from a kind of incomplete knowledge, from the grasp of faith, and proceeds toward, but never quite reaches, complete understanding.

The Figurative Level:
The Moral and Doctrinal Meanings of Reading and Interpretation

What begins to emerge is that for both Augustine and Hugh, rules of reading and interpretation have a significance beyond the literal. They choose to give their account of Christian education in terms of a program of secular and sacred reading not only because that is literally the main task before the Christian who must read the texts of Scripture and the philosophers. But they also choose it in order to invest the tasks of reading and interpretation with another level of meaning; living a Christian life, for Augustine and Hugh, constitutes 'reading' the signs correctly, neither taking signs for things nor taking signs for the wrong things. Furthermore, as both make clear, functioning as a Christian theologian means trafficking in signs rather than things, signs which bear an imperfect and uncertain relationship to the things they attempt to represent.

Augustine uses the language of signs to designate and warn against the sins of idolatry and superstition, pride and concupiscence, all of which are types of non- or misinterpretation of signs, of the aimless wandering of misinterpretation, or premature arrival when we fail to interpret. Augustine even describes the degree of our sinfulness by the number of removes from 'things' our understanding and affections are, resting in signs, or worse, signs of signs.

Augustine leads us to the connection between moral and hermeneutic failure first by interspersing moral lessons with interpretive principles. In book 2, after a discussion of unknown figurative signs and the figurative meaning of numbers in Scripture, Augustine describes the superstitions surrounding music and the superstitious practices of augury and astrology; these accounts are followed by a listing of nonsuperstitious human disciplines and institutions, all falling under the account of signs, some instituted by human beings, others by God.[46] Thus superstitions are defined not only as false sciences in contrast with true physics and astronomy but also as signs wrongly related to things.[47] Pride too is a kind of mistaken interest in signs, the placing of value on one's ability to understand and manipulate signs rather than to know and love things.[48] Augustine further equates a failure to take Scripture figuratively with the taking of signs for things and with the inability to raise the mind from corporeal to spiritual things.[49] This imprisonment in the corporeal, in signs as if they were things, is concupiscence. Idolatry is also the taking of signs for things; here Augustine distinguishes between the Jews and the Gentiles, between those who deify the works of God as opposed to those who deify the works of humans. The Jews' tendency to reify their practices of worship is a result less of the taking of the sign for the thing than of an inability to interpret the signs they enact, Augustine argues; the Gentiles, on the other hand, tended to worship the images as gods rather than as images of gods.[50] So they are taking the wrong things as signs of God by taking the signs themselves as gods. Christian freedom, in contrast to both, is defined as interpreting as signs the practices the Jews did not understand the meaning of, and as the destruction of the signs the Gentiles worshiped as idols, that is, as things.[51]

However, the relationship between signs and things in morality is just as complex as it is in Scripture itself; as in Scripture, everything may not be taken literally, and knowing what to take figuratively and what literally depends on previous knowledge and moral formation. Augustine explains that the superstitious may seem to have the false relationship between signs and things they hold confirmed as a kind of punishment so that they will be further enmeshed in their errors.[52] So the superstitious can seem to be religious, can look as if they have correctly understood the relationship between signs and things. Further, those who act in a more restricted way than is customary toward 'things' of the world Augustine says may be either temperate or superstitious; those who use material things excessively may be either vicious or signifying something.[53] Thus not only is moral (or immoral) activity capable of functioning as a sign of something else altogether, the outward act, which is a sign of the real and inner morality of the act, has a complex and ambiguous relationship to the 'thing' it signifies. Augustine underlines this point enumerating some of the ways in which the outward act can be mismatched to its significance; someone may use one wife lustfully and another use many chastely, may eat plain food gluttonously and gourmet feasts virtuously, may conform to or transgress the customs of clothing with vice or virtue.[54]

Augustine does not deny the connection and even resemblance between sign and thing, he only reminds us that this relationship is not one-to-one, that, as he remarks more than once, things may be similar to each other in a multiple number of ways; hence, "we must not take it as prescribed that since something signifies something by similitude in one place, we should believe that it always signifies the same thing."[55] Thus though Augustine defines justice and holiness in terms of the ability to assess or interpret things as related to God, this assessment is neither absolute nor certain.[56] The things of this world are signs we may fail to interpret correctly, and even our own acts toward these signs are themselves signs which may only ambiguously reflect our character and our acts.

Augustine takes this schema to its logical conclusion, subjecting his own text to the consequences of the complicated and uncertain principles of interpretation he articulates. Just as there is no closed set of correct interpretations for Scripture, and no fixed and objective set of correspondances between actions and true moral value, so Augustine's own text cannot pretend to provide the accurate or complete set of rules for the interpretation of Scripture. He makes his text reflect this reality, undermining the text's possibility to be a thing or even to represent things. Its constant message is a reminder that just as Christians may not take signs for things, the world for God, we also cannot make (but have an unfailing tendency toward making) our own texts into things, our own understandings and theories into fixed and complete truth.

That Augustine will be constantly robbing us of our fixed notions and, thus, preventing us from reifying our own understanding is clear from the opening of book 1. Augustine defines a thing as that which is not used to signify something else "like wood, stone, and cattle, and so on." But immediately he adds, "but not that wood which we read that

Moses cast into bitter waters . . . nor that stone which Jacob placed on his own head, nor the animal [*pecus*] which Abraham sacrificed for his son."[57] Of course, he is in one sense merely pointing out the possibility of figurative meanings, of things to function as signs, but in another sense he is destabilizing our pretentions to definition, qualifying our ability to capture things with our understanding.

Further, the observation that things are also signs is followed by the reminder that signs are also things, that written and spoken words are sounds and shapes; thus all signs are things, though not all things are signs.[58] But even when he turns to a description of things which are not also signs (God), the distinction between signs and things self-destructs. For though he says the Trinity is a thing, not a sign, he adds the following complication: "if, however, it is a thing and not the cause of all things or both a thing and a cause."[59] Thus either God is the *only* thing, all else is a mere sign; or God is exactly *not* a thing because he is unlike the things we see and touch around us but is the cause of things; or he is both thing and cause. All these descriptions of God can be true only because of an ambiguity of the distinction between signs and things. In the normal context of 'thing' in the created world, everything, even signs, is a thing, but if we call God a thing, we change the context, and we must simultaneously take away this designation from created things and make them signs. Moreover, even in the sense that the Trinity is a thing, Augustine denies the possibility of creating a sign which might designate this thing, claiming not even to have spoken about God but merely of having wished to speak, or, having spoken, of not having said what he wished to say.[60] Thus do signs and things defy Augustine's attempt to fix them as one or the other.

Augustine's advice to the reader of Scripture is also a lesson in the lack of ultimate ground for our 'reading', the lack of a system or set of principles, of any *thing* on which to build our interpretations. A brief example. When Augustine is discussing strategies for dealing with problems of translation, he gives a series of examples to show how to deal with discrepancies, but he refuses to let his examples solidify into rules. First he takes different translations to illuminate one another, then he takes different translations as unrelated but equally valid, and last he argues that one translation is simply false.[61] No overarching guidelines are given for knowing which strategy is the *correct* one except the principle of charity because there can be no final, complete set of rules for reading. This is what seems to be behind Augustine's presentation of Tyconius's rules, which he prefaces with a remark that undercuts their claim to truth; these rules do not help us with all difficult passages, Augustine notes, and other methods may be used, and even Tyconius himself uses methods not authorized by his own rules.[62] The same must be true (and Augustine is the first to say it) of his own attempt in *DDC* to offer guidelines for reading Scripture.

If this is true for our reading of Scripture, how much more must it be true for our reading and writing of secular texts? In both, we must constantly correct our tendency to take them as things or even as signs which adequately represent things, such that the need for further interpretation and understanding is closed off. Thus a multiplicity of hermeneutic strategies, like a multiplicity of meanings in Scripture, is not accidental to Augustine's theological project. And so Augustine must in the polemical preface admonish not only those who misread Scripture but also those who will misread him, those who in different ways will reify his text and find it wanting. These readers, he says, "should cease to blame me and should entreat God to supply them with the light of the eye. For if I can move my finger to point at something, I cannot give light to their eyes, by means of which either my pointing itself or that which I want to show can be perceived."[63] I can only offer and myself be a sign, Augustine seems to say; all things and the ability to see them are from God.

Again Hugh follows in this tradition of making the Christian life a life of reading, and of reminding us that that reading skill must also be applied to the texts we write and read to understand the world. And again, the difference in Hugh seems to be in a formalization of those insights. The first step in making the life of reading and interpretation a version of the moral life and vice versa is accomplished by setting up moral requirements for reading and making those moral requirements mirror and inform the life of reading. The most important of these requirements is humility, which Hugh understands in academic terms as openness to all learning and to learning from others.[64] No book is without some merit, according to Hugh, and what one does not presently understand may not be a reflection of its unintelligibility but rather of our own abilities.[65] Thus humility seems to correspond to, and to recommend, attention to the literal level, to the lack of presumption which allows one to read what is given; no one, Hugh admonishes, should disdain to at least read any book. The remaining moral requirements for the life of reading—eagerness, quiet, scrutiny, parsimony, and a sense of exile—Hugh describes as pertaining alternately to discipline and to practice, corresponding to the levels of doctrine (allegory) and morality (tropology) in Scripture.[66]

Hugh finds this same threefold pattern in the soul and in its path toward understanding. The first power of the soul, like the literal level, is the condition and ground of the rest, Hugh explains, that which gives life to the body. The second is the power of sensation, which Hugh associates with knowledge and judgment; it is analogous to the allegorical level whose fruit is doctrine.[67] The third is the power of reason; Hugh seems to think of reason as active in using the knowledge it discovers, and in seeking and gaining knowledge of what is beyond its experience, so it is analogous to the tropological level in its knowledge of, and direction toward, action.[68] Mirroring the twofold purpose of Scripture—the dissemination of knowledge in the literal and allegorical levels, and the production of virtue in the tropological—the reasoning soul, Hugh tells us, has two functions, grasping the natures of things and acting on that understanding.[69]

But the moral and the hermeneutic are not just related in having the same two tasks and three levels; they also have symmetrical narrative structures. Just as Hugh describes progress in reading as moving from the historical and literal to the figurative and spiritual, so he thinks of our educational progress as from a study of words in the trivium to things in the quadrivium, and from the secular arts (the study of the works of foundation) to sacred study (the study of the works of restoration). Similarly, he plots our moral progress as moving from an immersion in and understanding of the things of this world toward an experience of this world as one of exile.

The most poignant description of the narrative structure common to reading and salvation occurs at the end of book 3, at the end of the account of secular reading leading into the account of the sacred. "Tender," Hugh begins, "is the one whose homeland is sweet; already strong, however, is the one to whom every soil is his homeland; but perfect is the one to whom the whole world is foreign soil."[70] In this journey the texts of the arts are for Hugh "foreign soil," merely, and at their best, signs pointing us onward, which the beginner, ignorant of both signs and things, "at home" only on her native soil must assimilate; the philosopher, the educated reader of secular texts, is "at home" with them and the world they portray; but for the truly wise, secular texts are foreign soil. As with the texts of the world, so with the world itself. Our moral progress does not skip the world, moving directly to God, any more than our education can skip grammar and logic, heading straight into physics, or our reading of Scripture omit the literal level for allegory and tropology; instead we travel through the world seeking to grasp its nature and value but move beyond this immersion to a sense of its emptiness and strangeness.

However, this linear structure for education / salvation is complicated in the same ways as Hugh's hermeneutic for Scripture. Hugh begins by describing moral progress as a kind of straight line ascending from study to meditation, prayer, activity, and contemplation; this structure seems to mirror the one Hugh began by constructing, but ultimately reshaped, for secular and sacred reading, moving directly from secular to sacred and from letter to spirit. What we need, Hugh contends, is an order and method for work so that we find our way through "the wood" of study and Scripture by the most direct route.[71] But just as Hugh revises the simple interpretive schema for Scripture, arguing for a kind of faith preceding a reading of literal level and a return to the literal level from the spiritual levels, so he bends the line of moral development into a more complex spiral:

> Our purpose ought always be to ascend, but because the mutability of our life is so great, we are unable to stand in the same place, and we are often constrained to look back at the things we have done, and, so that we do not lose the place we occupy, from time to time we repeat what we have done.[72]

Thus, Hugh continues, we are sometimes forced to descend in order to ascend, ascending for its own sake and descending for the sake of ascending.[73] But if we must go back in order to go forward, progress is in a radical sense relativized and our place along that line must be constantly reevaluated. Just as Hugh's hermeneutic for Scripture refuses to let us rest in either the letter or the spirit, the literal or figurative meanings, so our 'reading' in a moral sense must move back and forth between signs and things, between secular and sacred texts, this world and thoughts of the next, as we are sent back and forth on a path that will deepen our understanding and make more profound our desire for the homeland.

This view is incarnated in Hugh's sacramental theology. The sacraments, for Hugh, are external and material signs of sacred things, efficacious because of the humility, instruction, and exercise they occasion. Because of this they are, I contend, the way to salvation which moves 'down' and 'back', if you will, in order to go 'up' and 'forward'. According to Hugh, the sacraments function by making that which divided us from God, the material and temporal, into the mediator of the distance sin has created, since sin is the rejection of higher things for lower, of spiritual things for material; the sacraments make us travel humbly back through the very instrument and expression of our fall. Next, Hugh explains, we are instructed through the sacraments in such a way that through the visible good of the sacramental sign, the invisible good we lost sight of through sin is returned to us. Lastly, exercise in the variety and multiplicity of the sacraments serves as remedy for the changeableness of our lives and affections, which, divided and misdirected, make us second Cains, wanderers without direction on earth. "We hunger and we fail," Hugh says of our fallen condition, "and we eat lest we fail, and yet if we ate always, we would fail; what is sought unto consolation is turned to pain."[74] In response, Hugh continues, "God provided multiplicity and variety and intermission, that the human mind in multiplicity might find exercise, in variety delight, and in intermission recreation."[75] Thus not only are we directed "down" and "back" to material things through which the sacraments operate, we are directed "outward" to variety and multiplicity of practices, so that our misdirected and divided attention is in effect cured by the very things which distracted and fragmented our affections.

But if progress is not always in the same direction and is sometimes made by going back, then beginning, middle, and end points are relative rather than absolute, and the foundation and superstructure unstable and shifting. And if the means to the desired end are multiple rather than single, then a necessary open-endedness characterizes the set of those means to salvation. And, once again, if this is true for the texts and practices prescribed by God, how much more must it be true for the texts and practices we devise, including Hugh's own? While less directly than Augustine, Hugh nonetheless takes account of these reflexive consequences of his own theses, that the lines of progress and division are complex and blurred, and that the paths toward truth are not one but many, by blurring his own distinctions and multiplying the means both in and beyond his own text to understanding and salvation.

Hugh's text is structured to maintain the division between secular and sacred writing, between the works of foundation and those of restoration, but these divisions are no sooner made than they are undermined. The opening schema of three books devoted to secular writing and three to sacred is undercut as each half of the book begins. Paraphrasing Boethius, Hugh's opening sentence on secular things reads, "Of all things to be valued, the first is wisdom, in whom the form of the perfect good stands"; it is this wisdom which the arts seek.[76] But Hugh, following Boethius, has a christological understanding of the Form of the Good, and of the Wisdom we seek.[77] These lines, 'originating' in Neoplatonic thought, are reinterpreted in a Christian sense.[78] They open the chapters on the secular arts and are the bridge into the story of their origin; thus does Christian truth predate and ground the discovery of the arts and writings of the pagan philosophers which in a literal sense precede Christianity.

Book 4, the first on sacred writing, on the other hand, uses its opening lines to disqualify the obvious ways one might try to distinguish sacred from secular writing. Texts whose subject is God, invisible things, or the future life are not necessarily sacred: pagan philosophers, Hugh says, write convincingly on these topics; Scripture, on the other hand, he warns, speaks almost completely of the present state of life and of the deeds to be done in it.[79] They differ because secular writings contain falsehood while Scripture does not, but this distinction reveals itself ultimately only at the level of interpretation. Further, given the hermeneutic for Scripture which Hugh articulates later in the *Didascalicon*, according to which the literal meaning may be absurd, it is a distinction which slips away almost as soon as it is given.[80] In *De sacramentis* this distinction, between secular and sacred writing as that between the works of foundation and of restoration, is immediately followed with the qualification that the restoration is not sufficiently explained without an account of the human fall, which in turn requires an account of human creation, and this of the creation of the whole world; thus the works of foundation are contained within those of restoration.[81]

Hugh's own work both finds its place and falls firmly between the cracks of the distinction between the secular and the sacred that is articulated in these works; its subjects are both the visible and invisible, the present and future life, both the texts concerning the arts and those of sacred Scripture, and his work's claim to truthfulness is somewhere between the sacred writings of the Bible and Fathers and those of pagan writers on the arts and philosophy.

Hugh not only undercuts and complicates his distinction but also multiplies the paths toward beatitude by inclusion of the writings of the Church Fathers and Doctors in the realm of sacred writings, making them, in a way, like the sacraments he multiplies in *De sacramentis*. The works of the Fathers and Doctors of the church are too many to be numbered; nonetheless, in each one, Hugh continues, "the full and perfect truth stands, though none of them are superfluous."[82] Thus Augustinian notions of the multiplicity of meanings and theologies are maintained and a place is created for Hugh's own work in this open-ended set. But the *Didascalicon* no sooner finds its place than it assures that its place and authority will be superseded by others added to this set.

The blurring of distinctions and complication of the path of progress in interpretation and toward salvation is not inconsistent with, but is rather required by, Hugh's sense of our ultimate exile in the world that for him, as for Augustine, is a "region of unlikeness." With the sense of exile comes the realization that the things around us have their value not for their own sakes but from their ability to remind us of our exile and of the homeland which we seek; they become, in Augustine's language, signs rather than things. The closest we come to 'things' for Hugh is a realization of the merely transitory nature of the world as signs, and as signs they must be interpreted and reinterpreted rather than possessed and consumed. It is a world in which all road maps are incomplete, all distinctions defeasible, and all rules exceptionable. Thus the path of restoration and salvation is, to use Hugh's metaphor, a path of reading but one on which the most profound error is to stop, to rest in the certainty of an account or interpretation while we remain in this life.[83] On such a journey for both Hugh and Augustine, texts (including their own), which are the articulations of our understandings of things, should be accorded the ambiguous reality of signs, of way stations, which do not contain their signified, nor carry us the distance written on their tickets. As such, they should neither be avoided in an immediate leap to the truth, abandoned in despair of ever reaching the truth, nor allowed to captivate us in a false homeland.

Notes

1. See, for example, Henri Marrou's famous objection to the composition of *DDC* in *Saint Augustin et la fin de la culture antique* (Paris, 1958), 61, and the later, at least partial, retraction appended to the same volume, 665–72. See also a summary of the debates over *DDC*'s status as an exegetical or rhetorical work and over the breadth of its intended audience as a specialized text for the training of clergy or as an outline of Christian culture for all Christians (E. Kevane, "Augustine's *De doctrina christiana*: A Treatise on Christian Education," *Recherches augustiniennes* 4 [1966]: 103–13).

Evaluations of Hugh's work have ranged from viewing it as, at its best, the forerunner of thirteenth-century scholasticism to a view of him as a "mere mystic." The range of such interpretations can be explained by Hugh's inclusion in a work like the *Didascalicon* of a wide range of materials—scholarly, moral, and spiritual—which taken partially would justify such diverse views; what I propose here is a reading of Hugh which accounts for something approaching the whole of his text. On Hugh as the precursor of scholasticism, see Martin Grabmann, *Geschichte der scholastischen Methode*, 2 vols. (Freiburg, 1911), 2:234; and Joseph Mariétan, *Le problème de la classification des sciences d'Aristote à saint Thomas* (Paris, 1901), 131. Barthélemy Hareau describes Hugh as a "mere mystic" in *Les oeuvres de Hugues de Saint-Victor* (Paris, 1886), 424. For a more moderate view, see Roger Baron, *Science et sagesse chez Hugues de Saint-Victor* (Paris, 1957); and Luce Giard, "Logique et système du savoir selon Hugues de Saint-Victor," *Thalès* 16 (1979–1981): 3–32.

2. *DDC* 1.3.3–5.5; and Hugh of St. Victor *Didascalicon* 1.1–2 (*Hugonis de Sancto Victore Didascalicon de studio legendi: A Critical Text,* ed. Charles Henry Buttimer [Washington, D.C., 1939]; *PL* 176:741C–743C). Hereafter, all citations to the *Didascalicon* refer to Buttimer's edition by book and chapter,

with *Patrologia Latina* volume and page number in parentheses; the title is abbreviated *Did*. All translations are my own unless otherwise noted.

3. *Did*. 1.5 (*PL* 176:745B).

4. DDC 1.4.4.

5. DDC 2.8.12–10.15.

6. DDC 2.14.23.

7. DDC 2.16.24.

8. DDC 2.16.25.

9. DDC 2.31.48–37.55.

10. DDC 2.19.29.

11. DDC 2.27.41.

12. DDC 2.28.42–30.47.

13. DDC 2.31.48–35.53.

14. DDC 2.2.2.

15. DDC 2.2.3.

16. DDC 2.25.39.

17. It is to emphasize the problematic and relative functioning of signs that have no necessary or natural connection to their referents that Augustine concentrates on the societal agreement and invention that allows these signs to function, not, as R. A. Markus seems to suggest in an earlier essay, because Augustine is naive about the degree to which we are formed by our sign systems as opposed to being autonomous creators of signs. See Markus's criticisms of Augustine's theory of signs in "St. Augustine on Signs," in R. A. Markus, ed., *Augustine: A Collection of Critical Essays* (New York, 1972), 77–78. But see his later position in "Signs, Communication, and Communities in Augustine's *De doctrina christiana*, in "*De doctrina christiana*": *A Classic of Western Culture*, ed. Duane W. H. Arnold and Pamela Bright (Notre Dame, Ind., 1995). Also it seems clear to me that Augustine does not seriously consider the possibility that words may function more like natural signs, that is, as symptoms having a necessary and causal relationship with their referents / causes, because he does not think this is a possible model for language and culture. As he makes clear in *DDC* and elsewhere, words and other *signa data* have a much more ambiguous and relative relationship to the things they signify than does smoke to fire.

18. DDC 2.39.58.

19. DDC 2.41.62.

20. *Did*. 1.4 (*PL* 176:744D).

21. *Did*. 1.5 (*PL* 176:745B).

22. *Did*. 1.11 (*PL* 176:749A–B).

23. Cf. R. W. Southern, *The Making of the Middle Ages* (New Haven, 1970), 172; and G. R. Evans, *Old Arts and New Theology* (New York, 1980), 63.

24. See DDC 2.8.13, 2.15.22; and *Did*. 4.2–16 (*PL* 176:778D–790A).

25. *Did*. 4.2. Cf. Hugh of St. Victor *De sacramentis* prologue.2 (*On the Sacraments of the Christian Faith*, trans. Roy J. Deferrari [Cambridge, Mass., 1951], 3).

26. *Did*. 5.6 (*PL* 176:749B–C).

27. *DDC* 3.1.1.

28. *DDC* 3.2.2. G. Istace recognizes Augustine's reliance on Scripture, especially on its "plainer" and more open passages, but fails to understand that it is not self-evident which passages are "plainer" and so may guide the rest; hence, even establishing which passages are "plainer" requires (once again) a prior appeal to the articles of faith ("Le livre Ier du *De doctrina christiana* de Saint Augustin," *Ephemerides Theologicae Lovanienses* 32 [1956]: 326).

29. For an argument against the plurality of literal meanings for Augustine, see François Talon, "Saint Augustin a-t-il réellement enseigné la pluralité des sens littéraux dans l'écriture?" *Recherches de science religieuse* 11 (1921): 1–28.

30. *DDC* 3.2.5. Cf. *DDC* 3.3.6.

31. *DDC* 3.10.14.

32. *DDC* 3.10.15.

33. *DDC* 3.15.23.

34. *DDC* 3.5.9.

35. *DDC* 3.27.38.

36. On the novelty of Hugh's emphasis on the literal level, see Beryl Smalley, *The Study of the Bible in the Middle Ages* (Oxford, 1957), 97–106; for the view that this emphasis on the literal level is neither as novel nor as strong as Smalley argues, see Henri Lubac, *Exégèse médiévale,* 2 vols. (Lyon, 1961), 1.2:357–59.

37. *Did.* 1.11 (*PL* 176:749D).

38. *Did.* 6.3 (*PL* 176:799D).

39. *Did.* 6.3 (*PL* 176:799D).

40. *Did.* 1.11 (*PL* 176:749B). Cf. Boethius *Commentaria in Porphyrium a se translatum* 2 (*PL* 64:73A–B; *CSEL* 48:139), cited as Hugh's source by Jerome Taylor, ed. and trans., *The Didascalicon of Hugh of St. Victor* (New York, 1961), 195, note 75.

41. *Did.* 6.3 (*PL* 176:801B).

42. *Did.* 6.11 (*PL* 176:808D); Augustine *De genesi ad litteram* 1.21 (*PL* 34:262).

43. *Did.* 6.4 (*PL* 176:801B–C).

44. *Did.*, ed. Buttimer, Appendix C, 134–35. According to Buttimer (pp. xvi and xxxi), this appendix on the three subsistencies of things (in the divine mind, in the human mind, and in the material world) appears in some classes of manuscripts as a preface to the whole *Didascalicon.* Taylor (*Did.,* trans., 152) thinks it might belong in book 1, after ch. 6, which is the discussion of the "three manners of things."

45. Cf. J. Ries, "La bible chez saint Augustin et chez les manichéens," *Revue des études augustiniennes* 9 (1963): 231–43. Ries examines the thesis that Augustine's theory of biblical exegesis and spiritual levels of meaning is a defense against Manichaeanism. Cf. *Did.* 3.4 (*PL* 176:768D–769C) and 6.4 (*PL* 176:804D–805B) for the dangers of ignoring the letter in order to construct one's own interpretations. Hugh's warnings may be a response to the excesses of those associated with Chartres and their emphasis on allegorical readings of both secular and sacred texts.

46. See *DDC* 2.17.27–24.37 on superstitions and 2.16.23–26 for problems surrounding unknown and figurative signs in Scripture.

47. *DDC* 2.22.34.

48. *DDC* 2.13.20; 2.37.55. In these passages Augustine mentions the pride of those in their learning of grammar and logic. The desire of those captivated by these kinds of study, Augustine explains, is for knowledge of signs rather than things, a kind of knowledge one must not mistake for "the truth of the beatific life."

49. *DDC* 3.5.9.

50. *DDC* 3.6.10–7.11.

51. *DDC* 3.8.12.

52. *DDC* 2.23.35.

53. *DDC* 3.12.18.

54. *DDC* 3.12.19–20.

55. *DDC* 3.25.35. Cf. 2.25.38.

56. *DDC* 1.27.28.

57. *DDC* 1.2.2.

58. *DDC* 1.2.2.

59. *DDC* 1.5.5.

60. *DDC* 1.6.6.

61. *DDC* 2.12.17.

62. *DDC* 3.30.42.

63. *DDC* prooemium.3.

64. *Did.* 3.13 (*PL* 176:773C–775A).

65. *Did.* 3.13 (*PL* 176:774B).

66. *Did.* 3.15 (*PL* 176:776C). That is, eagerness, scrutiny, and sense of exile are parts of practice; and humility, quiet, and parsimony, of discipline.

67. *Did.* 1.3 (*PL* 176:743B–744A).

68. *Did.* 1.3 (*PL* 176:744A–B).

69. *Did.* 1.3 (*PL* 176:744C). On Scripture's role to instruct us in doctrine and to furnish us with morals, see *Did.* 5.6 (*PL* 176:749B–C).

70. *Did.* 3.19 (*PL* 176:778B).

71. *Did.* 5.5 (*PL* 176:793C–794A). Cf. *DDC* 1.36.41. Augustine uses the same metaphor, i.e., of reading as a kind of travel which one may undertake by means of the road or through a field which less directly leads to the same place. However, Augustine emphasizes that both arrive in the same place, at an interpretation which builds up charity, while Hugh emphasizes the inefficiency of the indirect routes. The contrast is one small sign of the greater structure and lesser tolerance of openness and multiplicity in Hugh as compared to Augustine despite their substantial agreement.

72. *Did.* 5.9 (*PL* 176:797D–798A). Cf. *DDC* 1.17.16: "Further, since we are on a road (*in via*) which is not a road of places but of affections, which is blocked off by certain thorny [plants] by the malice of our past sins . . ."

73. *Did.* 5.9 (*PL* 176:797D–798A).

74. Hugh of St. Victor *De sacramentis* 1.9 (trans. Deferrari, 157–58).

75. Hugh of St. Victor *De sacramentis* 1.9 (trans. Deferrari, 158).

76. *Did.* 1.1 (*PL* 176:741C). Cf. Boethius *De consolatione philosophiae* 3, pros. 10.

77. *Did.*, trans. Taylor, 175, note 1.

78. *Did.* 4.1 (*PL* 176:777C). See Giard, "Logique et système du savoir," 22–23, on the Neoplatonic origins of Hugh's opening statements on wisdom and philosophy.

79. *Did.* 4.1 (*PL* 176:777C).

80. Cf. above, The Literal Level: The Role and Method of the Arts and Scripture.

81. Hugh of St. Victor *De sacramentis* prologue.2–3 (trans. Deferrari, 3–4).

82. *Did.* 4.2 (*PL* 176:779C–D).

83. Thus, neither Augustine nor Hugh would claim to have articulated "the principles implement[ing] the very indefectibility of the teaching church" nor to have located and contained "the distilled essence of Christian culture," as Augustine has been described by Kevane as doing ("Augustine's *De doctrina christiana*," 132–33). Quite the contrary.

From Theory to Practice:
The *De doctrina christiana* and the Exegesis of Andrew of St. Victor

MICHAEL A. SIGNER

More than half a millennium passed between the completion of the *De doctrina christiana* (*DDC*) by Augustine, the bishop of Hippo, and the composition of commentaries on the Hebrew Bible by Andrew of St. Victor, abbot of Wigmore. It is difficult to imagine a greater contrast than the embattled Augustine with the broad intellectual scope of his literary output of both theoretical and pastoral treatises and the quiet routine of study and prayer at St. Victor Abbey in twelfth-century Paris, or at Wigmore Abbey in Herefordshire where Andrew produced commentaries on the Hebrew Bible *secundum litteram*. Nevertheless, an examination of Andrew's exegetical writings reveals hermeneutical tensions which are latent in the *DDC* and its approach to the language of the Hebrew Bible or Christian Old Testament. These tensions, which are based on the relationship between the language of the biblical text and the community which transmits and interprets it, reflect a dispute between Augustine and Jerome about the "original" language of the Hebrew Bible that continues to plague Christian exegetes down to the twentieth century.

Since Augustine's motivation for writing the *DDC* may, as Charles Kannengiesser has written, have resulted in part from the bishop's desire to establish himself as a reliable interpreter of Sacred Scripture, he would have to contend with both components of the Christian canon—Old and New Testaments.[1] The relationship between these two documents was by no means settled within the Church. Evidence of this problem may be discerned in Augustine's discussion of the scriptural canon in the second book of *DDC* which indicates some disagreement about the books which were accepted for use as authorities in theological argument.[2]

Quotations from the Hebrew Bible and New Testament in *DDC* reveal a seamless web between the two testaments.[3]

Augustine is conscious of the distinction between the two Testaments for purposes of comprehending the true nature of signs and things. While he admitted his own lack of knowledge of Hebrew, he did insist that when determining the meaning of any passage in Scripture it was important to understand the original languages, Hebrew and Greek.[4] However, he makes it quite clear that a correct interpretation must be grounded in more than philological parsing of individual words but in the broader context of *caritas.*

> Whoever thinks that he understands the Divine Scriptures or any part of them so that it does not build the double love of God and of our neighbor does not understand at all. Whoever finds a lesson there useful to the building of charity, even though he has said what the author may have shown to have intended in that place has not been deceived nor has he been lying in any way.[5]

The rule of love—the "inner teacher" as R. A. Markus has shown—guides the exegete, who is permitted to err in the precise comprehension of the original language, because fulfillment of the higher commandment of love will place appropriate limits on his interpretation.[6]

What seems to be crucial for Augustine is that linguistic meaning is determined by social context and understood through convention.[7] In *DDC* 2.14.21 he presents a hermeneutical situation where the reader of Scripture is impeded by an unknown word or expression. Augustine urges him to "consult one who speaks those languages." Thus a speaker of the language—one who lives it—may be a reliable source of information. And further, when unfamiliar words in our language are memorized, as Augustine urges, we can have the opportunity to expand our linguistic horizon, "when one more learned [than we] appears who may be questioned."[8]

In expounding the literal sense of Sacred Scriptures, Augustine calls upon the reader to learn the ancient languages, Hebrew or Greek. Translations and manuscripts guide the interpreter in the search for meaning.[9] There is, however, a hierarchy of the languages in which Scripture has been transmitted or translated that ultimately leads to the correct interpretation for the reader. Of all the Latin texts the *Itala* is to be preferred because "it adheres to the words and is at the same time perspicacious regarding meaning."[10] Latin texts of both Old and New Testaments are to be amended by Greek translations.[11]

In this same passage, he avers that with respect to the Old Testament the Septuagint is to be preferred over the Hebrew because "in all the more learned Churches it is now said that this translation was so inspired by the Holy Spirit that many men spoke as if with the mouth of one."[12] The fundamental reasons for preferring the Septuagint is its acceptance by the "learned Churches" and that its seventy authors spoke as one. This unity of expression urged Augustine to declare:

> Who would compare any other authority with this or prefer another? But even if they conferred and arrived at a single opinion on the basis of common judgment, is it not right and proper for any man, no matter how learned, to seek to emend the consensus of so many older more learned men?[13]

The Septuagint seems to represent a divinely inspired source for spreading the gospel's message of salvation prior to the Incarnation. In contrast with this universally available Greek text, Augustine identifies the Old Testament text in the Hebrew language with the Jewish nation which was recalcitrant to share its truth.

> Even though something is found in the Hebrew versions different from what they [the Seventy] have set down, I think that we should cede the divine dispensation by which they worked to the end that the books which the Jewish nation refused to transmit to other peoples, either out of envy or for religious reasons, might be revealed so early by the authority and power of King Ptolemy to the nations which in the future were to believe in our Lord.[14]

This passage reveals Augustine's interpretation of the *Letter of Aristeas to Philocrates* within the Christian tradition.[15] In contrast with his understanding, the text of the letter itself describes King Ptolemy as filled with blandishments and gifts for the Jerusalem Temple and as finding the sages sent to him by the high priest of the Temple to be worthy companions at his symposium. The letter reveals no reluctance at all on the part of the Jews to provide translators for King Ptolemy.[16] *DDC* adds an anti-Jewish dimension to the story of the translation in that it warns against consulting the Hebrew text because the Jews either through jealousy (*invidia*) or religious reasons (*religio*) refused to communicate the message of Scripture to the Gentiles. This negative assessment of the Jewish attitude toward the text of the Bible appears in only one other Christian author, John Chrysostom (347–407). In his *Homilies on Matthew* 5.2, Chrysostom contrasts the superior value of the Septuagint to all the other Greek translations of the Hebrew because those who made them remained Jews after the coming of Christ and had veiled the clear meaning of the prophecies.[17]

One might suppose that the statements about the Septuagint in *DDC* would predispose its reader toward reliance on the Greek rather than the Hebrew. This predisposition would be precisely Augustine's argument when describing the Septuagint in his later work *De civitate Dei* 18.43–44 (written after 418). In that passage, Augustine does not accuse the Jews of being unwilling to share the Hebrew text of their Scriptures out of jealousy (*invidia*).[18] However, in another passage which describes a discrepancy between the Hebrew and Septuagint codices over the length of Methuselah's years he advances an argument of those who accuse the Jews of changing their Hebrew codices because they were jealous of Christians since the interpretation of the Law and Prophets had been transferred to them. Although he does not endorse the argument, he allows his reader "to adopt [it] according to his own judgment."[19]

It would be fair to claim at this point that Augustine holds a position about the Hebrew language different from his stance toward the Jewish community which utilized the Hebrew text of the Bible as the basis for its interpretation. The Hebrew language is significant for the Christian interpreter. In the very next section of *DDC* 2.16.23 Augustine underscores the importance of understanding Hebrew names as a source of biblical enigmas.[20] However, book 2 would seem, on the whole, to exclude consultation directly with Jews and their Hebrew text of Scripture as devices which are likely to result in a true interpretation for Christians.

In book 3, where Augustine discusses the literal sense, this linguistic boundary is reinforced. Augustine focuses attention on the importance of determining the literal sense based on properly construing the language of the passage.

> Only rarely and with difficulty may we find ambiguities in the literal meaning of the scriptural vocabulary which may not be solved either by examining the context which reveals the authors intention or by consulting a text in an earlier language.[21]

However, for Augustine, there was the danger that the Christian reader might understand the sign literally. He condemns those who would take "figurative expressions as though they were literal and do not refer the things signified to something else" (*DDC* 3.5.9). Two examples, the Sabbath and the sacrifices of the biblical cult, function as the things which must refer beyond themselves to more profound Christian truths. Failure to transcend things is, from Augustine's perspective, "servitude of the spirit." In *DDC* it is precisely "servitude" which the Christian exegete is charged to surmount.[22]

In the next section (*DDC* 3.6.10) he continues the theme of "servitude," turning to the Jewish people whose "servitude was different from that of others, since they were subjected to temporal things in such a way that the One God was served in all these things." In the divine dispensation such activity was permissible until the Incarnation. Alluding to 2 Cor. 3:6 and then to Rom. 8:6, Augustine demonstrates that the Law acted as a tutor or pedagogue and was horribly oppressive until Christ came to reveal its true meaning.[23]

In three consecutive sections of book 3 Augustine moves from the need to know languages in order to understand the biblical text to a condemnation of the Jewish community whose knowledge of Scripture limited their understanding of signs to things. Thus, book 3 reinforces the ideas expressed in book 2: the Hebrew Bible for the Church has its divinely revealed message carried by the chosen community. This is not restricted to a single language, and the Septuagint carries the higher truth. After the Incarnation the Jews are in error and not reliable consultants for the Christian exegete.

We can see then that books 2 and 3 of *DDC* provide another perspective on the differing attitudes toward Hebrew language and consultation with Jews. This conflict is also reflected in the correspondence between Jerome and Augustine.[24] The focus for much of their argument was Jerome's commitment to the *Hebraica veritas* rather than the Septuagint for his translation of the Scriptures into Latin. The first letter from Augustine, written in 394/395, requested Jerome not to return to the Hebrew when translating the Old Testament but to adhere to the Septuagint as corrected by Origen. He requested Jerome to insert diacritical marks so that one could immediately mark the difference from the Hebrew. What attracted Augustine to the Septuagint was its expression of harmony of mind and spirit.[25]

In his letter of 403, Augustine again focused on Jerome's reliance upon *Hebraica veritas*.[26] This letter, in contrast to his previous missive, appeals to contemporary ecclesial concerns rather than to the antiquity and harmony revealed in the Septuagint translation. Augustine avers that if Jerome's rendering of the Hebrew into Latin were to gain general acceptance, it would bring division between the Greek and Latin churches. He supported the potential reality of this schism by citing an incident from his own experience. In a church in Tripoli the local bishop had adopted Jerome's version of Jonah 4:6 rather than that of the Septuagint. The Greek-speaking members of the community objected to the reading, and the bishop consulted with local Jews who "either from ignorance or from spite, answered that the words in the Hebrew manuscript were correctly rendered in the Greek version and in the Latin one taken from it."[27] Consultation with Jews produced only further confusion, and Augustine reports that the bishop corrected Jerome's translation.

What should be noted is that when reading the letter of 405 against the arguments in books 2 and 3 of *DDC* one can observe that Augustine's basis for interpreting Scripture is ecclesiastical unity and consensus. Part of this process seems to be the exclusion of the Jews from the process of consultation. From the perspective of the *DDC* the Jews are restricted to a single language and are ignorant of appropriate hermeneutical rules. Within the perspective of Augustine's letter, they are perverse and sow confusion in Christian communities.

Needless to say, Jerome's response to Augustine was quite angry. For him the *Hebraica veritas* represented truth. His advice to Augustine to leave him to be alone in his monastery and to tend his flock reflects the ecclesial dimension of their approaches.[28] Both men understood their work to be for the good of the Church. Jerome's consultation with Jews and his learning Hebrew were not gestures of philo-semitism but efforts to respond effectively to the Jewish arguments about scriptural interpretation.[29] I do not believe it is appropriate to claim that Jerome's more "open" attitude toward consulting Jews may be ascribed to his living as a part of a Christian minority in Bethlehem while Augustine lived in an area with fewer Jews. There were Jews present in North Africa during the fifth century even though it is difficult to trace their level of learning. What seems to be at issue here is an approach to language and its interpretation. One has the impression, based on the prefaces to his commentaries, that for Jerome the original text and language was the starting point for investigations of interpretation and meaning. It would seem that for Augustine in the *DDC* the meaning of the text derived from its inner spirit which is transmitted within a community guided by the *regula fidei* of love. For that reason, he excluded the possibility of discovering true interpretation from a people who failed to accept the Incarnation as their hermeneutic axial point. The tradition of the believing community as contained within the Septuagint text determined the proper interpretation of Scripture for the reader of *DDC*.

Echoes of the discussion between Augustine and Jerome about *Hebraica veritas* may be discerned in the writings of the scholars at St. Victor Abbey in twelfth-century Paris. Their interpretations of the Hebrew Bible were grounded in a rereading of the Fathers.[30] This can be clearly documented at St. Victor, whose library contained multiple volumes of Augustine, Jerome, Origen, and Gregory.[31] Andrew, who was there after 1125 as a student of Master Hugh and taught from 1141 to 1147 and 1154 to 1163, would have had his choice.[32] For example, Andrew seems to have read widely from the Heptateuch commentary, citing Jerome more often than Augustine. But he clearly knew and cited Augustine's

Quaestiones in Heptateuchum (sixty-three times) and *De Genesi ad litteram* (forty-five times). They are followed in decreasing order by citations from *De Genesi contra Manichaeos, De civitate Dei, Contra Faustum Manichaeum,* and *Ennarationes in Psalmos.* There are no citations from *DDC* in Andrew's commentary on the Heptateuch.[33] The parallels between these citations from Augustine and their parallels in the *Glossa ordinaria* may provide yet another link between the Abbey of Saint Victor and the gloss.[34]

Andrew discerned his role as an exegete primarily as an explorer of the literal sense. He was by no means closed off from preaching. There was preaching at St. Victor, and when he was abbot at Wigmore in Herefordshire he preached to the unruly monks who threw him out in 1147 but then begged him to return in 1163.[35] Perhaps this phrase from his Ezekiel commentary sums up his attitude about preaching: "It is often the perversity of the listeners which closes the mouths of the preachers."[36] Basically, Andrew liked working on his own.

> I keep watch for myself; I work for myself consulting my poverty which cannot always have commentaries and glossed books to hand. I have collected together what is scattered and diffused through them pertaining to the historical sense and have concentrated it as it were into one corpus. Lastly, if I could discover anything on the prophets whom I decided to study with special care because of their obscurity or on other books of the Old Testament as the Jews or certain others and my own study showed it to me or as God revealed it (for sometimes he grants even this to his servants), I thought it good to insert it lest what had been usefully learnt should be forgotten.[37]

This passage from Andrew's prologue to the commentary on the Minor Prophets sets out his idiosyncratic program as an exegete. First, he consults commentaries and "glossed books" [*libros glossatos*] with respect to the historical sense, gathering them into a single collection. If something remains unclear, Andrew will consult the Jews who were available in Paris. Finally, he is not reluctant to add that he may derive his own insights which, of course, he attributes to God.

Books, Jews, and personal insight seem to be at quite a distance from the ideal Christian exegete and preacher described in *DDC*. There is no mention of a theory of translation; no appeal to the *regula fidei*. We get the sense more of Jerome than Augustine. Yet that would be an overstatement. Andrew focused entirely on the historical sense. He neatly sidesteps all the doctrinal landmines of the spiritual sense by leaving that to others.[38] He had, at best, only a rudimentary knowledge of Greek, so that he could not match Jerome's erudition. His knowledge of Hebrew has been seriously questioned by Avrom Saltman and, more recently, by William McKane.[39] Yet his commentaries are filled with comments which read *in hebraeo dicit*. More significantly, one discovers the comments which begin with *traditio hebraeorum* or *hebraei dicunt*. Andrew appears to be following the spirit of the dictum we read earlier from *DDC* about reading and memorizing unfamiliar passages so that one can ask the speaker of the language what the meaning might be.[40] For Andrew, direct contact with the Jews was the most reliable source for understanding the Old Testament.

Andrew's interest in contemporary Jews may have derived from his belief that scriptural books focused on the narrative about the people they describe. The prologue to the commentary on Genesis describes Moses as an author who was forced to give "heavy and harsh commandments" to the people of Israel who were an untutored people, lax from soft living and many pleasures in Egypt. His purpose is to educate his hearers to a more careful observance of the Law. He accomplishes this goal by providing the many great riches of heavenly favor. The acts of creation are a blessing suited to this untutored people. This means that the creation focuses on "what was done for man and for man's use." The state of the people liberated from Egypt was such that this idolatry would have been encouraged had there been open mention of the Trinity. However, Andrew claims that the Trinity is suggested (*insinuare curavit*) in all God's works: "power in creating things from nothing, wisdom in deposing and guiding them, goodness in sustaining and cherishing."[41]

The human focus of the biblical text is carried into Andrew's discussion of prophetic revelation. In contrast to his colleague Richard, who wanted to know how the beasts in the vision appeared, Andrew concentrated on what the significance of the animals was for Ezekiel, and what it taught the people for whom he wrote it.

> The prophet [Ezekiel] had called the creatures of the vision "beasts" so that they might be conceived merely as wild animals and hence of very little concern for man; the men for whom this vision was written would heed it little since they would have nothing in it that was related to them. Therefore, the prophet added, "This was their appearance. There was the likeness of a man in them." (Ez. 1:5)[42]

Andrew appreciated that the actions of the prophets and their gestures were a means to communicate the divine word.

> *Turn your face toward Sidon and prophesy against her.* Not only the words of the prophets but even their actions and dress are prophetic, as Scripture states with respect to Isaiah, "Go and walk barefoot." The position and

direction of the face of the prophet towards Sidon signifies the harm and misfortune which will befall her.[43]

This passage supports Andrew's argument that there is a direct relationship between human speech and action that elucidates meaning. This may provide an additional explanation for the link he made between the Hebrew of the biblical text and his own Jewish interlocutors. Joining human speech and action as a key to interpreting ancient texts may provide a more theoretical perspective for what Beryl Smalley once claimed was the motivation of Christian hebraists to consult with Jews—"The Jew appealed to him as a kind of telephone line to the Old Testament."[44] This perspective encouraged Andrew to present contemporary Jewish mourning customs as an explanation for the directions given by God to Ezekiel upon the death of his wife.[45] The "straight feet" of the beasts which are described in Ezekiel's first vision are explained as the basis for the posture which Jews assume when they pray the Eighteen Benedictions (*'Amidah*) as part of the daily liturgy.[46]

Andrew was aware of the boundaries of Jewish explanations which were acceptable.[47] He acknowledged that his Jewish contemporaries identify Christians with the biblical Esau.[48] His Jewish informants shared with him their sense of living in exile, since all lands outside of Israel are considered "dead."[49] Despite the derogatory remarks by Richard with respect to Andrew's exegesis of the Emanuel passage in Isaiah 7:14, Andrew knew and affirmed that Jewish messianic hopes are foolish.[50] For Andrew, Jews were gullible to believe that they would be restored again to their land and that their Temple cult would be restored. He simply quoted Horace, "Credat hoc Iudaeus Apella."[51]

Andrew's path to this exegetical approach was set by his teacher Hugh whose treatise, *De Scripturis et scriptoribus sacris,* on the interpretation of Scripture has been discussed elsewhere in this volume by Grover A. Zinn, Jr.[52] The commentaries by Andrew seem to reflect, in addition, a goodly amount of the practical advice in Hugh's *Didascalicon*. Andrew also quotes Hugh's propaedeutic works, such as *De grammatica*.[53] These works seem to have been the factor which mediated Andrew's approach to the glossed books and commentaries from which he read Jerome and Augustine.[54]

What seems very clear at this point is that Andrew differed sharply from Augustine on the nature of biblical language. Augustine's *regula fidei* provided a metalanguage for the transmission of the Holy Spirit— a *langue*, as it were. This meant that any word or phrase—the *parole*, to pursue the image—had to be in concord with the metalanguage of love. Any community which did not believe in the incarnation could not continue providing appropriate information because its perspective would be distorted. For Andrew of St. Victor the hierarchy was quite the opposite. Like Jerome, he believed that the original language of the Old Testament was Hebrew. Therefore, the Jewish community in any era could provide access to it whether or not they possessed correct belief. It would be unfair to label Andrew an antiquarian or a detached philologist. He was committed to, and knew the limits of, successful engagement. Christian teaching had to be built on the firm foundation of the biblical letter, no matter how deep one had to dig for it.

Notes

1. Charles Kannengiesser, "The Interrupted *De Doctrina Christiana*," in Duane W. H. Arnold and Pamela Bright, eds., *"De doctrina christiana": A Classic of Western Culture,* Christianity and Judaism in Antiquity 9 (Notre Dame, Ind.: 1995), 3 ff.

2. DDC 2.7.12 (CCSL 32:39, lines 6–20) elaborates the importance of the judgment of the Church for canonicity. In the section which follows (2.7.13 [CCSL 32:39–40, lines 21–55]), Augustine describes the books of the canon and their authors. He claims that Ecclesiasticus and Wisdom have been ascribed to Solomon, but written by Jesus ben Sirach, but they are to be considered authoritative because they have been received as such by the Church, "qui tamen quoniam in auctoritatem recipi meruerunt." This passage is discussed again in *Retractationes* 2.4.30 (ed. A. Mutzenbecher, CCSL 57:93, lines 11–15) where Augustine casts doubt upon Jesus ben Sirach as author of both books. On the canonization of Scripture in the early church, see Hans van Campenhausen, *The Formation of the Christian Bible,* trans. J. A. Baker (Philadelphia, 1972). The relationship between the Hebrew Bible and New Testament is discussed by J. Danielou, *From Shadow to Reality: Studies in the Biblical Typology of the Fathers* (London, 1960); and H. DeLubac, *Exégèse médiévale: Les quatre sens l'écriture,* 4 vols. (Paris, 1959–1964).

3. A survey of the scriptural citations in the *Index Locorum* of the CCSL edition indicates that Augustine quotes both Hebrew Bible and Christian Scriptures in the same passages without distinguishing between them.

4. For Augustine's knowledge of Hebrew, one may consult B. Blumenkranz, *Die Judenpredigt Augustins* (Basel, 1946), 70–82, where he cites *Epistulae* 101.4 and *Contra Faustum Manichaeum* 12.37 as evidence. The problem of languages as a source for knowledge of things and signs may be discerned from DDC 2.11.16 (CCSL 32:42, lines 1–25); and 2.12.17 (CCSL 32:42–43, lines 27–31).

5. DDC 1.36.40 (CCSL 32:29).

6. R. A. Markus, "Saint Augustine on Signs," in *Augustine: A Collection of Critical Essays,* ed. R. A. Markus (New York: 1972), 61–85.

7. R. A. Markus has developed the social context of Augustine's theory of signs in his essay, "Signs, Communication, and Communities in Augustine's *De*

doctrina christiana," in Arnold and Bright, eds., *"De doctrina christiana": A Classic of Western Culture.*

8. Note that Augustine suggests that the living language—one which is spoken and heard as well as read—is important for understanding: "Si autem ipsius linguae nostrae aliqua verba locutionesque ignoramus, legendi consuetudine audiendique innotescunt" (*DDC* 2.14.21 [*CCSL* 32:46–47]).

9. *DDC* 2.11.16 (*CCSL* 32:42).

10. *DDC* 2.15.22 (*CCSL* 32:47).

11. *DDC* 2.15.22 (*CCSL* 32:47): "Et latinis quibuslibet emendandis graeci adhibeantur"; and *DDC* 2.15.22 (*CCSL* 32:48, lines 26–33): "Latini ergo, ut dicere coeperam, codices veteris testamenti, si necesse fuerit, graecorum auctoritate emendandi sunt et eorum potissimum, qui cum Septuaginta essent, ore uno interpretati esse perhibentur. Libros autem novi testamenti, si quid in latinis varietatibus titubat, graecis cedere oportere non dubium est, et maxime qui apud ecclesias doctiores et diligentiores reperiuntur."

12. *DDC* 2.15.22 (*CCSL* 32:47): "Qui iam per omnes peritiores ecclesias tanta praesentia sancti spiritus interpretati esse dicuntur, ut os unum tot hominum fuerit."

13. *DDC* 2.15.22 (*CCSL* 32:47–48): "Quis huic auctoritati conferre aliquid necdum praeferre audeat? Si autem contulerunt ut una omnium communi tractatu iudicioque vox fieret, ne sic quidem quemquam unum hominem qualibet peritia ad emendandum tot seniorum doctorumque consensum aspirare oportet et decet."

14. *DDC* 2.15.22 (*CCSL* 32:48): "Quamobrem etiamsi aliquid aliter in hebraeis exemplaribus invenitur quam isti posuerunt, cedendum esse arbitror divinae dispensationi, quae per eos facta est ut libri quos gens Iudaea ceteris populis vel religione vel invidia prodere nolebat, credituris per dominum gentibus ministra regis Ptolemaei potestate tanto ante proderentur."

15. On the development of the legend of Septuagint translation, see "The Septuagint Legend after Aristeas," in *Aristeas to Philocrates (Letter of Aristeas),* ed. and trans. M. Hadas (New York, 1973), 73–78. Also "Le developpement de la legende," in A. Pelletier's introduction to *Lettre d'Aristee à Philocrate,* ed. A. Pelletier, *Sources Chrétiennes* 89 (Paris, 1962), 73–95.

16. For the argument of the letter, see Aristeas *Letter* 5–6 (*Sources Chrétiennes* 89:123–143) and 11 (*Sources Chrétienne* 89:191–231).

17. John Chrysostom *In Mattheum Homiliae* 5.2 (*PG* 57:57).

18. *De civitate Dei* 18.43 (ed. B. Dombart and A. Kalb, *CCSL* 42–43:638–40). The major emphasis in these passages is on the harmony and unity of the seventy translators. For Augustine this implied that the Septuagint represented the Holy Spirit: "Quia sicut in illis vera et concordantia dicentibus unus pacis Spiritus fuit, sic et in istis non secum conferentibus et tamen tamquam ore uno cuncta interpretantibus idem Spiritus unus apparuit" (p. 640).

19. *De civitate Dei* 15.11 (*CCSL* 43:467–68): "Iudaeos vero, dum nobis invident, quod lex et prophetae ad nos interpretando transierint, mutuasse quaedam in codicibus suis, ut nostris minueretur auctoritas. Hanc opinionem vel suspicionem accipiat quisque ut putaverit."

20. *DDC* 2.16.23 (*CCSL* 32:48–49): "Sic etiam multa, quae ab auctoribus eorundem librorum interpretata non sunt, nomina hebraea non est dubitandum habere non parvam vim atque adiutorium ad solvenda aenigmata scripturarum, si quis ea possit interpretari. Quod nonulli eiusdem linguae periti viri non sane parvum beneficium posteris contulerunt, qui separata de scripturis eadem omnia verba interpretati sunt . . . et quaecumque alia in illa lingua nobis sunt incognita nomina, quibus apertis et interpretatis multae in scripturis figuratae locutiones manifestantur."

21. *DDC* 3.4.8 (*CCSL* 32:82): "Rarissime igitur et difficillime inveniri potest ambiguitas in propriis verbis, quantum ad libros divinarum scripturarum spectat, quam non aut circumstantia ipsa sermonis, qua cognoscitur scriptorum intentio, aut interpretum conlatio aut praecedentis linguae solvat inspectio."

22. *DDC* 3.5.9 (*CCSL* 32:82–83): "Nam in principio cavendum est, ne figuratam locutionem ad litteram accipias. Et ad hoc enim pertinet, quod ait apostolus: "Littera occidit, spiritus autem vivificat. . . . Qui enim sequitur litteram, translata verba sicut propria tenet neque illud, quod proprio verbo significatur refert ad aliam significationem. . . . Ea demum est miserabilis animi servitus signu pro rebus accipere; et supra creaturam corpoream oculum mentis ad hauriendum aeternum lumen levare non posse."

23. *DDC* 3.6.10 (*CCSL* 32:83–84): "Quia tamen servitus in Iudaeo populo longe a ceterarum gentium more distabat, quandoquidem rebus temporalibus ita subiugati erant, ut unus eis in omnibus commendaretur deus. Et quamquam signa rerum spiritualium pro ipsis rebus observarent nescientes, quo referrentur, id tamen insitum habebant, quod tali servitute uni omnium, quem non videbant, placerent deo. Quam custodiam tamquam sub paedagogo parvulorum fuisse scribit apostolus. Et ideo qui talibus cum iam tempus revelationis eorum venisset, ferre non potuerunt atque inde calumnias, quod sabbato curaret, moliti sunt principes eorum populusque signis illis tamquam rebus adstrictus non credebat deum esse vel a deo venisse, qui ea, sicut a Iudaeis observabantur, nollet attendere." These arguments are discussed by Blumenkranz, *Die Judenpredigt Augustins.*

24. This brief summary of the correspondence is based upon J. N. D. Kelly, *Jerome* (New York, 1975), 217–20, 263–72, 317–18; and H. D. F. Sparks, "Jerome as Biblical Scholar," and F. Bonner, "Augustine as Biblical Scholar," in P. R. Ackroyd and C. F. Evans, eds., *Cambridge History of the Bible,* vol. 1: *From the Beginnings to Jerome* (Cambridge, 1970), 517–62. For a more complete discussion of Jerome and the Hebrew Bible, see A. Kamesar, *Jerome, Greek Scholarship, and the Hebrew Bible* (Oxford, 1993). Kamesar's excellent study of Jerome's relationship to LXX and Hebrew was not available when I wrote this essay.

25. Augustine *Epistulae* 28.2–3 (ed. A. Goldbacher, *CSEL* 34:105–8). Kelly, *Jerome,* 217–18.

26. Augustine *Epistulae* 71.3–6 (*CSEL* 34:250–55).

27. Augustine *Epistulae* 71.5 (*CSEL* 34:253): "Factus est tantus tumultus in plebe maxime Grecis arguentibus et inflammantibus calumniam falsitatis et cogeretur episcopus—Oea quippe civitas erat—Iudaeorum testimonium flagitare,

utrum autem illi imperitia an malitia hoc esse in Hebraeis codicibus responderunt quod et Graeci et Latini habebant atque dicebant."

28. Augustine *Epistulae* 75:22 (CSEL 34:322–24).

29. Kelly, *Jerome*, 158–69.

30. B. Smalley, *The Study of the Bible in the Middle Ages*, 3rd. ed. (Oxford, 1984), 37–82 for the Schools; 83–195 for the Victorines. DeLubac, *Exégèse médiévale*, presents the most thorough evidence for the continuities and discontinuities between patristic and medieval exegesis; vol. 3, ch. 4–5 (287–435), focuses on the twelfth century and the Victorines.

31. *Le catalogue de la bibliothèque de l'Abbaye de Saint-Victor de Paris de Claude de Grandrue 1514*, Introduction by G. Ouy and V. Gerz–von Buren (Paris: 1983); see also author-title index under Augustine, Gregory, Jerome, and Origen.

32. Smalley, *Study of the Bible*, 117–19. A more comprehensive documentation of Andrew's life is now to be found in R. Berndt, *André de Saint-Victor (1175): Exégète et théologien*, Bibliotheca Victorina 2 (Paris and Turnhout, 1991), 17–49.

33. Andrew of St. Victor *Expositio super Heptateuchum* (ed. C. Lohr and R. Berndt, CCCM 53, "Index locorum auctorum," 236–37). See also Berndt, *André de Saint-Victor*, 219–21.

34. Berndt, *André de Saint-Victor*, 221, provides a caution with respect to our knowledge of Andrew's part in the gloss, because the manuscript in the Victorine library derives from the thirteenth century. However, M. T. Gibson ("The Place of the *Glossa ordinaria* in Medieval Exegesis," in M. D. Jordan and K. Emery, Jr., eds., *Ad Litteram: Authoritative Texts and Their Medieval Readers*, Notre Dame Conferences in Medieval Studies 3 [Notre Dame, Ind., 1992], 5–27) and G. Lobrichon ("Une nouveauté: Les gloses de la Bible," in P. Riche and G. Lobrichon, *Le moyen âge et la Bible*, Bible de tous les temps 4 [Paris, 1984], 95–140) seem to place one of the final stages of redaction at St. Victor. Gibson (21) claims, "In an earlier essay, I flew the kite that the *Glossa Ordinaria* was organized for the school of St. Victor. That kite may be a rather more substantial craft. The educational philosophy of St. Victor falls in very easily with the *Glossa Ordinaria* even to the point of requiring some such correlation of patristic exegesis and biblical text."

35. On the life of the community at St. Victor, see L. Jocque, "Les structures de la population claustrale dans l'ordre de Saint-Victor au XII siecle: Un essai d'analyse du *Liber Ordinis*," in J. Longiere, ed., *L'Abbaye parisienne de Saint-Victor au moyen âge*, Bibliotheca Victorina 1 (Paris and Turnhout, 1991), 52–95.

36. Andrew of Saint Victor *Expositio in Ezechielem* ad 3.36 (ed. M. A. Signer, CCCM 53E:28, lines 143–44).

37. Smalley, *Study of the Bible*, 121–23 (translation here, at 123; Latin, transcribed by Smalley, at 377, lines 9–21).

38. This would appear to be the case from the structure of his commentaries. Despite Andrew's reluctance to provide formal discussions of doctrinal issues, there are passages which focus on theological questions. See Berndt, *André de*

Saint-Victor, ch. 7, "Le chemin de la théologie chez André de Saint-Victor," 275–311.

39. A. Saltman, "Pseudo-Jerome in the Commentary of Andrew of St. Victor on Samuel," *Harvard Theological Review* 67, 3 (July 1974): 195–253. William McKane, *Selected Christian Hebraists* (Cambridge, 1989), 42–75. My own assessment of Andrew's Hebrew knowledge may be found in the introduction to *Expositio in Ezechielem* (CCCM 53E:xxi–xxxii).

40. DDC 2.14.21 (CCSL 32:46–47): "Quae si ex alienis linguis veniunt, aut quaerenda sunt ab earum linguarum hominibus aut linguae eaedem, si et otium est et ingenium, ediscendae aut plurium interpretum consulenda conlatio est. Si autem ipsius linguae nostrae aliqua verba locutionesque ignoramus, legendi consuetudine audiendique innotescunt."

41. Smalley, *Study of the Bible*, 131–32. I have utilized her translation with some additions of my own. The Latin text may be found in Smalley, 375–77, and in Andrew of St. Victor *Expositio super Heptateuchum* (CCCM 53:4–5).

42. Smalley, *Study of the Bible*, 139. Andrew of St. Victor *Expositio in Ezechielem* 1.5 (CCCM 53E:12, lines 324–30).

43. Andrew of St. Victor *Expositio in Ezechielem* 28.21 (CCCM 53E:118, lines 303–10).

44. Smalley, *Study of the Bible*, 362. Amos Funkenstein describes one of the Christian approaches toward Jews in twelfth-century Europe as "non mutare cum tempore," in *Perceptions of Jewish History* (Berkeley, 1993), 172–96. This portion of his book is a revision of his earlier Hebrew essay, "Changes in the Patterns of Christian Anti-Jewish Polemics in the 12th Century," *Zion* 33, 3–4 (1968): 125–44.

45. Andrew of St. Victor *Expositio in Ezechielem*, editor's introduction (CCCM 53E:xxx–xxxi) and the commentary, at 24.17 (CCCM 53E:109, lines 19–25): "Septem sunt vel potius octo in quorum mortuorum luctu Iudei faciunt que hic fieri vetantur: uxor sive maritus, pater et mater, filus et filia, frater et soror. *Calciamenta*, in luctu nudis pedibus incedunt. *Nec cibos lugentium.* Lugens a sepultura rediens primo die non in sua sed alicuius amicorum suorum domo reficitur. Ora quoque lugens velat eo saltem die ut pauca loquitur sed nec per eam septimanam barbam tondent."

46. Andrew of St. Victor *Expositio in Ezechielem* 1.7 (CCCM 53E:13, lines 355–62): "Sunt et de hebreis etiam qui pedes eorum rectos pedes equaliter sine omni obligatione iunctos exponunt, hinc traditionem que iunctis sine omni excessione et inequalitate pedibus illos orare compellit, exordium habuisse asserentes, non enim orantibus illis, licet aut sura femori aut cruri crus superimponere aut alterum ultra alterum pedem extendere." It should be noted that this practice is mentioned in the Babylonian Talmud *Berakhot* 10b, and was part of the Jewish liturgical customary of Northern France, *Mahzor Vitry* (ed. S. H. Horovitz [Jerusalem, 1963], 15).

47. Smalley, *Study of the Bible*, 156–67; Andrew of Saint Victor *Expositio in Ezechielem*, editor's introduction (CCCM 53E:xxxii–xxxvii); Berndt, *André de Saint-Victor*, 263–68.

48. Andrew of St. Victor *Expositio in Ezechielem* 17.24 (CCCM 53E:83, lines 99–104): "Lignum prius sublime et virens quod a domino humiliandum et siccandum predicitur posteritatem Esau genus, videlicet, omnes quod secundum illos nos sumus hebrei significare autumnant. Bona que ligno prius humili et arido promittuntur ad se retorquentes."

49. Andrew of St. Victor *Expositio in Ezechielem* 32.24 (CCCM 53E:133, lines 94–100): "*Terra viventium.* Hec quam nos viventes incolimus. Dicitur terra autem mortuorum interiora terre ubi defunctorum corpora condita iacent. Vel infernus qui in medio terre creditur esse solet appellari. Vel terra quod iam Hebreorum populus ex Egipto eductus inhabitabat terra viventium dici potest, comparatione gentium que sicut non esse, ita non vivere reputate sunt—in Hester legitur: Ne tradas sceptrum tuum hiis qui non sunt."

50. Richard of St. Victor *De Emmanuele* (PL 196:607). This argument has now been thoroughly examined by Berndt, *André de Saint-Victor,* 294–307.

51. Andrew of Saint Victor *Expositio in Ezechielem* 43.17 (CCCM 53E:178, lines 113–17): "Sed absit credere quod facta mortuorum resurrectione rursus templa construantur et altaria, rursus victimarum in templo renovetur immolatio, rursus iudaicarum iustificationem et ceremoniarum fiat renovatio. Avertat deus hec credere a sanctorum menta pia. Credat hoc Iudeus Apella."

52. PL 175:9–28. See also this volume, above, Grover A. Zinn, Jr., "The Influence of Augustine's *De doctrina christiana* upon the Writings of Hugh of St. Victor."

53. The relationship between Andrew's exegesis and Hugh of St. Victor is described by Berndt, *André de Saint-Victor,* 177–93. However, a more thorough study of this relationship remains a desideratum.

54. It seems that there were only three manuscripts containing examples from *DDC* in *Le catalogue de la bibliothèque de l'Abbaye de St.-Victor de Paris de Claude de Grandrue* (p. 528). There is no indication which would show that Andrew had access to them.

Reflections on the Place
of the *De doctrina christiana*
in High Scholastic Discussions
of Theology

JOSEPH WAWRYKOW

The thirteenth century witnessed an explosion of interest in the formal aspects of the discipline of theology, its practitioners often incorporating into their systematic treatises detailed reflections on the essential characteristics of the discipline. In this essay, I will examine a selection of these programmatic statements on theology[1] from the second half of the century in order to determine the contribution of the *De doctrina christiana* (*DDC*) to thirteenth-century understandings of "theology."[2] To what extent have such theologians as Thomas Aquinas and Henry of Ghent employed the *DDC* in describing the theological enterprise?[3]

On the face of it, answering this question might appear to be an unprofitable undertaking. Many of the issues that are raised in these treatments of the discipline of theology—the host of problems associated with the affirmation of the scientific character of the discipline, for example—are peculiarly thirteenth-century concerns, and the resolution of the problems is frequently framed in language foreign to Augustine.[4] What, then, could the *DDC* possibly have had to contribute to thirteenth-century investigations of this discipline? Or to put it even more bluntly, was the bishop of Hippo not left behind in the euphoria of the recovery of Aristotle?

Examination of these texts reveals, however, that Augustine continued to exert a considerable influence on thirteenth-century accounts.[5] Despite shifts in terminology and the expansion of the repertoire of sources, there is nevertheless a great continuity between the Augustine of the *DDC* and my thirteenth-century theologians. In unison with Augustine, these authors see the basic task of theology in fundamentally the same way— as the recovery, interpretation, and proclamation of God's truth. And, again with Augustine, these theologians are agreed about the principal locus of the revelation of this truth—the canonical Scriptures, in which the triune character of God, the end of the human person in God, the way to God through union with Jesus Christ in faith, hope, and charity have all been revealed.[6] In this light, it is completely understandable that many of Augustine's insights in the *DDC* about God's revelation in Scripture and about the appropriate means for the reception of this revelation have found their way, implicitly and explicitly, into thirteenth-century accounts of the discipline of theology. To anticipate the following discussion, first of Aquinas and then of Henry, the Augustine of the *DDC* was indeed a respected and prominent voice in thirteenth-century treatments of theology.

I. Thomas Aquinas and the *De doctrina christiana*

Thomas Aquinas offers accounts of theology in three of his works.[7] The earliest of these, the first version of the opening question of his *Scriptum* on the *Sentences* of Peter Lombard, is, for our purposes, the least satisfactory: although, as I will suggest towards the end of this section on Aquinas, there are probably a few implicit references to the *DDC* here, Thomas does not explictly cite the *DDC* in this question of the *Scriptum*.[8]

The next work in which he addresses the nature and scope of theology is, however, more promising. In terms of Thomas's different accounts of theology, the second question of his *Expositio* on the *De trinitate* of Boethius is distinctive. Whereas in the *Scriptum* and in the opening question of the later *Summa theologiae* the discussion of the theological enterprise is securely and insistently situated against the background of God's revelation, in the second question of the *Expositio*, Thomas more or less simply presupposes that Christian truth comes from God, allowing instead the consideration of theological *function* to dominate from the outset. In particular, the work of the human agent, the theologian, here provides the principal focus for Thomas's analysis of theology. Hence, in the successive articles of the question, Thomas asks whether the theologian should inquire into the truths of God (a. 1), whether the theologian can build a science on the basis of the truths that are held by faith (a. 2), whether the theologian can employ rational argument, taken over from the philosophers, in the explanation of faith (a. 3), and, finally, whether the theologian should employ new or obscure words in the exposition of faith (a. 4).[9] The *DDC* figures in the third and fourth articles. Should the "science of faith" employ rational argument? Can the philosophers contribute to the theological enterprise? In article 3,

Thomas picks up the thread of the analysis first offered in article 1. There, he had disallowed rational argument when the aim of such argument is to demonstrate the truths of faith and so replace "faith" by "knowledge."[10] But he had allowed inquiry geared at deepening the understanding of what is affirmed by faith and defending the faith from external attack. In article 3, Thomas simply repeats that the insights of the philosophers cannot be used as if to demonstrate the faith but can be used in its defense and explication.[11] In one of the arguments of the *sed contra* of this article, Thomas employs the *DDC*. To justify this limited role of rational argument in the theological enterprise, Aquinas quotes the passage of *DDC* 2[12] where Augustine notes that some philosophers have spoken truly and that Christians are thus fully warranted in appropriating these truths, especially since the philosophers hold these truths as unjust possessors—in other words, since the pagan philosophers probably came across these truths through the Hebrew Scriptures, Christians are justified in reappropriating these insights for Christian ends.

The use of the *DDC* in article 4 of question 2 of the *Expositio* is much more interesting, and indeed the entire article revolves around Augustine's comments on the proclamation of Christian truth in *DDC* book 4. The issue Thomas raises in article 4 is peculiar to the *Expositio* on Boethius and when approached from Thomas's other programmatic statements about theology is in fact surprising. In asking about the place of "new and obscure words" in the theological discipline, one might very well expect him to focus on the value of ambiguity in the Scriptures inspired by God. As in the later *Summa theologiae* I.1.9, Thomas would then observe how obscure scriptural language is in fact beneficial for believers, inasmuch as the recovery of meaning in obscure passages requires effort on the part of the interpreter and, as Thomas implies, people value more highly that for which they must work the hardest.[13] In reality, however, article 4 of question 2 of the Boethius commentary manifests relatively little interest in the use of "new and obscure words" in *Scripture*.[14] Rather, Thomas offers here a justification for the use of "new and obscure words" by the *expositor* of Scripture— that is, the thirteenth-century theologian and preacher. Thomas's guiding principle is that the expositor must proclaim only what is beneficial for his audience. Now, the core truths of the Christian religion are of benefit to everybody. Hence, the expositor, in both oral and written work, must proclaim these truths to all and do so in a way that these truths of the first order are conveyed clearly to all—after all, God reveals these truths in Scripture to make possible human salvation, and the human expositor in turn contributes most fittingly to the prosecution of God's ends by conveying these necessary truths in as clear a form as possible. On the other hand, adds Aquinas, there are other truths found in Scripture that are not necessary for human salvation and which are potentially confusing and thus destructive of Christian faith. When it comes to such truths, the expositor must be careful to take account of his audience. If uncultivated listeners are present, the preacher will simply stay away from mention of such truths, being content to proclaim—and in a clear way—the truths necessary for salvation. The *written* work of the expositor of Scripture, however, must be more sophisticated. Written work can fall into the hands not only of the learned, who can handle obscure and potentially confusing truths, but of the uncultivated as well. The writer will strive to be useful to both types of reader and so will treat these truths in obscure language. In this way, the unsophisticated reader will be shielded from the danger while the more cultivated and curious reader will struggle to discern the meaning. After delineating this teaching, Thomas then concludes the corpus of this article by quoting the pertinent paragraphs of book 4 of the *DDC*, thereby proclaiming the Augustinian origin of this excursion into obscurity.[15]

The first question of the *Summa theologiae* marks a considerable advance over the second question of the Boethius *Expositio*. In the opening question of the *Summa,* explicit citation of the *DDC* has fallen away, as part of a general streamlining of authorities in this work. The *DDC* nevertheless maintains a presence in Thomas's final discussion of the theological discipline. Not only does Thomas here restore the treatment of theological function to its proper setting, emphasizing the *revelation* that stands at the basis of theological work and only then delving into theological function. The opening question also offers a more thorough account of the scriptural locus of this revelation, going beyond in this respect the parallel treatment in the earlier Parisian *Scriptum* as well.[16]

In the final articles of the first question (*ST* I.1.9–10), in which Thomas discusses scriptural language and meanings, the contact between Augustine's *DDC* and the *Summa* is at its most profound. The difficult ninth article especially warrants close scrutiny. I propose to evaluate the teaching of this article on the symbolic[17] and metaphorical language of Scripture that operates at the literal level of meaning from two angles:[18] from the perspective of modern critical theory and by taking account of the post-scriptural sources upon which Thomas relies.

First, modern disputes about metaphor shed light on the tension inherent in Thomas's comments in *ST* I.1.9 about the value of metaphor. As Janet Martin Soskice observes in her important *Metaphor and Religious Language,*[19] contemporary theorists advance widely differing estimations of metaphor. For some, metaphor is merely "ornamental," expressing in colorful, imageful language what could be expressed in "plain words." In this view, metaphor is by no means essential for the conveying of meaning; indeed, the restatement in plain language of the truths conveyed in metaphor as a rule would mark a considerable gain in precision. In "emotive" accounts of metaphor, the conveying of meaning is at best of secondary importance and often is simply ignored; the focus in such accounts is shifted to the affect that imagery can have on readers. In "incremental" theories of metaphor, finally, the conveying of meaning retakes center stage, and the claim is advanced for the nonreducible, essential character of metaphorical language. As in Soskice's own description of metaphor,[20] metaphor expresses the otherwise inexpressible. What is said via metaphor about one "thing," understood in a broad sense to cover not only discrete objects but physical and mental states, can only be said in terms suggestive (to a skilled speaker of the language) of some other "thing"; the use of metaphor thus permits a genuine increase in our knowledge of the first "thing."

Thomas's own discussion of the metaphorical language of Scripture can be viewed with profit from the perspective of this contemporary debate.[21] Thomas evinces in *ST* I.1.9 only a moderate interest in defining metaphor. He is content with some vague comments, scattered throughout the article: in metaphor, something is passed on under a similitude;[22] in the metaphors of Sacred Scripture, divine and spiritual things are passed on under corporeal similitudes;[23] in Scripture, divine things are described under the figures of less noble bodies;[24] in similitudinous language, words are not used in their proper sense.[25] Taking as his point of departure the basic fact of the presence of symbolic language in Scripture, Thomas concentrates on limning the "value" of scriptural metaphor, which he asserts in a number of contexts. Thus, in *ST* I.1.9 ad 3, he offers three reasons why spiritual truths are expressed in Scripture under the figures of lower, rather than noble, creatures;[26] in ad 2, he notes some "religious" reasons for scriptural metaphor.[27] Indeed the *corpus* of this article is wholly devoted to arguing the value of scriptural metaphor, offering a combination of epistemological and religious observations. Here Soskice is especially helpful; one might say that in the "reasons" of the *corpus*, Thomas anticipates—or at least, seems to anticipate—the contemporary debate between adherents of an "incremental" and of an "ornamental" account of metaphor.[28]

On the one hand, in the first reason for metaphor in Scripture that is raised in the *corpus* Thomas seems committed to the irreducible, essential character of metaphor. The suitability of scriptural metaphor is apparent on epistemological grounds. People come to intelligible truth through sensible objects. God is a most skilled teacher, providing for each type of being according to its nature. Thus, in the Scripture of sacred doctrine, which is designed to convey to people the truths necessary for salvation,[29] it is convenient for God to pass on scriptural truths through scriptural metaphor.[30] This argument for the value of metaphor would appear to be of universal application, that is, applies to all human beings—the beginning of all human knowledge lies in the evidence provided by the senses; metaphor would, therefore, convey meaning otherwise unattainable.

On the other hand, the other, more palpably "religious" reason advanced in the *corpus* for scriptural metaphor would seem more in keeping with an ornamental view of metaphor. The truths of Scripture are proposed to all human beings, including the simple. Thus, it is convenient for sacred doctrine to propose spiritual things under corporeal similitudes so that the rude, who are incapable of grasping intelligible things in themselves, might nevertheless come to know what is required for salvation.[31] Unless we are to take "rude" as referring to all human beings (as contrasted with more sophisticated beings, the angels)—and there would seem to be no good reason to do so—this second assertion of the value of metaphor is of decidedly more limited application: it applies only to more simple-minded, less sophisticated people. Moreover, it is tempting to see the second reason of the *corpus* as undercutting the first, undermining Thomas's affirmation of the need for metaphor. Should we complete Thomas's thought in this second reason, inferring that for other beings—the more sophisticated—metaphor is in fact not required? To them, perhaps, religious truth could be "given straight," freed of its metaphorical veil.

The second reason of the *corpus* would appear to find its echo and amplification in the second response. *ST* I.1.9 ob. 2 had questioned the appearance of metaphor in Scripture on the grounds that similitudes obscure truth; since sacred doctrine is directed to the manifestation, not the obscuring, of truth, it would be better not to have similitudes in Scripture.[32] In response, Thomas insists that metaphor need not be in conflict with the desire for clarity. If we look at the human authors of Scripture, there is no danger that by their use of similitudes they will have botched or altered God's truth: in revealing this truth to them, God has raised them to the direct cognition of these transcendent truths, to which they are faithful in their symbolic rendering.[33] More importantly, in terms of the readers of Scripture, similitudinous language will not obscure God's truth: for, as Thomas adds here, "those things which are passed on under metaphor in one passage of Scripture are expounded more expressly (*expressius*) in other passages."[34] As with the second reason of the *corpus*, our initial inclination is to doubt Thomas's full commitment, implied in the first reason of the *corpus*, to the necessity of metaphor in sacred doctrine.

That there is a tension in this article is beyond question. It can be conceded that Thomas has been too abrupt in the enumeration of reasons for metaphor. But, that the first and second reasons of the *corpus* are ultimately incompatible, or that the claim made in *ST* I.1.9 ad 2 is irrevocably at odds with the first reason, or that Thomas at bottom favors an ornamental view of metaphor—all these seem more doubtful. For one thing, it is useful to recall that in such articles of the *Summa*, Thomas is simply reporting exemplary arguments which individually and together show the plausibility of some state of affairs. Is scriptural metaphor appropriate? Yes, given the way that (all) people know; yes, given the predilection of some people for the imageful. At any rate, it would appear ludicrous to think that Thomas has been so inept that immediately after arguing for the necessity of metaphor he would undercut his point by (supposedly) arguing that in fact only some really "need" metaphor. Rather, the second reason cannot be at odds with the first; it simply offers *another* reason why scriptural metaphor is valuable. Nor does the claim advanced in ad 2 necessarily commit Thomas to an ornamental view of metaphor, denying the incremental view offered in the first reason of the *corpus*. That would follow only if Thomas were drawing an absolute contrast between metaphorical and nonmetaphorical language and were assuming that all metaphorical language is necessarily obscure. But, it is by no means clear that *expressius* needs so be taken. The present claim should be read in the light of the first reason of the *corpus*. *Expressius* covers much. It undoubtedly includes those passages employing perfection terms, terms which according to Thomas are predicated analogically of God and creatures. But, it is also likely that *expressius* refers as well to other metaphorical locutions.[35] In given situations, the point of a metaphor will be difficult to grasp and there will be a danger of taking it the wrong way. Recourse to other metaphorical expressions, plainer in their intent, will help greatly in overcoming the difficulty. Given the principal interest of this response, the claim of *ST* I.1.9 ad 2 is unexceptional and compatible with the first reason of the *corpus*. Thomas wants to guarantee clarity; in the present claim he wants to assure his readers that the obscurity attendant on some metaphorical expressions is not insurmountable. There are ways of grasping the meaning of the new meaning conveyed metaphorically, of even the most difficult metaphorical expressions.

Thomas's comments in *ST* I.1.9 ad 2 about the "more express" scriptural statements suggest, in turn, a second approach to the ninth article: it will be fruitful to consider the post-scriptural authorities on which Thomas's presentation is based. Without denying the contribution of others, Thomas would appear most indebted to two principal authoritative sources for this analysis of metaphorical language. One—the Pseudo-Dionysius of the opening chapters of the *Celestial Hierarchy*—Thomas openly acknowledges. Thomas turns repeatedly to the Pseudo-Dionysius throughout *ST* I.1.9: the three reasons in ad 3 for God using lower corporeal figures are taken over from the *Celestial Hierarchy*'s second chapter; he insists, on the basis of its first chapter, that figures do not destroy the divine revelation conveyed by them;[36] and he anchors the first reason of the *corpus*, that metaphor is convenient in Scripture because of the way that people know, by an appeal, not to Aristotle, but again to Pseudo-Dionysius's opening chapter.

Thomas is less obvious in his approach to his other major source in article 9 of question 1 and does not cite it explicitly; the contribution of *DDC* however, is nevertheless pronounced. In particular, Thomas seems to have had *DDC* 2.6 in mind in composing this article. Before turning to detailed proposals for overcoming the obscurities of Scripture created by unknown and ambiguous signs, Augustine provides in *DDC* 2.6 some general reflections on the value of obscure passages in Scripture: the work required to resolve their difficulties is an effective counter to pride; the struggle to overcome these difficulties frees us of disdain (what we have to work for, we appreciate the more); the similitudinous language that proves difficult (at least initially) also has the capacity to delight us.[37] While there is undoubtedly some overlap in this regard between these reasons and the various reasons that Thomas takes over from Pseudo-Dionysius in *ST* I.1.9,[38] what really captures our attention in *De doctrina* 2.6 is Augustine's final comment. After enumerating the various benefits of scriptural obscurity, Augustine assures his reader that such obscurity poses no threat to clarity (and so to the human salvation that is facilitated by reading Scripture); for, he concludes, "hardly anything may be found in these obscure places which is not found plainly said elsewhere."[39] Other than eliminating any possible exceptions (Thomas provides an across-the-board assurance), Thomas has simply replicated this claim in *ST* I.1.9 ad 2.

Not only the ninth article betrays a reading of the *DDC* or the effort to incorporate the concluding insight of *DDC* 2.6. This particular passage lies behind the tenth article as well. In *ST* I.1.10, the focus has shifted from the figurative language that operates at the literal level of meaning, the topic of the ninth article, to the different levels of meaning found in Scripture. The basic teaching of the *corpus* is, for a medieval, wholly unremarkable. Thomas asserts that there are many levels of meaning that are conveyed by Scripture. At the first level, the words of Scripture convey a literal meaning (*res*) intended by the author of Scripture. This *res* in turn can point to other *res* that render spiritual truth also intended by the author of Scripture. In this analysis, Thomas is very much aware of the prowess of the principal author of Scripture: God alone not only can make words point to *res* but also have this literal *res* point to other, "deeper" *res* as well, in the latter demonstrating God's providential control over history. Indeed, to the extent that there is any novelty in the tenth article—and even in this regard there are significant anticipations in the earlier tradition[40]—it comes in the first response, in which Thomas insists on the primacy of the literal level of meaning. Picking up on his teaching in *ST* I.1.8 c., in which he had depicted the argumentative character of sacred doctrine, Thomas notes in *ST* I.1.10 ad 1 that in sacred doctrine, argument proceeds solely on the basis of the literal, not the spiritual, sense.

In the first response Thomas in fact reveals anew his reading of *DDC* 2.6. He adds that reliance on the literal sense alone does not mark a diminution in scriptural meaning and the consequent impoverishment of sacred doctrine. There will be no loss to sacred doctrine in forfeiting the spiritual sense in argument, for the literal and spiritual senses of Scripture are ultimately identical. The spiritual sense discernible in a given passage of Scripture is identical with the literal sense elsewhere in Scripture. As Thomas puts it: "nothing that is necessary to faith is contained under the spiritual sense which Scripture elsewhere does not manifestly (*manifeste*) pass on through the literal sense."[41] There are, of course, differences in verbal form between this statement and *DDC* 2.6 and even *ST* I.1.9 ad 2; that Thomas has repeated the teaching of *DDC* 2.6, this time with explicit reference to the relations of spiritual and literal meaning, remains nevertheless evident.[42]

It is worthwhile pondering this "double use" of *DDC* 2.6. Why has Thomas felt the need to state the Augustinian sentiment twice, once of the figurative language operative at the literal level (*ST* I.1.9 ad 2), again of the literal and spiritual levels of meaning (*ST* I.1.10 ad 1)? The repetition is in all likelihood due to Thomas's own sense that Augustine has spoken imprecisely at points in books 2 and 3 of *DDC*, especially in the consideration of "figurative" locutions. In these books, Augustine is principally concerned with the "obscure" passages of Scripture. In his analysis, obscurity arises from either unknown or ambiguous signs; he treats the former in book 2.10 ff., the latter in book 3 (entire). Augustine offers as well a further distinction: unknown and ambiguous signs can each be divided into signs that are "literal" and signs that are "figurative." For Augustine, a sign is a thing which causes us to think of something beyond the impression the thing itself makes upon the senses.[43] "Literal" signs designate those things on account of which they were instituted; signs are "figurative" when the thing which we designate by a literal sign is used to signify something else.[44] For the most part, when he speaks in books 2 and 3 of "figurative" signs, Augustine is thinking of signs that point to another, deeper level of meaning, one distinct from the literal. This is certainly the case in *DDC* 2.6, in his ruminations on the pleasure associated with encountering similitudinous language in Scripture; as example, he provides an allegorical reading of some verses from the Song of Songs (ch. 4). In such instances, Augustine can even speak of expressions that signify *translate ac mystice*.[45] Yet, elsewhere in these books Augustine offers as examples of figurative speech, locutions that, in Thomas's eyes, do not point to a distinct, nonliteral sense but work at the literal level. Thus, at least some of the examples provided in *DDC* 2.16 of unknown figurative signs would be metaphorical according to Thomas.[46] The single affirmation in *DDC* 2.6, meant to apply in a global, undifferentiated way to all figurative language, is acceptable in Augustine. But, once a more nuanced view of "figure" is attained, once one has distinguished more carefully between figurative expressions that are literal and the "figures" that point to other meanings, the Augustinian insight must be recalled twice: once, to insist on the identity of the literal and spiritual meanings (*ST* I.1.10 ad 1); the other, to cover the figurative language that conveys literal meaning (*ST* I.1.9 ad 2).

Read from the perspective of the thirteenth century, there is even some Augustinian warrant for this duplication, for the more nuanced application of the final sentence of *DDC* 2.6. In *DDC* 3.26, Augustine is trying to show the utility of interpreting one scriptural passage in the light of others. He shows how an obscure metaphorical expression can be explicated in the light of a more patent metaphor, and in the course of this analysis recalls 2.6: "in those places where things are used openly we may learn how to interpret them when they appear in obscure places."[47] As used by Augustine, this is but a proof of the validity of the general insight articulated at the end of 2.6. But, by virtue of this more nuanced undertanding of "figurative" language and figurative / spiritual meaning, *DDC* 3.26 opens the door to Thomas's restatement of the final sentence of *DDC* 2.6 in the distinctive contexts covered by the ninth and tenth articles of *ST* I.1. In addition, *DDC* 3.26 offers further support to the interpretation of *expressius* in *ST* I.1.9: *DDC* 3.26 notes specific examples of metaphorical usage explaining (more obscure) metaphorical usage, which examples Thomas may well have had in mind in *ST* I.1.9 ad 2.

There are perhaps two additional points in both the Parisian *Scriptum* and the *Summa* at which Thomas makes implicit reference to the *DDC*.

The first comes in his reflections on the subject matter of the discipline of theology.[48] For Thomas, the subject matter of "theology" or "sacred doctrine" is God, primarily, and all other things (creatures) as these are shown by divine revelation to stand in relation to God as to their beginning or end. In presenting his own view of the subject matter of sacred doctrine, Thomas notes in turn some alternate proposals—some have thought that the subject matter of theology is the "whole Christ." Similarly, without naming a sponsor of the view, Thomas notes that some claimed that the subject matter of theology is *res et signa*. In the present context, Thomas most likely has the *Sentences* of Peter Lombard in mind; however, since the *Sentences* were organized—according to Peter's explicit comments[49]—along the lines suggested by the *DDC*, Thomas's rejection of this description of the subject matter as too general and vague extends to Augustine's work itself.

The other possible reference in the *Scriptum* and the *Summa* to the *DDC* comes in Thomas's account of the use of argument in sacred doctrine.[50] As in the *Expositio* on Boethius, so in the *Summa* and *Scriptum* Thomas is careful to distinguish between appropriate and inappropriate uses of reason in theology. One cannot *prove* the truths of faith by rational argument; one must simply accept these truths in faith. However, given faith, there is nevertheless a place for rational argument in the theological enterprise, to defend the faith and to explicate it, including drawing from the first principles of faith (that is, the truths revealed by God that are necessary for salvation) some secondary conclusions. As the only example of this latter use of argument in theology, in both the Parisian *Scriptum* and the *Summa* Thomas points to Paul's arguing in 1 Corinthians 15 from the resurrection of Christ to the general resurrection of the dead. In citing this particular example, Thomas is conceivably following the Augustinian precedent in book 2 of the *DDC*,[51] where Augustine refers to 1 Corinthians to show the use of argument in the Scriptures.[52]

II. Henry of Ghent and the *De doctrina christiana*

In Aquinas, then, the use of the *DDC* is relatively subtle. When we turn to Henry of Ghent, however, the presence of the *DDC* in thirteenth-century theology becomes much more palpable. Henry's discussion of *theologia* in his great *Summa* of ordained questions is quite remarkable.[53] He has produced an account of theology that dwarfs every other in the thirteenth century, in size if not necessarily in insight. The sheer length of this treatment of *theologia* is due to more than Henry's doggedness as an investigator, to his unwillingness to leave any aspect of a topic unexplored. It is especially the consequence of Henry's preference for explicit citation, for amassing often-lengthy quotations of important authorities in support of his own teaching. Henry, of course, favors a wide range of authorities: in addition to Augustine, he will turn to Pseudo-Dionysius, to Ambrose, to Damascene. And the DDC is not his only Augustine. Henry makes frequent use of a wide variety of Augustinian writings, including the De trinitate and De civitate Dei. Yet, it is clear that DDC holds a special place in Henry's teaching about theologia. He invokes the DDC throughout these articles, quoting from each book as well as the prologue in support of his most fundamental insights about theologia.[54]

Henry is an extremely perceptive reader of the DDC, incorporating into his own study of theologia the key passages of this Augustinian work. Thus, he recalls the basic distinction between res et signa;[55] notes the further division of res into res that are enjoyed and res that are used;[56] quotes with approval the Augustinian justification for retrieving as from unjust possessors the best in pagan culture.[57] Henry is also familiar with Augustine's motive for the composition of DDC, the overcoming of the obscure passages of Scripture,[58] and seconds Augustine in rebuking those who would question the need for training in order to grasp God's teaching in Scripture.[59] Henry also refers to Augustine's "organizational comments" in the DDC on at least two occasions, using to good effect Augustine's comments about the two parts of the treating of Scripture, the discovery of truth and the passing on of truth. The second reference to these organizational comments is especially striking. In the transitional paragraph that introduces article 20, in which Henry examines the possibilities of speech about God and divine things, his description of his project is cast in distinctively Augustinian terms: having discovered in the earlier articles how Scripture is to be used and known and having shown that theology is a science about God and divine things, it is now necessary to proceed to the passing on of these truths about God.[60] Quite possibly Henry sees in this lengthy account of theologia the thirteenth-century restatement of the DDC; in this conceit, his own articles 6–19 would supplant Augustine's books 1–3, his article 20, book 4.

In general, Henry employs De doctrina in conjunction with other authorities, Augustinian and non-Augustinian. On occasion, however, an entire question can be composed of a series of quotations from DDC. Thus, in a. 20, q. 4, in which he asks about the eloquence of the preacher, he weaves together in quick succession a series of quotations from different books of the DDC, from Augustine's insistence on the proper aim of preaching, the edification of the audience, and the consequent need to express Christian teaching in an understandable way even if this requires the sacrifice of classical standards of eloquence, through the definitions of solecism and barbarism offered in book 2.13.19 (departures from customary usage which are necessary at times to guarantee the conveying of meaning), to a final recognition that the conveying of meaning need not always be opposed to the requirements of eloquence—the ideal, indeed, would be to teach Christian truth eloquently.[61] The arrangement is far from haphazard. Henry fairly renders Augustine, bringing to the surface the internal connections linking these quotations from different books of the *DDC*.

Henry's teaching about scriptural language and meaning mirrors Thomas's in *ST* I.1.9 and 10. With Thomas, Henry affirms a multiplicity of meanings, with the spiritual founded on the literal.[62] Henry also agrees with Thomas about metaphor: as in Aquinas, metaphor works on the literal level.[63] And, the spiritual and literal senses are ultimately identical, agreeing on the matters crucial to the faith; the spiritual meanings of Scripture do not create or add to the truths central to the Christian religion announced by God at the literal level.[64] All that differentiates Henry from Thomas is the tenor of his approach to scriptural language and meanings. In *ST* I.1, as we have seen, Thomas's use of explicitly cited authorities is kept to a minimum and, as is the case of the *DDC* in *ST* I.1.9–10, Thomas is quite capable of leaving sources significant for his thought simply unacknowledged. For his part, however, Henry in characteristic fashion devotes considerable space to delineating the traditional sources which constitute the foundation of his teaching. Thus, to secure his points about the value of obscure passages in Scripture and about the basis of the Christian confidence that even the most obscure passage need not prove intractable, Henry quotes the relevant comments of Augustine. Indeed, in a. 16, q. 9, ad 2, he quotes *DDC* 2.6, entire, including Augustine's important final sentence.[65] Whether Henry's explicitness is an advance is difficult to decide. On the one hand, Thomas's manner of proceeding assumes a reader of greater theological culture, one capable of supplying the appropriate text, in this case the *DDC*.[66] On the other hand, it is by no means evident that in every case this is a safe assumption—missing the undertones of *DDC* in *ST* I.1.9–10 may not be an exclusively modern danger. With Henry, however, there is no doubt: not only does he advance his teaching; he explicitly produces the texts on which that teaching is based. At bottom, Henry may be more realistic.

III. The "Rule of Faith"

One final facet of thirteenth-century introductions to theology reveals most vividly the significance of the *DDC* for Henry, and indeed for

Thomas and Bonaventure as well: the common subscription to the "rule of faith" (*regula fidei*) which both delineates the essential content of faith and governs the subsequent inquiry into the Word of God in Scripture. In actual fact, two distinct, yet related, issues must be addressed in considering the place of the "Augustinian rule of faith" in thirteenth-century theological reflection: the exact meaning of "rule of faith," and the claim of a specifically *Augustinian* provenance of the rule in thirteenth-century theological discourse.

With regard to the meaning of "rule of faith," Augustine and his thirteenth-century successors are in fundamental agreement. As employed at strategic moments in the *DDC*[67] and as seconded by these later authors, the "rule of faith" is a rich and multifaceted concept and covers both divine initiative and human response. The rule denotes, on the one hand, God's revelation of the truths necessary for salvation: in Scripture God has revealed both the transcendent end of human existence (life with God in heaven) and the way to this end (conformity with Christ). By this revelation, then, God has established the possibility for a distinctly Christian form of life. The realization of this possibility, on the other hand, also entails correct human response; this response is, I am convinced, similarly covered by the notion of the "rule of faith." Correct human response proceeds on a number of levels. At its most basic, the appropriate response is expressed in faith and love: to attain salvation, we must affirm God's Word and live in accordance with it. At a different level, one more pertinent to the present question, the reception of God's Word also requires considerable investigation and reflection. Scripture is not without its difficulties, and the point of discrete texts is not always immediately evident. In its meditation on the Word of God in Scripture, however, the believing community has learned how to distinguish what is essential in the biblical books from what is not. Through its reflection on the clear passages of Scripture, the community has come to a consensus about the core elements of God's revelation in Scripture (and so about the foundation of Christian existence), codifying this consensus in its various credal statements. From the perspective of the rule, then, it is thus possible to approach problematic passages in Scripture with greater confidence, seeking to acquire an understanding of these texts that would conform to the most important aspects of God's revelation. Indeed, armed with the "rule of faith," one is now prepared to plumb ever more intelligently the depths of God's message as this is expressed throughout the whole of Scripture. And so, for both Augustine and these thirteenth-century theologians, assimilation of the rule is decisive for the fruitful reception of God's Word.

But it is one thing to discern the fundamental identity between the Augustinian and the thirteenth-century "rule of faith." It is quite another to ascribe the presence of the rule in thirteenth-century theology and exegesis to the special influence of the *DDC*. After all, a skeptic might observe, the notion of a "rule of faith" which governs Christian existence and shapes the reading of Scripture is neither original nor peculiar to Augustine. The "rule of faith" as I have described it here was employed by some Christians by the end of the second century, and Augustine himself was in all likelihood indebted to earlier theologians for his recognition of the hermeneutical value of the rule.[68] And, after Augustine, in the medieval West the "rule of faith" was simply in the air, its prominence undoubtedly fostered by Augustine's use of the concept but hardly due exclusively to it.

With regard to Aquinas, there is some weight to this observation. Earlier, I argued that in *ST* I.1.9–10 Thomas is especially concerned to do full justice to the insights of Augustine in *DDC* 2.6 ff. In that case, Thomas's recognition of the value of the "rule of faith" might very well be due to the Augustinian impulse. On the other hand, as I also observed, Thomas does not explicitly note that these articles provide his own commentary on the material in the *DDC*; and, accordingly, he does not explicitly ascribe his "rule of faith" to an Augustinian source. Of course, it is useful to note here that in his systematic reflections on the "rule of faith" as it figures in theology, Thomas simply remains silent on his source for this concept.[69]

With Bonaventure, however, we are on somewhat firmer ground, although we cannot be absolutely certain that Bonaventure has taken the rule over from Augustine. In the prologue of the *Breviloquium*,[70] Bonaventure's lengthiest explicit citation of the *DDC*, in which he paraphrases Augustine on how figurative signification is to be distinguished from proper, comes immediately after one of Bonaventure's recommendations of the "rule of faith" as the guide in the study of Scripture. And indeed, this makes sense: only if one knows what is crucial to God's message in Scripture can one determine when it is necessary to pass to a figurative reading. Now, in his recommendation of the "rule of faith," Bonaventure does not refer to any earlier author, but the close proximity to the citation of Augustine on the application of the rule makes it plausible that Bonaventure here too has been influenced by the Augustinian use of the rule.

For his part, however, Henry is without the reticence of Aquinas and Bonaventure on the origin of his "rule of faith." Not only does he insist, throughout these questions on theology, on the value of a thorough schooling in the rule;[71] Henry explicitly points to the Augustine of the

DDC as his source for this insight. A favorite technique for exploring the usefulness of the "rule of faith," by which the interpreter becomes more sensitive to the nuances and dimensions of God's word in Scripture, is simply to quote the pertinent passages scattered throughout the *DDC* on the "rule of faith."[72] Hence, the skeptic may be right in noting that the rule is in the air in thirteenth-century theological circles. But, at least in the case of Henry of Ghent, it is precisely under the aegis of the great Augustine that the "rule of faith" has entered theological discourse.

Henry's reception of the Augustinian "rule of faith" is in fact complete, extending even to an aspect of the teaching of the *DDC* that has received increasing attention from Augustinian scholars.[73] Against those who assert that the interpretation of Scripture according to the rule must entail a closed system, a relatively limited range of acceptable meanings, scholars point to those passages in the *DDC* in which Augustine stresses the indeterminacy of some scriptural texts and proclaims the value of multiple interpretations of the same text. Scripture's goal is the overcoming of cupidity and the promotion of charity. In a given case it may be unclear how precisely the scriptural passage promotes charity, and expositors may legitimately propose widely differing readings. Augustine accepts this multiplicity, even allowing that the ultimate Author of Scripture may have envisioned and provided for each of these diverse interpretations of the same text.[74] There is a tendency in the scholarship to think that Augustine is unusual in this regard, that his openness to multiplicity disappears in subsequent authors.[75] Whatever the truth for other medieval theologians,[76] this is not the case for Henry. He not only allows for multiple interpretations; he insists on the point, quoting in support of this claim—and at length—the passages in the *DDC* where Augustine most eloquently testifies to the power of God to teach people in a variety of ways through a single scriptural passage.[77]

Notes

1. I have consulted the following thirteenth-century works in the preparation of this article: Thomas Aquinas *Scriptum super libros Sententiarum magistri Petri Lombardi, In I* prologue, question 1 (ed. P. Mandonnet [Paris, 1929]); Aquinas *Expositio super librum Boethii De trinitate* question 2 (ed. B. Decker [Leiden, 1955]); Aquinas *Summa theologiae* part 1, question 1 (Ottawa, 1953); Henry of Ghent *Summa quaestionum ordinariarum* articles 6–20 (ed. I. Badius [St. Bonaventure, N.Y., 1953 reprint of the 1520 edition]).

In references to Thomas's *Summa theologiae* (*ST*), the roman numeral gives the part; the remainder of the citation renders in turn the question, article, and part of article. In Henry's *Summa*, the article (a.) marks the more comprehensive unit, which is further divided into questions (q.) and their parts. The subdivisions of this level—parts of the question for Thomas, parts of the article for Henry—are abbreviated ob. (objections, usually numbered), sed contra (comments to the contrary), resp. (*responsio*, the body of the article), ad (replies to objections, usually numbered). Additional abbreviations used here are bk. (book), c. (corpus), dist. (distinction), qc. (*quaestiuncula*), sol. (*solutio*).

This essay is not meant to be exhaustive. My aims are rather simple: to show that the *DDC* continued to be used in the second half of the thirteenth century and to depict some of the different forms this use might take. In making the case for the continued importance of *DDC*, I have eschewed examining authors who are known for their special affinity for Augustine, such as those Franciscan authors who are rather loosely styled "Augustinians" (see below, note 3, as well). Rather, I have confined this study to the most important secular theologian of the late thirteenth century at Paris and the great Dominican who, again rather loosely (and, I would add, incorrectly) is often seen in the historiography as at odds with Augustine—Henry's and Thomas's extended and at times creative use of the *DDC* suffices to make the point of the continued prominence of the work.

2. I am interested here in the role of the *DDC* in some thirteenth-century accounts of the technical discipline of theology. The thirteenth-century analysis of this discipline can at times be advanced in the course of the consideration of other, related topics. Thus, while Henry of Ghent writes at great length about *theologia* in this sense in his *Summa quaestionum ordinariarum*, in his *Summa theologiae* Thomas Aquinas discusses this technical discipline as part of his analysis of the broader concept, *sacra doctrina*. In Thomas's *Summa*, *sacra doctrina* and the technical discipline of "theology" are not identical; *sacra doctrina* includes this "theology" but also covers God's revelation, patterned on God's self-knowledge, which is conveyed in Scripture. Indeed, in the opening question of the *Summa* Thomas refers to *theologia* only twice: in *ST* I.1.1 ad 2, when he speaks of a *theologia* that pertains to *sacra doctrina*, and in *ST* I.1.7 sed contra, where he glosses *theologia* by *sermo de Deo*. Students of Aquinas have not always recognized the difference between *sacra doctrina* and "theology." See, for example, the translation of *ST* I.1 in the Blackfriars edition; there, *sacra doctrina* is regularly (mis-)translated as *theology*, thus obscuring the subtlety of Thomas's teaching. I will address more closely the organization and shifting perspectives of the different thomistic discussions of "theology" later in the text.

3. A study of the use of *DDC* in introductions to theology offered by Bonaventure in such works as the prologue of the *Breviloquium*, the *Commentaria in quatuor libros Sententiarum*, and the *De reductione artium ad theologiam* would also be of interest. However, in the interests of developing the description of the teachings of Thomas and Henry, I have concentrated on their works. At the end of this article, I shall consider briefly the Augustinian provenance of Bonaventure's rule of faith.

4. For orientations to thirteenth-century discussions, see M.-D Chenu, *La théologie comme science au XIIIe siècle*, 3rd ed. (Paris, 1957); U. Köpf, *Die Anfänge der theologischen Wissenschaftstheorie im 13. Jahrhundert* (Tübingen,

1974); and A. Lang, *Die theologische Prinzipienlehre der mittelalterlichen Scholastik* (Frieburg, 1964). For a stimulating discussion of Augustine's ideas about *sapientia* and *scientia,* with some consideration of the Augustinian contribution to the thirteenth-century treatment of theology as a science, see T. Deman, "Composantes de la théologie," *Revue des sciences philosophiques et théologiques* 28 (1939): 386–434. Talk of *scientia* is not entirely foreign to Augustine; thirteenth-century writers eagerly turned to such passages as *De trinitate* 14.7, in which Augustine attributes various functions to this *scientia.*

5. That the *DDC* was available at Paris in the thirteenth century is beyond question. See, e.g., Richard H. Rouse, "The Early Library of the Sorbonne," in M. A. Rouse and R. H. Rouse, *Authentic Witnesses: Approaches to Medieval Texts and Manuscripts,* Publications in Medieval Studies 17 (Notre Dame, Ind., 1991). In an appendix, Rouse has published two leaves from the Sorbonne catalogue of c. 1275; for the *DDC,* see pp. 401, 402. See as well the stationer's *taxatio* from c. 1275 printed in H. Denifle and A. Chatelain, eds., *Chartularium Universitatis Parisiensis,* vol. 1 (Paris, 1889), 645; the *DDC* is listed among the items available for copying. On the early manuscript distribution, see M. M. Gorman, "The Diffusion of the Manuscripts of Saint Augustine's *De doctrina christiana* in the Early Middle Ages," *Revue bénédictine* 95 (1985): 12–24.

6. Aquinas insists on the primacy of canonical Scripture and its sufficiency for essential truths of the Christian religion in such texts as *ST* I.1.8 ad 2. Henry's appreciation of the canon is expressed, for example, in his *Summa* a. 8, q. 6 ad 2 and a. 16, q. 8 resp. For Augustine's emphasis on canonical scripture, see *DDC* 2.8. 12–13.

7. The earliest is the *Scriptum* on the *Sententiae* of Peter Lombard prepared at Paris; James A. Weisheipl (*Friar Thomas d'Aquino: His Life, Thought, and Works* [Washington, D.C., 1983], 358), dates the Parisian *Scriptum* to 1252–1256. The date of the *Expositio* of Boethius's *De trinitate* is uncertain; Weisheipl (482) dates it to 1252–1259. Thomas began the *Summa theologiae* in 1266. To this list may be added the prologue of the recently identified second version of the opening book of the *Scriptum,* which Thomas prepared at Rome. For this identification of the Roman *Scriptum,* see Leonard Boyle, "Alia lectura Fratris Thome," *Mediaeval Studies* 45 (1983): 418–29. Thomas worked on this just before beginning the *Summa theologiae.* In terms of the use of the *DDC,* the Roman *Scriptum* fails to mark an advance on the Parisian, and for the sake of completeness I will simply observe in the notes the parallels between the two versions. There is as yet no critical edition. I am grateful to Professor Mark D. Jordan of the Medieval Institute, University of Notre Dame, for providing me with a transcript of the prologue.

8. As in *ST* I.1, the topic of *In I* prologue, q. 1 of the Parisian *Scriptum* is *sacra doctrina* (see the introductory paragraph to the entire question). In this question, Thomas asks in turn whether besides the physical disciplines another doctrine is needed (a. 1), whether only one such doctrine is needed (a. 2), what kind of thing it is (a. 3, qc. 1: Is it practical or speculative? a. 3, qc. 2: Is it a science? a. 3, qc. 3: is it a *sapientia?*), whether God is its subject (a. 4), and how

it proceeds (a. 5). In the fifth article, Thomas covers a wide range of material, corresponding roughly to all that is treated in the later *ST* I.1, 9–10. As in *In I* prologue, q. 1, a. 5 ad 3, Thomas can refer to *theologia;* he even speaks (*In I* prologue, q. 1, a. 2 ad 3) of the *theologus.*

The prologue of the Roman *Scriptum* falls into four articles: it asks in turn whether this *doctrina* is a *scientia* (a. 1), whether God is its subject (a. 2), whether it is practical (a. 3), and how it proceeds (a. 4, which further comprises four *quaestiunculae,* on the manner of its procedure, the transcendent nature of its truths, and the place of both philosophical and "saintly" authorities in this discipline). As in the earlier version of the *Scriptum* and the later *ST* I.1, Thomas here views the theological discipline in close proximity to its source, the revelation of God in Scripture.

9. *Expositio* q. 2, a. 1: "utrum divina liceat investigando tractare"; a. 2: "utrum de divinis possit esse aliqua scientia"; a. 3: "utrum in scientia fidei quae est de deo liceat rationibus philosophicis et auctoritatibus uti"; a. 4: "utrum sint obscuris et novis verbis divina velanda." Thomas entitles the *Expositio* q. 2, "de manifestatione divinae cognitionis," with the emphasis placed on the human agent's manifestation of this *cognitio.* The *scientia fidei* is referred to as *sacra doctrina* in a number of places: see q. 2, a. 3 c., ad 5, and ad 8. It is called *theologia* in a. 3 ad 7. In this question, Thomas leaves the human practitioner of this *scientia* without designation; the word *theologian* employed in the text is justified by the equivalence in this work between *scientia fidei* and *theologia.* Despite the difference in perspective, there is some overlap with the Roman *Scriptum* (for example, a. 4, qc. 2 and qc. 3 find their echo in the *Expositio* q. 2, a. 1 and 3.

10. See, e.g., *Expositio* q. 2, a. 1 ad 5. See as well the warnings in the body of the article; Thomas is especially concerned about the danger of presumption in theological inquiry.

11. *Expositio* q. 2, a. 3 c.: "Sicut enim ea quae sunt fidei non possunt demonstrative probari, ita quaedam contraria eis non possunt demonstrative ostendi esse falsa, sed potest ostendi ea non esse necessaria. Sic ergo in sacra doctrina philosophia possumus tripiciter uti. Primo ad demonstrandum ea quae sunt praeambula fidei, quae necesse est in fide scire, ut ea quae naturalibus rationibus de deo probantur, ut deum esse, deum esse unum et alia huiusmodi vel de deo vel de creaturis in philosophia probata, quae fides supponit. Secundo ad notificandum per aliquas similitudines ea quae sunt fidei, sicut Augustinus in libro De trinitate utitur multis similitudinibus ex doctrinis philosophicis sumptis ad manifestandum trinitatem. Tertio ad resistendum his quae contra fidem dicuntur sive ostendendo ea esse falsa sive ostendendo ea non esse necessaria."

12. See *Expositio* q. 2, a. 3 sed contra 5, where *DDC* 2.40.60 is cited.

13. *ST* I.1.9 ad 2: "ipsa etiam occultatio figurarum utilis est ad exercitium studiosorum." It is intriguing to observe how seldom Thomas refers in *ST* I.1 to the human agents involved in *sacra doctrina* and the theological discipline. In addition to the present text, see especially I.1.8 ad 2, where Thomas discusses the hierarchy of authorities in sacred doctrine and mentions the human authors

of Scripture and the doctors of the church; I.1.9 ob. 2, where he notes that a reward is promised to those who make God's truth manifest, i.e., to expositors of Scripture. The passage at I.1.6 ad 3, in which Thomas contemplates the kind of wisdom involved in *sacra doctrina*, might also be consulted. Yet, in the *Summa* it is striking how often Thomas will pass up the opportunity to make explicit reference to human agents. Thus, in *ST* I.1.8 c., in the consideration of the argumentative character of *sacra doctrina*, he allows that there is argument in sacred doctrine. But, he does not refer to those who do the arguing—that is, theologians. Instead, he speaks of *sacra scriptura* arguing with its opponents. Thomas's relative inattention in the later *Summa* to the human agent reflects, I would think, his focus in that work on God as the principal agent of sacred doctrine and recognition that people (the human authors of Scripture, the interpreters of Scripture, the contemporary "theologian") play but a thoroughly subordinate role in sacred doctrine.

14. Thomas does, however, consider that and adjacent topics later in the *Expositio*, in q. 6, a. 2–3.

15. *Expositio* q. 2, a. 4, c.: "Sed in collocutione potest fieri distinctio, ut eadem seorsum sapientibus manifestentur et in publico taceantur. Unde dicit Augustinus in IV De doctrina Christiana: 'Sunt quaedam quae vi sua non intelliguntur aut vix intelliguntur, quantolibet et quantumlibet quamvis plenissime dicentis versentur eloquio, quae in populi audientiam vel raro, si aliquid urget, vel numquam omnino mittenda sunt.' Sed in scribendo non potest talis distinctio adhiberi, quia liber conscriptus ad manus quorumlibet venire potest, et ideo sunt occultanda verborum obscuritatibus, ut per hoc prosint sapientibus qui ea intelligunt et occultentur a simplicibus qui ea capere non possunt. Et in hoc nullus gravatur, quia qui intelligunt, lectione detinentur, qui vero non intelligunt, non coguntur ad legendum. Unde Augustinus dicit in eodem libro: 'In libris qui ita scribuntur, ut ipsi sibi quodammodo lectorem teneant, cum intelliguntur, cum autem non intelliguntur, molesti non sunt volentibus legere, non est hoc officium disserendi, ut vera, quamvis ad intelligendum difficillima, ad aliorum intelligentiam perducamus.'" The reference is to *DDC* 4.9.23.

16. The ten articles of *ST* I.1 may be grouped as follows: article 1 asks about the necessity of *sacra doctrina*, articles 2–7 take up its scientific character (including whether it is practical or speculative), and articles 8–10 examine the ways and procedures of *sacra doctrina*. Article 8 limns the place and basis of argument in this science; articles 9 and 10 look at scriptural language and meanings, respectively. As compared with the corresponding articles of the two versions of the *Scriptum*, these final articles of *ST* I.1 mark a considerable improvement; the analyses of *ST* I.1.8–10 adopt a more leisured pace and are therefore less confusing.

17. In the heading of the ninth article itself, Thomas asks whether Sacred Scripture ought to use metaphor. However, in his comments introducing *ST* I.1, Thomas asks whether this doctrine ought to use metaphor or "symbolic locutions." The latter way of putting the ninth article reflects Thomas's special debt to Pseudo-Dionysius.

18. I defer recounting Thomas's working definition of *literal* meaning until the discussion of *ST* I.1.10; the warrant for this is Thomas's own practice in a. 9 and 10 of the first question of the *Summa*.

19. Janet Martin Soskice, *Metaphor and Religious Language* (Oxford, 1985), see especially ch. 3.

20. Soskice provides this working definition of metaphor: "Metaphor is that figure of speech whereby we speak about one thing in terms which are seen to be suggestive of another" (*Metaphor and Religious Language,* 15).

21. Soskice's discussion of Aquinas on metaphor is itself fragmentary. However, her treatment of one of Thomas's non-Christian sources is helpful; she shows that by his comments in the *Poetics,* Aristotle need not be taken as thinking of metaphor in exclusively ornamentalist terms (*Metaphor and Religious Language,* ch. 1). For a good discussion of *ST* I.1.9, see M. Corbin, *Le chemin de la théologie chez Thomas d'Aquin* (Paris, 1974), 857–67. Corbin perceptively insists on the symmetry between this article and the first article of *ST* I.1, in which Thomas argues for the necessity of sacred doctrine.

22. *ST* I.1.9 sed contra: "tradere autem aliquid sub similitudine est metaphoricum."

23. *ST* I.1.9 c.: "Sacrae Scripturae divina et spiritualia sub similitudine corporalium tradere . . . in Sacrae Scripturae traduntur nobis spiritualia sub metaphoris corporalium . . . spiritualia sub similitudinibus corporalium proponantur." See as well *ST* I.1.9 ad 2.

24. *ST* I.1.9 ad 3: "magis est conveniens qoud divina in Scripturis tradantur sub figuris vilium corporum quam corporum nobilium." See as well the next note, for the verb employed in the text.

25. *ST* I.1.9 ad 3: among the reasons that vile figures should be employed is that there is less chance that divine things and the figures will be confused; for, "manifestum . . . apparet quod haec secundum proprietatem non dicuntur de divinis; quod posset esse dubium, si sub figuris nobilium corporum describeretur divina." See as well *ST* I.1.10 ad 3, in which Thomas addresses the related notion of parable. Parable, he says, is contained under the literal sense: "nam per voces significatur aliquid proprie et aliquid figurative." *ST* I.1.10 ad 3 makes explicit what article 9 takes for granted, that metaphor works at the literal meaning of Scripture. In Aquinas, *literal* covers locutions in which words are used in their proper sense and locutions where they are used figuratively. The closeness of Thomas here to Soskice is apparent: as she does, so Thomas is thinking of an extended use of words, which goes beyond their proper (normal) application.

26. In *ST* I.1.9 ad 3, he lists the following reasons for expressing spiritual truth through vile figures: it lessens the likelihood that divine things and their figures will be confused; it corresponds more closely to our knowledge of God in this life (what God is not is more manifest to us than what God is); and it preserves divine truths from the unworthy.

27. In *ST* I.1.9 ad 2, he observes that the *occultatio* that is connected with the use of figure is useful for the exercise of the studious and for preserving these truths from the derision of the unfaithful.

28. In her own fleeting references to Thomas, Soskice in fact cites the second reason of the body of ST I.1.9 (*Metaphor and Religious Language*, 24). However, in the corresponding note (166, n. 3), she allows that there is more to Thomas on metaphor.

29. Thomas's presentation of the first reason of ST I.1.9 c. assumes our familiarity with the teaching of ST I.1.1 c. on the necessity of sacred doctrine.

30. ST I.1.9 c.: "Deus enim omnibus providet secundum quod competit eorum naturae. Est autem naturale homini ut per sensibilia ad intelligibilia veniat, quia omnis nostra cognitio a sensu initium habet. Unde convenienter in Sacra Scriptura traduntur nobis spiritualia sub metaphoris corporalium."

31. ST I.1.9 c.: "Convenit etiam Sacrae Scripturae, quae communiter omnibus proponitur secundum illud Ad Rom. 1:14: 'Sapientibus et insipientibus debitor sum,' spiritualia sub similitudinibus corporalium proponantur, ut saltem vel sic rudes eam capiant, qui ad intelligibilia secundum se capienda non sunt idonei."

32. ST I.1.9 ob. 2: "Haec doctrina videtur esse ordinata ad veritatis manifestationem; unde et manifestatoribus eius praemium promittitur. . . . Sed per huiusmodi similitudines veritas occultatur. Non ergo competit huic doctrinae divina tradere sub similitudine corporalium rerum."

33. ST I.1.9 ad 2: "ut mentes quibus fit revelatio, non permittat in similitudinibus permanere, sed elevet eas ad cognitionem intelligibilium; et per eos quibus revelatio facta est, alii etiam circa haec instruantur." Here, Thomas resumes the teaching of ST I.1.8 ad 2, in which he details the hierarchy of authorities, including the human authors of Scripture, in *sacra doctrina*.

34. ST I.1.9 ad 2: "Unde ea quae in uno loco Scripturae traduntur sub metaphoris, in aliis locis expressius exponuntur" (trans. in text mine). Thomas completes the second response by adding the two reasons mentioned in note 27, above, for the religious benefit of metaphorical language in Scripture.

35. It goes well beyond the scope of this essay to explore the various ways in which analogical predication and metaphorical locution differ in Thomas. To get some sense of the difference, however, one might contemplate such phrases as "God is good" and "the arm of God." In the first, a perfection is affirmed of God; in the other, a claim is advanced metaphorically. The latter will be evident to a reader versed in Christian truths. Even without attending to any additional context, "arm of God" cannot be taken in the proper sense of "arm"—God lacks physical characteristics. See ST I.1.10 ad 3 for this example; and I.13.3, 6 and 9 for Thomas's more extended reflections on the difference between analogical predication and metaphor. I will return to the notion of "being versed in Christian truths" later in the essay, in the consideration of the place of the Augustinian *regula fidei* in high scholastic discussions of fruitful scriptural exegesis.

36. ST I.1.9 ad 2.

37. DDC 2.6.7–8: "Quod totum provisum esse divinitus non dubito ad edomandam labore superbiam et intellectum a fastidio revocandum, cui facile investigata plerumque vilescunt. . . . quare suavius videam, quam si nulla de divinis libris talis similitudo promeretur, cum res eadem sit eademque cognitio, difficile

est dicere et alia quaestio est. Nunc tamen nemo ambigit et per similitudines libentius quaeque cognosci et cum aliqua difficultate quaesita multo gratius inveniri."

38. For example, in the claim that the *occultatio* by figures exercises the studious.

39. *DDC* 2.6.8: "Nihil enim fere de illis obscuritatibus eruitur, quod non planissime dictum alibi reperiatur" (trans. in text Robertson, 38).

40. When he makes the same point in the *Expositio super librum Boethii De trinitate* q. 2, a. 3 ad 5, Thomas cites in support both Peter Lombard (*Sententiae* 3, dist. 11) and Pseudo-Dionysius (Epistle 9). The Pseudo-Dionysian text is also cited in the Roman *Scriptum, In I* prologue, q. 1, a. 5 sol. In *ST* I.1.10 ad 1, Thomas cites a saying of Augustine (in Epistle 93).

41. *ST* I.1.10 ad 1: "nihil sub spirituali sensu continetur fidei necessarium, quod Scriptura per litteralem sensum alicubi manifeste non tradat" (trans. in text mine).

42. See as well *DDC* 2.9.14, where Augustine repeats his earlier claim: "In his enim, quae aperte in scripturis posita sunt, inveniuntur illa omnia, quae continent fidem moresque vivendi, spem scilicet atque caritatem, de quibus libro superiore tractavimus. Tum vero facta quadam familiaritate cum ipsa lingua divinarum scripturarum in ea, quae obscura sunt, aperienda et discutienda perfendum est, ut ad obscuriores locutiones illustrandas de manifestioribus sumantur exempla et quaedam certarum sententiarum testimonia dubitationem incertis auferant."

43. *DDC* 2.1.1: "Signum est enim res praeter speciem, quam ingerit sensibus, aliud aliquid ex se faciens in cogitationem venire."

44. *DDC* 2.10.15: "Propria dicuntur, cum his rebus significandis adhibentur, propter quas sunt instituta. . . . Translata sunt, cum et ipsae res, quas propriis verbis significamus, ad aliquid aliud significandum usurpantur." See as well the end of book 3 (3.37.56), in which Augustine similarly distinguishes literal and figurative: "in verbis propriis . . . ubi res ut dicuntur intellegendae sunt, sic in translatis . . . ubi aliud ex alio intellegendum est." As in these passages, in his reflections about different kinds of signs, Augustine is drawing the distinction between *propria* and *translata*. However, elsewhere in the *DDC* Augustine can use *figurata* and related forms as synonyms of *translata*. See, for example, 2.16.24; 2.30.47; 3.5.9. *DDC* 3.12.20 is especially interesting, for Augustine distinguishes here between what can be taken *historice ac proprie* and what is taken *figurate ac prophetice*.

45. See *DDC* 2.16.25.

46. See the counsel in *DDC* 2.16.24 to learn the natures of animals, stones, plants in order to appreciate scriptural similitudes fully. See as well 3.11.17: here, Augustine cites some Scripture, notes that in these passages there are some words that are employed in a "transferred" sense, but adds that they are not so many that they obscure the sense or make an allegory of the kind that he normally thinks of when he refers to locutions as "figurative." Finally, in his treatment of the tropes of Scripture, including metaphors (in 3.29.40), Augustine offers examples that for Thomas would fall under the literal meaning of Scripture.

47. *DDC* 3.26.37: "Ubi autem apertius ponuntur, ibi discendum est, quo-modo in locis intelligantur obscuris" (trans. in text Robertson, 101).

48. *ST* I.1.7 c.; the parallel discussion in the Parisian *Scriptum* occurs in *In I* prologue, q. 1, a. 4 ob. 3 and ad 3, and the *solutio* of a. 4.

49. See Peter Lombard, *Sententiae in IV libros distinctae* bk. 1, dist. 1 (ed. I. Brady, 3rd ed. [Rome, 1971]).

50. See *ST* I.1.8 c.; the Parisian *Scriptum, In I* prologue, q. 1, a. 5 ad 4; the Roman *Scriptum* a. 1 c. Note that in the Roman *Scriptum,* Thomas offers a second example of scriptural argument: the prophets argue to the penalties imposed on the impious from the justice of God.

51. *DDC* 2.31.49 ff.

52. There may be an additional implicit reference to the *DDC* that is peculiar to the discussion of the theological discipline in the Parisian *Scriptum:* see *In I* prologue, q. 1, a. 3, sol. 3, where Thomas quotes Isaiah 7:9 ("Nisi credideri-tis, non intelligetis"), "secundum aliam litteram"; this may recall Augustine's treatment (*DDC* 2.12.17) of two translations of this verse.

53. Henry of Ghent (d. 1293) *Summa quaestionum ordinariarum*. The treat-ment of *theologia* in articles 6–20 runs from fol. 42r to fol. 122v in the Badius edition. Henry has organized this discussion according to the four Aristotelian causes. For a recent approach to these articles, see A. J. Minnis, "The *accessus* Extended: Henry of Ghent on the Transmission and Reception of Theology," in Mark D. Jordan and Kent Emery, Jr., eds., *Ad Litteram: Authoritative Texts and Their Medieval Readers* (Notre Dame, Ind., 1992), 127–50. Minnis focuses on the relationship between divine activity and authority and the (fallible) human agents involved in various ways in *theologia*. I am grateful to Professor Emery for discussing with me some of the finer points of Henry's method. For an orientation to the literature on Henry and to some of the major issues in Henry research, see Steven P. Marrone, *Truth and Scientific Knowledge in the Thought of Henry of Ghent* (Cambridge, Mass., 1985).

54. The *DDC* is explicitly cited over fifty times in these articles of the *Summa quaestionum ordinariarum*. In quoting the *De doctrina,* Henry usually gives the book from which he is drawing. On occasion, he will attempt a more precise reference, specifying that he is quoting "from the beginning" or "from the end" of a given book. Only rarely does Henry fail to indicate the book of the *DDC;* rare too is the confusion in his reference of one book for another.

In the following list I give Henry's explicit references. I have put in parentheses the book of the *DDC* to which he refers; where necessary, I also provide a corrected reference: a. 6, q. 3 resp. (*DDC,* no book specified); a. 6, q. 3 ad 2 (*DDC* 2); a. 7, q. 6 resp. (*DDC* 2, cited twice); a. 7, q. 7 resp. (*DDC* 2); a. 7, q. 9 resp. (*DDC* 2); a. 7, q. 12 contra (*DDC* 2); a. 7, q. 12 resp. (*DDC* 1); a. 7, q. 12 resp. (*DDC* 4); a. 7, q. 12 resp. (*DDC* 2); a. 7, q. 12 resp. (*DDC* 2); a. 7, q. 12 resp. (*DDC* 4, "in principio"); a. 7, q. 12 resp. (*DDC* 2); a. 8, q. 2 ob. 2 (*DDC* 4, "cap. XIII" = ch. 15); a. 8, q. 3 ob. 3 (*DDC* 1 and 2); a. 8, q. 4 ad 2 (*DDC* 1 = prooemium); a. 10, q. 1 resp. (*DDC* 1); a. 10, q. 2 resp. (*DDC* 3); a. 11, q. 7 contra (DDC 3 = *DDC* 2); a. 11, q. 7 resp. (*DDC* 3); a. 12, q. 2

resp. (*DDC* 1 = *DDC* 2); a. 12, q. 2 resp. (*DDC* 1; the second use of *DDC* is introduced by saying it is "in fine eiusdem" (from the end of the same book)—it is from book 1, but the first quotation in this question was misattributed); a. 12, q. 3 resp. (*DDC*); a. 12, q. 5 resp. (*DDC* 3, "in principio"); a. 12, q. 5, in response to the first argument to the contrary (*DDC* 2, "in fine"); a. 12, q. 8 resp. (*DDC* 4); a. 13, q. 2 ad 2 (*DDC* 2); a. 13, q. 3 resp. (*DDC* 3); a. 13, q. 5 resp. (*DDC* 2); a. 13, q. 8 ob. 2 ("post principium" = prooemium); a. 13, q. 8 resp. (*DDC* 2); a. 13, q. 8 resp. (*DDC* 2); a. 13, q. 2 ob. 1 (*DDC* 2); a. 16, q. 3 resp. (*DDC* 1); a. 16, q. 4 resp. (*DDC* 2); a. 16, q. 6 resp. (*DDC* 1); a. 16, q. 6 resp. (*DDC* 3); a. 16, q. 8 resp. (*DDC* 3); a. 16, q. 9 resp. (*DDC* 4); a. 16, q. 9 ad 2 (*DDC* 2); a. 17, q. 2 resp. (*DDC* 2); a. 17, q. 1 ob. 2 (*DDC* 1 = prooemium); a. 18, q. 2 resp. (*DDC* 3, "in principio"); a. 18, q. 3 ob. 2 (*DDC* 3); a. 19, q. 1 ob. 10 (*DDC* 1); a. 19, q. 1 ad 10 (*DDC* 1); a. 20, introductory paragraph (*DDC* 1); a. 20, q. 1 ob. 2 (*DDC* 2); a. 20, q. 3 resp. (*DDC* 2, "cap. II" = ch. 6); a. 20, q. 4 resp. (*DDC* 4); a. 20, q. 4 resp. (*DDC* 4); a. 20, q. 4 resp. (*DDC* 4); a. 20, q. 4 resp. (*DDC* 3); a. 20, q. 4 resp. (*DDC* 2); a. 20, q. 4 resp. (*DDC* 4); a. 20, q. 4 resp. (*DDC* 4, "in principio"); a. 20, q. 4 resp. (*DDC* 4).

There are also some implicit references to the *DDC*. See a. 8, q. 1 ob. 1, where he defines *uti;* a. 13, q. 8 ad 2, where he notes, in the light of ob. 2, the account of Antony in *DDC*; a. 18, q. 3 resp., where he reports the account of Philip and the eunuch which in a. 18, q. 1 ob. 2, he explicitly attributes to the *DDC*; and a. 19, q. 2 resp., where he distinguishes *res et signa*.

55. See Henry *Summa* a. 19, q. 1 ob. 10, where he recalls *DDC* 1.2.2.

56. Henry refers to *DDC* 1.2.3 in *Summa* a. 19, q. 1 ad 10.

57. See, for example, Henry *Summa* a. 7, q. 9 resp., where he refers to the precedent of those such as Hilary and Cyprian who converted from paganism and brought their learning to Christianity (*DDC* 2.40.61); and a. 13, q. 2 ad 2, where he recounts the Augustinian version (*DDC* 2.28.43) of the source of Plato's knowledge (the reading of Jeremiah).

58. See in particular Henry *Summa* a. 13, q. 8 resp.

59. See, for example, the use made by Henry (e.g., *Summa* a. 8, q. 4 ad 2; a. 11, q. 1 resp.) of Augustine's mention (in the prooemium of the *DDC*) of the centurion's recourse to Peter to learn more about the faith.

60. Henry *Summa* a. 20, introductory paragraph: "Quoniam ut ait Aug. I de doct. cristiana, res quibus utitur omnis tractatio scripturarum sunt modus inveniendi quae intelligenda sunt, et, modus proferendi quae intellecta sunt, invento igitur quae et qualia ex sacra scriptura intelligenda, sive cognoscenda sunt—quomodo scilicet theologia sit scientia de deo et de rebus divinis et quomodo Deus et divina in ea sunt intelligenda et cognoscenda—sequitur videre quomodo de deo et divinis in ista scientia locutio sit habenda, et ita quomodo intellecta de eis sunt proferenda." The other reference to the organizational comments in *DDC* 1.1.1 comes in a. 7, q. 12 resp.

61. As is clear from the list provided in note 54, above, there are eight quotations of the *DDC* in this question of Henry's *Summa*. The third and the

eighth are quite lengthy: in the former, he pieces together statements from *DDC* 4.10.24, 4.9.23 (not, however, the part of the paragraph employed by Thomas in the discussion of "new and obscure words" in the *Expositio* on Boethius's *De trinitate*) and, again, 4.10.24; in the latter, he repeats, with only a few omissions, 4.5–7. Other references in a. 20, q. 4 resp. are to 4.3.4, 4.11.26, 3.3.7, 2.13.19 (on solecism and barbarism), and 4.2.3.

62. That Henry affirms many levels of meaning in Scripture is apparent in the *Summa* at a. 15, q. 3 resp., and a. 16, q. 2 ad 1. In a. 16, q. 5 ad 1, he explains the connection between the spiritual and the literal senses.

63. See Henry *Summa* a. 16, q. 3 ad 1 and ad 5, where the point is made explicitly. It should be noted that in the former text, Henry confirms his teaching by reference to the opening chapters of Pseudo-Dionysius's *Celestial Hierarchy*.

64. See below, on the "rule of faith." It may very well be that the spiritual sense will introduce details not found at the literal level in the recounting of Christian truths. Yet there is considerable distance between such details and the central, defining beliefs (about Trinity, incarnation, beatific end) of the Christian religion. While the details may add color to the account, only the central, defining beliefs are absolutely essential to Christianity and are without doubt clearly articulated at the literal level of the scriptural text.

65. Henry also quotes *DDC* 2.6 at length, including its important final sentence, in the *Summa* at a. 20, q. 3 resp.

66. For the memorial devices that would facilitate such recollection, see the ground-breaking and suggestive work of Mary Carruthers, *The Book of Memory: A Study of Memory in Medieval Culture* (Cambridge, 1990). Carruthers evinces particular interest in Thomas's own well-developed abilities to retain and recall what he has read.

67. See, for example, *DDC* 2.7.10, in the discussion of the knowledge that one will seek to acquire in the seven-step ascent to God; and 3.2.2–5, where Augustine speaks explicitly of the *regula fidei* and its role in the interpretation of Scripture. As the cross-references there suggest, the entire first book of the *DDC*, on the *res*, is in fact about the Augustinian "rule of faith," which is both the point of Scripture and the guide for the fruitful interpretation of Scripture. See in this regard the neat summary provided by Augustine in *DDC* 1.35.39 on the plenitude and end of Scripture, the twofold charity.

68. For the earlier use of the *regula fidei*, see, e.g., Irenaeus *Adversus haereses* 1.10.1–2 and 3.1–2 (ed. A. Rousseau and L. Doutreleau, under the title *Contre les hérésies, Sources chrétiennes* 211, 264 [Paris, 1974–1979]); Tertullian *De Praescriptione Haereticorum* 13 (ed. E. Kroymann, *CSEL* 70). For a superb introduction, from the perspective of New Testament scholarship, to the rule of faith in relation to the formation of the canon and the evolution of early baptismal creeds, see Nils A. Dahl, "Trinitarian Baptismal Creeds and New Testament Christology," in Donald H. Juel, ed., *Jesus the Christ: The Historical Origins of Christological Doctrine* (Minneapolis, 1991), 165–86. For a brief introduction to the early rule of faith, see Georges Florovsky, "The Function of Tradition in the Ancient Church," in *Bible, Church, Tradition: An Eastern Orthodox View* (Belmont, Mass., 1972), 73–92.

69. For Thomas's use of the *regula fidei* in the *Summa,* we must turn to the treatise on faith in the secunda secundae, which parallels and supplements the discussion of *sacra doctrina* in *ST* I.1. He speaks of the rule of faith, and its expression in creeds and Scripture, in such passages as II–II.1.9 ob. 1 and ad 1; see as well ad 2.

70. Bonaventure *Breviloquium* (*Opera omnia,* vol. 5 [Quaracchi, 1891], no. 6, pp. 207–8).

71. For references in Henry to the *regula fidei,* see, e.g., *Summa* a. 16, q. 3 resp. and a. 18, q. 1 (in response to the second argument to the contrary).

72. See Henry *Summa* a. 7, q. 6 resp.; a. 8, q. 3 ob. 3; a. 12, q. 2 resp.; a. 13, q. 5 resp.; a. 13, q. 8 resp.; a. 16, q. 3 resp.; a. 16, q. 4 resp.; a. 17, q. 2 resp. In a. 16, q. 5 ad 1, Henry refers to the *regula Augustini* for determining when scriptural passages ought to be read mystically and not literally.

73. See in this regard J. J. O'Donnell, "The Authority of Augustine," *Augustinian Studies* 22 (1991): especially 9 and 26, note 7; and E. Ann Matter, *The Voice of My Beloved: The Song of Songs in Western Christianity* (Philadelphia, 1990), ch. 3 (especially the documentation on 77–78, n. 12).

74. The pertinent texts are *DDC* 1.36.40–41 and 3.27.38.

75. See O'Donnell, "Authority of Augustine," 26, note 7: "there is also in Augustine what is often for moderns a surprising vein of licit multiplicity of interpretation. For him the *regula fidei* as guide of interpretation was a much less explicit, detailed, and risky matter than it later became for western Christians, and so we get the development in the *Confessiones* (12.14.17 ff.) of the idea that an interpretation of scripture may be erroneous as regards the author's intent but correct if it remains in accord with the will of God; the same idea underlies the generosity that permeates the interpretative precepts of *De doctrina christiana.*" It is unclear when O'Donnell thinks that the *regula fidei* became more constricting; perhaps it is in fact a post-medieval development.

76. Apart from his difficult comments at the end of *ST* I.1.10 c. (a statement that has often been seen as entailing a plurality of meanings established at the literal level by the divine author; see as well the Roman *Scriptum* a. 4, qc. 1 ad 3, on the plurality of the literal sense), the issue does not arise for Thomas in his discussions of the technical discipline of theology. For his openness to a multiplicity of *interpretations* of discrete passages, however, one must consult his various biblical commentaries, where he makes clear that in given instances it is impossible to decide for one interpretation in the tradition over others.

77. See Henry *Summa* a. 16, q. 6 resp. (where he cites *DDC* 1.36) and a. 16, q. 6 resp. (where he refers to *DDC* 3.27–28).

Is the *De doctrina christiana* the Source for Bacon's Semiotics?

THOMAS S. MALONEY

Eight hundred seventy-one years after Augustine presented the outlines of a semiotics in book 2 of his *De doctrina christiana*, Roger Bacon proposed a semiotics in a chapter called *De signis* in his *Opus maius* of 1267.[1] He later claimed on two occasions that his division of signs is what Augustine taught in the *DDC*.

In the *Opus tertium* of 1267 Bacon says that he has already taken steps "to point out the modes of signifying, just as Augustine teaches in the second and third books of the *De Doctrina christiana*: that some signs are natural and some are given by a soul."[2] In 1292, the last year of his life, Bacon recapitulated the *De signis* in part 2 of his *Compendium studii theologiae*, where he expands somewhat on his original claim:

> Granted that before I saw the book of blessed Augustine *On Christian Doctrine* I fell upon a classification of signs by dint of my own discovery (which I later found in the beginning of the second book of *On Christian Doctrine*), I say with his authority, granted I explicate his statements with reasons and examples, that according to [him] a sign is either from nature or given by a soul.[3]

Karin Margareta Fredborg speaks of Bacon's theory of imposition—the way sounds get attached to things as their names—and his division of signs and seems to say that Bacon's claim to originality in the *Compendium* was about both imposition and division and is not to be taken too literally, precisely because the *Compendium* shows "a fuller reading and a more ready acknowledge[ment] of Augustinian sources" than does the *De signis*.[4] Similarly, Jan Pinborg seems not only to endorse Bacon's claim in the *Opus tertium* to be doing what Augustine did but also to propose an even wider dependence—of Bacon as "taking as his over-all frame of reference the semiotics outlined in Augustine's *DDC*."[5]

In favor of Fredborg and Pinborg's reading of Bacon, one must also point out that, according to Pinborg,

> Generally, the Augustinian inspiration did not [a]ffect medieval discussions on logic; Bacon is here an interesting exception, a fact which is further underscored by his drawing also on the *De dialectica* and the *De magistro* which is a quite exceptional thing to do for a medieval logician.[6]

And to this I would add that Bacon is also seen to refer three times to book 2 and seven times to book 4 of the *DDC* in other chapters of the *Opus maius*.[7]

The view of Fredborg and Pinborg, I take it, is that Bacon's semiotics is in some fundamental sense derivative from Augustine's semiotics in the *DDC*. I, on the other hand, would like to propose that a close look at three of the major features of their semiotics—their definitions of *sign*, their initial divisions of signs, and a certain facet of the origin of what are ordinarily called conventional signs—reveal the kind of differences that count significantly against Fredborg and Pinborg's claims of derivation and Bacon's claim to be doing what Augustine was doing, and to argue significantly for Bacon's claim to originality. In this paper, then, I shall compare Augustine and Bacon on these three features of their semiotics.[8] I shall conclude with what I would call a plausible reconciliation of Bacon's claims to be doing what Augustine did and yet to have discovered his division of signs without Augustine's help.

I. The Semiotics of Augustine and Bacon

1. THE DEFINITION OF SIGNS

In book 2 of the *DDC* Augustine provides a definition of a sign that will become very popular throughout the Middle Ages. A sign, he says, is "a thing which causes us to think of something beyond the impression the thing itself makes upon the senses."[9] This definition restricts signs exclusively to things that can affect the senses, things, as he says, that can leave an impression on the senses.

Now if we look at Bacon's *Opus maius* we find a significantly different definition of a sign. According to Bacon a sign is "something that, once presented to a sensory faculty or an intellect, designates something to [that] intellect."[10] Whereas Augustine's definition does not permit him to consider anything nonmaterial to be a sign, Bacon's significantly less restrictive definition allows that nonmaterial things can be signs.[11]

A comparison of the two definitions of a sign shows that in a very fundamental sense Bacon's definition is not the same as Augustine's and that the difference counts against taking the *DDC* as Bacon's source.

2. THE INITIAL DIVISION OF SIGNS

The second point of comparison between the two semiotics is the initial division of signs that each author proposes. In book 2 of the *DDC* Augustine distinguishes between what he calls natural signs and given signs (*signa naturalia* and *signa data*), and, perhaps, reference to the examples he uses is the best way to explain the distinction that is operative. Among natural signs, he says, are smoke indicative of fire, tracks indicating a passing animal, and facial expressions spontaneously revealing certain emotions like anger and sadness. These examples lead him to define natural signs as "those which, without any act of the will or desire to signify, make us aware of something beyond themselves."[12] Curiously, he does not in this immediate context give any explicit examples of the other class of signs, namely, given signs, though it is clear from the definition he does provide and from the subsequent use he makes of this class that what he principally has in mind are the gestures and words (verbal or written) by which people communicate their thoughts to one another. For example,

> Given signs are those which living creatures give to one another for the purpose of conveying, insofar as they are able, the motions of their minds or something which they have sensed or understood. Nor do we have any other reason for signifying, that is, for giving [such a] sign, except for bringing forth and transferring to another mind the action of the mind in the one who makes the sign.[13]

Now it is careless of Augustine to start off his definition of this class of signs by saying that "living creatures" (*viventia*) are their authors, because this could include plants and animals as well as humans. Nevertheless, he quickly makes it clear that it is humans that are the givers of these signs—people, "we," as he says, who have minds (*animus*) and thoughts (*motus animi*) and things understood (*intellecta*), which one person communicates to another (*id quod animo gerit*), for a purpose (*ad demonstrandos*)—and this is the most important point to keep in mind for the contrast to be made with Bacon's approach in the *Opus maius*.[14]

Augustine does not come right out and say that given signs come about only by action of the human will. One is left to infer this as the proper contrast with natural signs because, as we have seen, these latter were pointedly said to signify "without any act of the will or desire to signify."[15] So I take it that the teaching of book 2 of the *DDC* is that all signs are initially divided on the basis of whether the human will is operative in establishing the connection between sign and significate: things that become signs without the operation of the human will are called natural signs; those which require it, given signs.

Having given his definition of given signs, Augustine points out that animals also use signs to communicate their desires (*appetitus animi sui*) to one another.[16] In the same breath he mentions facial expressions or cries of pain, surely the same kind of sign as the facial expression of anger and sadness we saw he clearly classified as a natural sign. But what he does not know, he says, is whether these expressions signify purposefully or not (*sine uoluntate significandi . . . an uere ad significandum*). That he is thoroughly stumped by these kinds of signs and does not want to sort them out is apparent when he says that this issue "is not in question here and does not pertain to our discussion, and we remove this division of the subject from this work as superfluous."[17] Something is very muddled here. On the one hand, we have already seen that he states explicitly that facial expressions of anger and sadness are natural, not given, signs, but on the other hand he professes ignorance of how to classify facial expressions or cries of pain.

Clearly, however, Augustine initially divides signs into those that do not involve an act of the human will and those that do, and, given this, on what is the parallel division of signs in Bacon's *Opus maius* based? Bacon tells us forthrightly: "Some signs are natural, some are directed to signify by a soul" (*ordinata ab anima*).[18] Natural signs are so called, he says, because "they are constituted signs by their very essence and not by the intent of a soul."[19] By contrast, then, the second class is made up of things that do not signify in virtue of their very essence but require the intervention of an animate agent to constitute them signs.

Now on the surface the distinction *naturalia / ordinata ab anima* bears a striking resemblance to Augustine's distinction *naturalia / data*. Both semiotics discriminate on the basis of the absence or presence of some kind of intent.

But here the similarity stops. Whereas Augustine (on interpretation) thinks of given signs taking origin only and exclusively from a rational mind, Bacon takes them to reflect the appropriate activity of an animal's sensitive soul as well. And the reason for this seems to be that he considers animal talk and involuntary displays of emotions—the very type of activities that Augustine refused to analyze and speak consistently about—to have semiotic properties closer to human language than to smoke and animal tracks.[20]

The semiotics of the *DDC* contains an initial and sole division of signs based on whether or not a rational mind is the cause of something becoming a sign. The *Opus maius*, on the other hand, reveals a highly complex set of divisions whose initial two classes are distinguished on the basis of whether or not a soul (*anima*, sensitive or rational) is such a cause. With this in mind, Bacon then subdivides natural signs into three subclasses, of which the first is further divided into two subclasses. He also subdivides signs directed by a soul into two subclasses, those that arise spontaneously or by instinct (like a facial grimace reflecting pain, or the cries of animals) and those that are constituted through an act of the human will and with a rational purpose (like human languages, flags, and advertisements). Here again the contrast shows that Bacon is not doing what Augustine did and counts heavily against any claim of derivation from the *DDC*.

3. SIGNIFICATION *AD PLACITUM*

The third area of comparison focuses on how Augustine and Bacon think of the way signification arises in the class of signs called by Augustine *signa data* and the subclass called by Bacon *signa ad placitum*, principally, that is, linguistic signs. In *DDC* 2.24 and 25, Augustine has occasion to make a few further remarks on the subject, and it is clear that he takes given signs to be the result of some sort of communal effort, the result, if you will, of a collective decision or agreement between the originator of the name or phrase and his/her audience.[21] Thus he says of words in different languages:

> Therefore just as all of these significations move men's minds in accordance with the consent of their societies, and because this consent varies, they move them differently, nor do men agree upon them because of an innate value, but they have a value because they are agreed upon.[22]

Moreover, he observes, there would be no need of translators "if those signs which actors make in their dances had a natural meaning and not a meaning dependent on the institution and consent of men."[23] These notions derive from his more general one that "all practices [including languages] which have value among men because men agree among themselves that they are valuable are human institutions."[24] For Augustine, then, the cause of given signs is some kind of collective effort or agreement between the sign giver and the interpreter.

Does Bacon's semantics reveal a similar collective dimension? On the contrary, for him the way words get attached to things is by an act called *imposition* that is described in extremely individualistic terms: words are imposed for things at the good pleasure of the one who institutes the names, thus giving rise to the name of this class as *signa ad placitum*, literally, "signs at one's own pleasure."[25] The most that can be said for any collective dimension to linguistic signification in Bacon's semantics is the lip service he pays to the fact that signification cannot occur unless an interpreter is present.[26] But having acknowledged the triadic elements of sign, significate, and interpreter essential to any kind of signification, he proceeds from the very earliest lines of his treatise on signs to ignore the role of an interpreter and emphasizes the efficient cause of language: the free will of the speaker.

On this account there seems to be sufficient difference between the two authors' semantics to support the claim that Bacon's is neither the same as, nor derived from, Augustine's. And this means that a comparison of the two semiotics on the issues of definition of a sign, initial division of signs, and the cause of *ad placitum* signification counts far more against a claim that Bacon's semiotics is derivative from Augustine's than for it.

II. Identification of Sources by Bacon

1. SOURCE OF DEFINITION

Having looked closely at the theories presented by the two authors, let us now look to see whether Bacon identifies any sources for his semiotics other than the retrospective, disputed references to Augustine mentioned at the beginning of this paper.

Bacon has been seen in the opening lines of the *De signis* to propose a definition of a sign that is significantly in clear opposition to Augustine's. But is there any evidence that he knows that it is Augustine's definition that he is opposing? It seems to me that there is. Just after stating his definition, Bacon explicitly acknowledges that he recognizes that it stands in contrast with the commonly accepted definition, what he calls the *vulgata descriptio*.[27] Now as far as I am aware, there was no other definition of a sign that merited that appellation more than Augustine's as presented in the *DDC*.[28] Hence I think it fair to say that in 1267 Bacon knew of Augustine's definition, consciously rejected it, and did this precisely because it would not allow to count as signs things which Boethius (mistakenly) thought Aristotle counted, namely, concepts of extramental things of which their concepts are likenesses. Hence we are also entitled to conclude that in the *Opus maius* Bacon was more concerned to be faithful to Aristotle than to Augustine, in spite of great respect for Augustine.

2. SOURCES FOR INITIAL DIVISION

Does Bacon say anything explicitly about his sources for his initial division of signs? Bacon pauses in the presentations of his semiotics in both the *Opus maius* and the *Compendium studii theologiae* to say a few words about the patrimony of that division. What he says is that he is rejecting as his starting point the distinction found in Aristotle's *Physics* between agents acting nonrationally and rationally, and is adopting that found in *On the Soul* between inanimate and animate activities.[29] This tells us that not only is Augustine not mentioned in a context expressly discussing the source of the initial division of signs in his semiotics, but also that the very distinction utilized by Augustine— nonrational/rational—is expressly rejected.

III. A Plausible Reconciliation

So, then, returning to our original question, What is to be said about Bacon's claims in the *Opus tertium* and *Compendium studii theologiae* to be doing what Augustine did and Bacon's simultaneous claim in the *CST* to have discovered his initial division on his own before finding it in the *DDC*?

I have tried to support the claim that Bacon's semiotics is sufficiently different from Augustine's that it is considerably more likely that it does not take origin from book 2 of the *DDC* than that it does, and I have appealed to four facts, a probability, and an inference to support this: (1) the fact that Bacon's definition of a sign allows for nonmaterial things to be signs whereas Augustine's does not; (2) the high probability that the *descriptio vulgata* of a sign rejected by Bacon was Augustine's, and the inference that Bacon knew this; (3) the fact that Bacon's initial division of signs is between animate and inanimate agents whereas on interpretation Augustine's is between rational and nonrational agents; (4) the fact that the cause of *ad placitum* signification in Bacon's semiotics is almost exclusively expressed in highly individualistic (Boethian) tones whereas in Augustine's it is given a highly conventional setting; and finally (5) the fact that Bacon states explicitly that his division of signs is based on a distinction found in Aristotle's *On the Soul* and rejects explicitly the distinction found in the *Physics*, the latter the same kind used by Augustine for his sole division.

In terms of a reconciliation of all claims and statements by Bacon about the origins of his semiotics I would propose the following as more probable than not:

Long before writing the *Opus maius*: "*De signis,*" Bacon came across Augustine's semiotics in book 2 of the *DDC*, found it to be the confusing tangle it still is, recognized the definition of a sign to be the favored one at that time and committed it to memory—a thing easily done and repeatedly reinforced every time he heard it mentioned by others in discussions on signs—and then proceeded to forget any of the details of that semiotics except the definition: he had no plans to be writing a treatise on signs at the time.

Sometime in the 1260s, but before the *Opus maius* of 1267, he had occasion to present a division of signs in an early version of part 2 of his *Communia naturalium,* and instead of simply passing on the classification found in the tradition of the *summulae* (which he himself had employed in his own *Summulae dialectices* of about 1252) and which was based on the distinction nonrational/rational, he drew on the distinction in Aristotle's *De anima* 2 between inanimate and animate agents and came up with a new classification of signs.[30] This he outlined in the *Communia naturalium* but did not develop.

In 1267 he wrote his *Opus maius* and in it was at pains to present a comprehensive treatise on signification. Recognizing that Augustine's definition would not allow him to be faithful to what he took to be Aristotle's notion that concepts were also signs, he formulated his own definition. In the course of this work he decided—possibly to avoid the charge of being too innovative—to incorporate the second and traditional way of approaching linguistic signs (one rooted in *Physics* 2) as a kind of overlay or secondary classification. Up to this point Augustine's classification of signs played no part in Bacon's thinking, as evidenced by omission of any reference to Augustine in those passages where patrimony is discussed and for which Augustine's "blessing" would surely have been thought a benefit.

At some point between the writing of the *Opus maius* and *Opus tertium*—both in the same year—the value of claiming Augustine's authority for his own division of signs occurred to him. His recollection of the details of Augustine's classification was fuzzy at best because he never had reason to give it detailed attention; because it was a confused tangle of claims and doubts; because there was just enough similarity between the names of their initial classes (*signa naturalia/data ab animo* [Augustine] and *signa naturalia/ordinata ab anima* [Bacon]), and because what he was doing in terms of his secondary, superimposed division and what Augustine was doing through his primary and sole division was sufficient to lull a very besieged man—he was under a second and now papal mandate to get the *Opus tertium* off to the pope immediately—into thinking that his and Augustine's initial divisions were actually the same.

By 1292, the year of Bacon's death and the writing of the *Compendium studii theologiae,* his recollection of the relationship of his semiotics to Augustine's was that expressed in the *Opus tertium,* which suggests that he never in the intervening years had occasion to return for a close look at book 2 of the *DDC*. The *Compendium*, which shows signs of being a hurried attempt to rework the material of the *De signis*, includes a few innovations and omissions, including the failure to even mention any definition of a sign, his own or Augustine's. While still claiming to be doing what Augustine was doing, he did want it abundantly clear, he tells us, that he discovered his division of signs before he found it in the *DDC*, the final pathetic plea of a great scholar for the recognition he thought he deserved and was never accorded in his lifetime.

This attempt at reconciliation of the claims avoids portraying Bacon as an out-and-out prevaricator, which I do not think he was, however conceited and given to inflating his own self-worth, and it accepts as quite possible that at some time prior to or in the early 1260s he read book 2 of the *DDC* but requires that he soon forgot its details, except the definition of a sign. It allows his claim in the *Compendium studii theologiae* to have discovered his new division of signs on his own be taken as true in the sense that he was not operating under any recollection of Augustine's division, and, upon a subsequent jogging of memory or a very hurried reading of book 2 of the *DDC* when writing the *Opus tertium*, he could understandably think that what he had done was sufficiently close to what Augustine did to claim Augustine's support. In this scenario the more troublesome question becomes what or who called his attention to the semiotics in the *DDC* in those hectic days in 1267 between the writing of the *Opus maius* and the *Opus tertium*?

Appendix:

Does Bacon's *vulgata descriptio* refer to DDC 2.1.1?

To prove that the *vulgata descriptio* referred to by Bacon in *De signis* 2 is indeed Augustine's definition from *DDC* 2.1.1. (for which, see the first definition presented in note 9), one must (1) clarify precisely the meaning of *vulgata* as used by Bacon; (2) show that the definition was not plausibly formulated by someone else, e.g., Aristotle, Boethius, the Stoics, the Epicureans, or Cicero; and (3) search the writings of the period, especially those of the liberal arts professors, and discover that Augustine's definition appeared in such a way as to meet the test of being *vulgata* in the sense defined. Short of such a thorough search the following points are to be noted:

1. If Bacon means by *vulgata* something like "the most often stated," then I think he has either characterized Augustine's definition incorrectly or is thinking of a definition other than Augustine's, though it would clearly include the notion that only things that can affect the senses can be signs. (Think, e.g., of Cicero's definition, for which see below, under 8.) A survey of the indexes of many of the major works of the period reveals that definitions having this additional feature are far less prevalent than those that lack it. Thus, e.g., in Aquinas's works we find several definitions of *sign* which, because of their lack of specificity, do not conflict with Bacon's need to allow concepts to be signs and hence do not qualify as the *vulgata descriptio* he has in mind: "Signum enim est, quod est institutum ad aliquid significandum" (A sign is something that has been devised to signify something) (*In 1am Sententiarum 1a expositio*); "Signum autem est, per quod aliquis devenit in cognitionem alterius" (A sign is that by which someone comes to a knowledge of something else) (*Summa theologiae* 3.60.4 c.); and "signum quantum in se est, importat aliquid manifestum quoad nos, quo manuducimur in cognitionem alicuius occulti" (In itself, a sign implies something known to us by which we are led to a knowledge of something unknown to us) (*In 4 Sententiarum* 1.1.1.1 ad 5).

2. Logicians, treating in their textbooks of names and verbs as sounds that signify as opposed to those that do not, had the perfect occasion to provide a definition of *sign*. Ordinarily they do not provide one, principally because they were following the pattern set by Boethius commenting on Aristotle's treatment in *On Interpretation* 2–3. Even Bacon does not provide one in his *Summulae dialectices* when he distinguishes between sounds that are signs and those that are not (see *SD* 2.1.1.19).

3. An interesting exception is the *Dialectica monacensis* from the last decades of the twelfth century, probably by an English master (see L. M. de Rijk, ed., *Logica Modernorum*, 2 vols. [Assen, 1967], 2.1:410–14) in which we find it said that a sign is "quod se offert sensui aliud relinquens intellectui" (what presents itself to a sensory faculty, leaving the other for the intellect) (414). The definition is mistakenly attributed to Aristotle, and the reference to the senses strongly represents a patrimony identical to the *vulgata descriptio* rejected in Bacon's *De signis* 2. For a brief sketch of Aristotle's theory of signs, see B. Darrell Jackson, *The Theory of Signs in Augustine's "De Doctrina Christiana,"* in R. A. Markus, ed., *Augustine: A Collection of Critical Essays* (Garden City, N.Y., 1972), 128–31.

4. In the *Summe metenses* of not later than 1220 (de Rijk, 2.1:452) one finds Augustine's definition, and accurately attributed: "ut Augustinus dicit, quod preter speciem sensibilem quam sensibus ingerit, aliud in

mente venire facit" (as Augustine says that, besides the sensible species which it leaves in the sensory faculty, it causes the other to come into the mind (482).

5. The definition in the *Dialectica monacensis* appears also in Bacon's *Compendium studii theologiae* 56. While it is unattributed there, it appears immediately after a reference to Augustine and is identified by Bacon as *communiter affimatur*, "the commonly held" definition.

6. Theologians required the notion of sign to treat of our knowledge of the will of God, the credibility of revelation (miracles), and sacraments. (See "Signe," in A. Vacant, E. Mangenot, and E. Amann, eds., *Dictionnaire de théologique catholique* [Paris, 1941], 14.2:2053–61.) Thus while Aquinas has been seen above to employ several definitions that do not imply that signs must be something that can affect the senses, when he contends that sacraments as signs must be such, he points out that the reason why Augustine defined *sign* the way he did in the *DDC* is because "primo et principaliter dicuntur signa quae sensibus offeruntur" (things which are presented to the senses are first and foremost called signs) (*Summa theologiae* 3.60.4 ad 1).

7. Surely it is not without significance that when Peter Lombard needs a definition of *sign* with which to introduce his treatment of sacraments in his *Sententiae* 4.1.3 it is none other than Augustine's that he employs (see College of St. Bonaventure, *Libri IV Sententiarum*, 2nd ed., vol. 2 [Grottaferrata, 1916], 746, no. 3). Perhaps it can even be said that the mere incorporation of that definition in what was to become so famous a book thereby assured it a kind of enduring presence and prestige that would have rendered the definition prominently public (*vulgata*) even had the *DDC* not been as well known in the twelfth and thirteenth centuries as it was.

8. It is possible that the definition Bacon has in mind is the one Cicero gives in his *De inventione* 1.30.48: "Signum est quod sub sensum aliquem cadit et quiddam significat quod ex ipso profectum videtur" (a sign is something apprehended by one of the senses and indicating something that seems to follow logically as a result of it) (Cicero *De inventione, De optimo genere oratorum, Topica*, ed. and trans. H. M. Hubbell [Cambridge, Mass., 1976], 86). While this definition has the reference to the senses in it that Bacon finds unacceptable, it would be far more difficult to show that this is the definition referred to as the *vulgata descriptio* than Augustine's.

So it seems to me that if Bacon means by *vulgata* in *vulgata descriptio* "the definition most often used or stated," then I think he is wrong: most discussions of signs did not require one to point out that nonmaterial things could be signs, and in consequence the "shortened" version was sufficient. But if he means something like "the most detailed, well known, and authoritative," then I think he is right to think of Augustine's (second) definition and that it indeed had those characteristics.

Notes

1. The works by Roger Bacon referred to in this paper appear in the following editions and are identified in the following way: *Summulae dialectices:* Alain de Libera, ed., "Les *Summulae dialectices* de Roger Bacon," parts 1–2, *Archives d'histoire doctrinale et littéraire du moyen âge* 53 (1987): 139–289, henceforth *SD* followed by paragraph number. *Opus maius:* John Henry Bridges, ed., *The "Opus maius" of Roger Bacon,* vols. 1 and 3 (1879–1909; reprint Frankfurt am Main, 1964), henceforth *OM* 1 and *OM* 3. *De Signis:* Karin Margareta Fredborg, Lauge Nielsen, and Jan Pinborg, eds., "An Unedited Part of Roger Bacon's *Opus Maius: De Signis,*" *Traditio* 34 (1978): 81–136, henceforth *DS* followed by paragraph number. *Opus tertium:* J. S. Brewer, ed., *Opus tertium,* in *Fr. Rogeri Bacon Opera quaedam hactenus inedita* (London, 1859; reprint Nendeln, 1965), 3–310, henceforth *OT* followed by page and line number. *Compendium studii theologiae:* Thomas S. Maloney, ed. and trans., *Roger Bacon: A Compendium of the Study of Theology* (New York, 1988), henceforth *CST* followed by paragraph number. All translations are mine unless otherwise noted.

2. *OT* 100.16–20: "Et quia haec non possunt sciri nisi homo sciat rationes et modos significandi ideo aggressus sum illos modos ostendere, sicut Augustinus docet in libro secundo et tertio *De doctrina christiana* quod signa quaedam sunt naturalia, et quaedam data ab anima." Three things need to be said about this claim: (1) Bacon first presents this division of signs in a part of his *Communia naturalium* that was written a little before the *Opus maius,* though published after it. (For the text, see Robert Steele, ed., *Opera hactenus inedita Rogeri Bacon,* 16 vols. [Oxford: Clarendon Press, (1905?)], 2:119.29–120.20; for comment on the relation of this text to that in the *Opus maius,* see *CST,* p. 10, n. 47.) (2) Whether one thinks of the remarks in the *Opus tertium* as directed to the *Communia naturalium* or to the *Opus maius* makes no difference to this paper. (3) The text in the *Opus tertium* can be interpreted to mean simply that Augustine and Bacon are both proposing a division of signs, or that what Bacon is proposing is what Augustine proposes. Since the former reading would provide no basis for an Augustinian "blessing" upon Bacon's work—that which is surely sought in this text—and the latter does, I take the second reading to express Bacon's intent.

3. *CST* 25: "Et, licet antequam vidi librum beati Augustini *De doctrina christiana,* cecidi per studium propriae inventionis in divisionem signorum, quam postea inveni in principio secundi libri De doctrina christiana, dico eius auctoritate, licet explico dicta eius ratione et exemplis, quod signum secundum [eum] est a natura vel datum ab anima." While this text admits of various readings, I take it to claim at least (1) that Bacon was not thinking of Augustine's division

of signs when he discovered the one he uses in the *De signis* 3, and (2) that his and Augustine's (initial) divisions are in some unstated, yet fundamental, sense the same.

4. She writes: "Bacon's immediate sources for details of his theory of imposition and his theory of conventional *versus* natural signs are difficult to trace. In the *Compendium Studii Theologiae* . . . he claimed that he had first devi[s]ed the theory himself, and only later found the same in St. Augustine (*DDC* 2.2–5). This statement should hardly be interpreted too literally. However, it remains a fact that the late *Compendium*, in comparison with the *De signis*, shows a fuller reading and a more ready acknowledge[ment] of Augustinian sources" (Karin Margareta Fredborg, "Roger Bacon on *impositio vocis ad significandum*," in H. A. G. Braakhuis, C. H. Kneepkens, and L. M. de Rijk, eds., *English Logic and Semantics: From the End of the Twelfth Century to the Time of Ockham and Burleigh,* Acts of the Fourth European Symposium on Mediaeval Logic and Semantics, Leiden-Nijmegen, 23–27 April 1979 [Nijmegen, 1981], 173). While the words "However, it remains a fact that" would seem to announce a contrast with what precedes, I doubt it is intended to do so. I take it, then, as her intended meaning that Bacon's claim to originality is in some fundamental sense false because of his increasing knowledge of Augustine.

5. Jan Pinborg, "Roger Bacon on Signs: A Newly Recovered Part of the *Opus maius*," *Miscellanea medievalia* 13: *Sprache und Erkenntniss im Mittelalter* (Berlin, 1981), 405. While the phrase "over-all frame of reference" is vague enough to admit of various meanings, to say something significantly important about the relation of Bacon's semiotics to Augustine's I take it to refer at least to their definitions of a sign and their initial division of signs.

6. Ibid.

7. For the references to book 2, see *OM* 3:30.3 and 1:178.7–12 and 180.3–6; (trans. Burke, 1:30, 198, and 199). For the references to book 4, see Eugenio Massa, ed., *Rogeri Baconis moralis philosophiae* (Zurich, 1953), 252.13–14; 258.25; 259.8–11, 11–13, 14–24; 262.3, 5–6, 6–7, 8–10; and 263.5.

8. There are, of course, other features on which the two semiotics could be compared. But it seems to me that, if they are significantly different in these three respects, one is justified is saying that they are fundamentally and sufficiently different to invalidate Bacon's claim to be doing what Augustine did and to count heavily against Pinborg's and Fredborg's apparent claim of derivation.

9. *DDC* 2.1.1 (*CCSL* 32:32.5–7; trans. Robertson, 34): "Signum est enim res praeter speciem, quam ingerit sensibus, aliud aliquid ex se faciens in cogitationem uenire." Something similar to this notion is expressed in other, less comprehensive, terms in *DDC* 1.2.2 (*CCSL* 32:7.11–12; trans. Robertson, 8–9): "signa, res eas uidelicet, quae ad significandum aliquid adhibentur" (they are things used to signify something).

10. *DS* 2: "Signum autem est illud quod oblatum sensui vel intellectui aliquid designat ipsi intellectui." For his complete notion of a sign, see below, note 27.

11. Bacon is very emphatic on the point because he wants to be able to consider concepts as signs of the things of which they are likenesses (see below, note 27). Once he makes the point, he makes no further use of it.

12. *DDC* 2.1.2 (*CCSL* 32:32.13–14): "quae sine uoluntate atque ullo appetitu significandi praeter se aliquid aliud ex se cognosci faciunt."

13. *DDC* 2.2.3 (*CCSL* 32:33.1–5): "Data uero signa sunt, quae sibi quaeque uiuentia inuicem dant ad demonstrandos, quantum possunt, motus animi sui uel sensa aut intellecta quaelibet. Nec ulla causa est nobis significandi, id est signi dandi, nisi ad depromendum et traiciendum in alterius animum id, quod animo gerit, qui signum dat."

14. B. Darell Jackson supports this interpretation when he points out that "terms like '*cogitatio*' and '*animus*' [in this context] are, nevertheless, primarily anthropological terms" ("The Theory of Signs in St. Augustine's *De Doctrina Christiana*," in R. A. Markus, ed., *Augustine: A Collection of Critical Essays* [Garden City, N.Y., 1972], 95; see also 113–15). The significance of this interpretation of the text quoted immediately above for the argument of this paper cannot be exaggerated. If Augustine intends *uiuentia, motus animi, animus gerens* and *ad demonstrandos* to include reference to all living creatures and/or their proper activities, or even just animals and humans, then Fredborg's and Pinborg's suspicion of Bacon's claim to originality is thereby supported: Bacon's and Augustine's initial division of signs would not be fundamentally different. And in this regard, see also below, note 16, where Augustine is seen to use *appetitus animi* and *motus animi* apropos of instinctual emotions in beasts and humans.

15. See above, note 12.

16. For this and what follows immediately see *DDC* 2.2.3 (*CCSL* 32:33.9–14): "Habent etiam bestiae quaedam inter se signa, quibus produnt appetitum animi sui. Nam et gallus gallinaceus reperto cibo dat signum uocis gallinae, ut accurrat; et columbus gemitu columbam uocat, uel ab ea uicissim uocatur; et multa huiusmodi animaduerti solent. Quae utrum, sicut uultus aut dolentis clamor sine uoluntate significandi sequantur motum animi, an uere ad significandum dentur, alia quaestio est et ad rem, quae agitur, non pertinet. Quam partem ab hoc opere tamquam non necessariam remouemus."

The Greeks sometimes made a distinction between *psyche* and *nous* whereby the former meant soul in the broad context of the principle of life (movement from within) and the latter the rational part of the human soul. These were sometimes rendered in Latin by *anima* and *animus*. It is clear, however, that Augustine in *DDC* 2.2.3 (*CCSL* 32:33.15–16) does not avail himself of this convention when he contrasts *motus animi* with *quae uere ad significandum dentur*: this is clearly intended to contrast the instinctive actions of an animal's soul with the rational action of human sign giving, and yet *animus* is said to be the cause of the former.

17. See above, note 16.

18. *DS* 3: "Signorum autem quaedam sunt naturalia, quaedam ordinata ab anima ad significandum."

19. *DS* 3: "Naturalia autem dicuntur, quia ex essentia sua et non ex intentione animae signi rationem recipiunt."

20. Apropos of Augustine's quandary about such signs, Bacon says in *CST* 36: "However, Blessed Augustine in the book mentioned [the *DDC*] is uncertain

as to whether cries like these of animals occur because of some intent of their souls (cum aliqua intentione animae). But it seems to me that they would come from intent (sed mihi videtur quod ex intentione fiant), because animals utter one kind of cry in one situation and a different [kind] in another. For example a hen utters one type of cry when she teaches her chicks to guard against a hawk and another when she calls them for food."

21. As far as I am aware the first to call attention to a contrast between what Augustine and Boethius have to say on this point is J. Engels, for which see his "La doctrine du signe chez Saint Augustin," *Studia patristica* 6, ed. F. L. Cross (Berlin, 1962), 366–73; and "Origine, sens et survie du terme boecien *secundum placitum*," *Vivarium* 1 (1963): 87–114. In the former, he concludes: "A curious fact: whereas the definition of a sign formulated by Augustine passed down through the Middle Ages, the collective aspect of the linguistic sign, although pointed out by him, has almost been eclipsed by the Boethian 'ad placitum'" (373). For the implications of this for translating *ad placitum,* see *CST,* "Introduction," 26–28.

22. *DDC* 2.24.37 (*CCSL* 32:60.19–22; trans. Robertson, 60–61): "Sicut ergo hae omnes significationes pro suae cuiusque societatis consensione animos mouent et, quia diuersa consensio est, diuerse mouent, nec ideo consenserunt in eas homines, quia iam ualebant ad significationem, sed ideo ualent, quia consenserunt in eas."

23. *DDC* 2.25.38 (*CCSL* 32:60.7–11; trans. Robertson, 61): "Illa enim signa, quae saltando faciunt histriones, si natura, non instituto et consensione hominum ualerent, non primis temporibus saltante pantomimo praeco pronuntiaret populo Carthaginis, quid saltator uellet intelligi."

24. *DDC* 2.25.38 (*CCSL* 32:60.4–6; trans. Robertson 61): "namque omnia, quae ideo ualent inter homines, quia placuit inter eos, ut ualeant, instituta hominum sunt."

25. These signs arise, says Bacon in *DS* 7: "ab anima cum deliberatione rationis et electione voluntatis, sive ad placitum, sive ex proposito, et huiusmodi est signum institutum ab intellectu ut linguae et idiomata et circulus vini et res expositae venditionis in fenestris venditorum positae pro signis" (from the soul with the deliberation of reason and choice of the will, i.e., at [one's] pleasure and for a purpose, and such is the sign instituted by the intellect like languages, dialects, the circle [that stands for] wine, and things displayed in store windows as things [that are] for sale). This individualistic tone is also preserved and emphasized in *CST* 81 when he speaks of the cause of the naming of composites as the "liberum arbitrium imponentis nomen secundum suae beneplacitum voluntatis" (the free will of the one imposing the name in accord with the good pleasure of his own will).

Bacon makes it clear in *CST* 97 that the paradigm of naming is the imposition of names at baptism and the naming of pets. Such reflect an explicit (or implicit) formula of the type "I name you 'John'." One should also point out that any medieval theory of naming should cover the solitary naming of all creatures by Adam, and it is not immediately clear how Augustine would explain his requirement of convention in that context.

26. *DS* 1: "Quia nisi posset aliquis concipere per signum, cassum esset et vanum, immo non erit signum" (Unless someone could conceive through a sign, it would be empty and useless; more, it would not even be a sign).

27. *DS* 2: "Signum autem est illud quod oblatum sensui vel intellectui aliquid designat ipsi intellectui, quoniam non omne signum offertur sensui ut vulgata descriptio signi supponit, sed aliquod soli intellectui offertur, testante Aristotle [*De interpretatione* 16a3–4], qui dicit passiones animae esse signa rerum quae passiones sunt habitus ipsi et species rerum existentes apud intellectum, et ideo soli intellectui offeruntur, ita ut repraesentant intellectui ipsas res extra" (A sign, moreover, is something which, once presented to a sensory faculty or an intellect, designates something to [that] intellect, because not every sign is presented to a sensory faculty, as Aristotle bears witness when he says concepts of the soul are signs of things; these concepts are the very habits and species of things [and] they exist within the intellect, and so present themselves only in such a way to the intellect as to represent to the intellect those very things outside [it]).

28. For support for this claim, see above, Appendix.

29. *DS* 13: "Aliter aut[em] in II *De anima* dividitur natura contra animam. Natura enim ut dicit movet in partem unam tantum, anima autem in omnem. Diceret aliquis quod voces animalium non sunt naturaliter significativae, et praecipue cum fiant ex intentione et ordinatione animae. Intelligendum est quod ibi sumitur 'natura' longe strictius quam in II *Physicorum*. Sumitur enim natura ibi pro sola virtute agente sine deliberatione ut in caelo et elementis et mixtis carentibus anima. Sed in II *Physicorum* universalius pro virtute agente sine deliberatione sive sit in rebus animatis sive inanimatis" (But nature is distinguished from soul in a different way in *On the Soul* 2, for nature, as it says, moves only one part at a time whereas soul all the different parts at once. One might say that the cries of animals do not signify by nature, and especially should they arise from the intent and direction of a soul. It must be understood that there *nature* is taken far more narrowly than in *Physics* 2. For there nature [is taken] for only a power acting without deliberation, as in the heavens and the elements and in compounds lacking a soul. But in *Physics* 2 [nature is taken] more broadly for a power acting without deliberation whether it be in the case of animate or inanimate things. And so soul may be understood under nature in one way, and although these signs exist by intent of a soul, this intent is natural and not rational).

If Bacon was in any sense thinking of Augustine's semiotics when he wrote these words, it would have offered the perfect opportunity to say that the distinction "natural / rational" was found not only in *Physics* 2 but also in *DDC* 2 and thereby reap whatever advantage he hoped to achieve by the later claim in the *Opus tertium;* no such acknowledgment is presented. What he does do in *De signis* 13 and the parallel text in *Compendium* 32 and 35 is to create a second way of classifying signs—this one in harmony with Augustine's—and, so to speak, to superimpose it upon his initial division. The result is two classifications that trade on an equivocation on the term *natural:* in the more fundamental one animal talk is not said to be natural (because here nature is distinguished from an animate agent); in the secondary one animal talk is classified as natural (because there nature is distinguished only from rational agents). Had Bacon proposed in the *Opus maius: De signis* and the *Compendium studii theologiae* only the second classification, or presented it as the initial division of signs, his claims in the *Opus tertium* and *Compendium* to be doing what Augustine was doing would at least be substantiated in respect to that part of his semiotics pertaining to the classification of signs. But recall that his definition of a sign is still different and the way he envisions signification *ad placitum*.

30. In a certain sense Bacon's traditional treatment of sound signs in his *Summulae dialectices* could be termed his first approach to semiotics, and what we have been discussing in this paper his second approach. Apropos of the *Summulae*, moreover, it should be noted that the inspiration for the distinction between rational and nonrational sound signs is Aristotle's *On Interpretation* 2–3 via Boethius's commentary on that work, and not the *DDC*. See *SD* 2.1.1.1–28, esp. 19–26.

De doctrina christiana and Musical Semiotics in Medieval Culture

KAY BRAINERD SLOCUM

The influence of Saint Augustine on musical theory and practice is a well-known aspect of medieval culture. The six books of his *De musica* were devoted to an explication of rhythm, metrics, verse, and number which provided both an aesthetic foundation and an aid to rhythmic practice during the Middle Ages. In addition, this work offered a view of musical expression which emphasized the use of rhythm and number as vehicles enabling one to ascend from the objects of sense to the apprehension of eternal truth.

This vision of music was further clarified in *De doctrina christiana*, where Augustine spoke of using "signs" so that the "invisible things" of God may be realized; by means of corporeal and temporal things comprehension of the eternal and spiritual may become possible. Using the principles put forth in this work, medieval philosophers and musicians developed a view of the function of music which derived not only from its possibilities as a sounding art but also from its metaphysical qualities, wherein it could act as a *speculum* of the universe, a means whereby one might apprehend the harmony of God's creation.

This essay will examine Augustine's theory of musical semiotics as presented in *DDC* and will also explore the influence of this tradition upon the musical philosophy of the thirteenth century, as exemplified in the writings of Saint Bonaventure and the musical theorist Jacques de Liège.

From the era of Saint Augustine until the fourteenth century, western European thinkers, artists, and musicians produced a variety of works which were characterized by a common philosophical foundation,

143

although they differed from one another in their individual forms. In seeking to define this ideological commonality or essence it is important to review briefly the concepts which differentiate the medieval attitude toward art and music from our own.

The most important difference lies in the changed meaning and function of the symbol. For the twentieth-century individual the symbol is an image that invests physical reality with poetic meaning. By contrast, the people of medieval Europe believed that the physical world had no reality except as symbol. For them everything was, to some degree, a manifestation of God—an image, vestige, or shadow of the creator. In other words, for us the symbol is the subjective creation of poetic fancy, but what we would call symbol was for medieval thinkers the only valid epistemological method. They were preoccupied with the symbolic nature of the world of appearances, for they believed that God had given to every created thing a cryptic meaning which could be read in the light of symbolism. The image, the word, and certain combinations of musical sound were perceived not as illusion but as revelation, for God was the beginning and also the goal of human knowledge. As Marcia Colish pointed out in *The Mirror of Language*, this "mental universe" was composed of standard preconceptions about the nature of reality which implied standard assumptions about the nature and methodology of knowledge and, as we shall see, of musical creation.[1]

During the Middle Ages educated people drew upon a common religious heritage and educational background in their attempts to understand and explain the function of the symbol as a pathway to knowledge of God. They had learned the basic techniques of the *trivium*, which provided them with linguistic skills, and they were also conversant with the disciplines of the *quadrivium*, which included the study of music. Hence, a symbolic theory of knowledge which included the concept of music as an epistemological relationship between God and human beings was a natural, and probably inevitable, outcome.

Integral to the development of musical semiotics was the Augustinian theory of signs as presented in book 2 of *DDC*. In a definition destined to become a fundamental tenet of medieval epistemology, Augustine described a sign as

> a thing (*res*) which causes us to think of something beyond the impression the thing itself makes upon the senses. Thus if we see a track, we think of the animal that made the track; if we see smoke, we know that there is a fire which causes it; if we hear the voice of a living being, we attend to the emotion it expresses; and when a trumpet sounds, a soldier should know whether it is necessary to advance or to retreat, or whether the battle demands some other response.[2]

Thus, for Augustine, a thing (*res*) was a sign precisely insofar as it stood for something to somebody. Indeed, as R. A. Markus has demonstrated, this triadic relation was essential to any situation in order for one element in it to function as a sign.[3]

Augustine expanded his definition by distinguishing two fundamental types of sign according to whether the relation of dependence was between the sign and the object or between the sign and the subject. The first type, *signa naturalia*, he defined as things, or events which

> without any desire or intention of signifying, make us aware of something beyond themselves, like smoke which signifies fire. It does this without any will to signify, for even when smoke appears alone, observation and memory of experience with things bring a recognition of an underlying fire.[4]

The second type, *signa data*, he defined in the following manner:

> conventional signs are those which living creatures show to one another for the purposes of conveying, insofar as they are able, the motion of their spirits or something which they have sensed or understood. Nor is there any other reason for signifying, or for giving signs, except for bringing forth and transferring to another mind the action of the mind in the person who makes the sign.[5]

Thus the thing or event which constitutes the conventional sign is the product of the sign maker's activity and owes its significance entirely to this. A sign of this kind might be called a "symbol," and would possess the determinate meaning or range of meanings which the sign maker's activity bestowed upon it.

Hence, for Augustine the meaning of *signa data* was exclusively conventional in nature. He argued that any expression, to be meaningful, presupposed a community established by users of the same language. Furthermore, he believed that people did not establish conventions for using signs with determinate meanings because signs already possessed significance ("quia iam valebant ad significationem"); they became meaningful solely because people established the conventions for their use ("ideo valent quia consenserunt in eas");[6] thus, "signs were not valid among men except by common consent."[7]

Among the signs by which people expressed their meanings to one another Augustine pointed to some which pertained to the sense of sight, more to the sense of hearing, and very few to the other senses.

> When we nod, we give a sign only to the sight of the person whom we wish by that sign to make a participant in our will. Some signify many things through the motions of their hands, and actors give signs to

those who understand . . . as if narrating things to their eyes. All of these things are like so many visible words. More signs pertain to the ears, and most of these consist of words. But the trumpet, the flute, and the harp make sounds which are not only pleasing but also significant, although as compared with the number of verbal signs the number of signs of this kind are few. For words have come to be predominant among men for signifying whatever the mind conceives if they wish to communicate it to anyone.[8]

Thus Augustine's theory of semiotics was mainly a theory of the meaning of words; it focused primarily upon linguistic signs.[9] Its application was not limited exclusively to verbal content, however, for he acknowledged the significance of musical sound functioning as symbol, and the theory which he provided was sufficiently comprehensive to include music as well as words, gestures, and expressions in the visual arts.

Augustine described the epistemological process as one in which the sign maker created an expressive sensuous form, and the observer had it furnished to him by the speaker, artist, or musician. It became a meaningful "language" for the observer insofar as he could reenact or interpret the expressive activity embodied in it. Understanding language—and Augustine used this word to include all forms of expressive activity from gesture to art and music—was a matter of interpreting to oneself noises heard or shapes seen according to immutable rules of truth. The awareness of these "rules" with regard to music presented a specific set of problems, as it does today, for music is a semiotic system without a semantic level. There were, as we have seen, musical "signs" with an explicit denotative value, such as trumpet signals in the army. More important, however, was the establishment of a common conceptual meaning, a conventional musical language, which was integrated with traditional procedures of composition to provide the theoretical canon for music in the Middle Ages. Several works of Augustine, including DDC, De musica, and De trinitate proved to be extremely valuable sources for the development of this attitude toward symbol.

Music formed an integral part of the culture of the medieval world: as musica practica it fulfilled a necessary role in the liturgy of the Church; as musica speculativa it formed an essential part of the education of the philosopher and theologian. Here, the metaphysical qualities of music were explored, whereby it could function as a speculum of the universe, a means through which the harmony of God's creation would become evident. In this conceptual framework the mathematical perception of music provided the symbols for a system of numerical relationships which unified the physical and metaphysical structure of the universe.

The propaedeutic effect of the study of music proceeded from the ability of the mind to apprehend the significance of numerical arrangements and value, which trained the intellect for the apprehension of ideal forms and aided in preparing the soul for a mystical union with God. In the words of Augustine,

> Music, making her way forth from some most intimate core of being ("*procedens quodam modo de secretissimus penetralibus musica*") has left her footprints, *vestigia*, both on our senses and on the objects of our sensation. We should follow these footprints to arrive at that intimate core, for that is the only way.[10]

The relationship between *musica practica* and *musica speculativa* was symbiotic; each developed by drawing upon the other. Thus, the Scholastic musical language exemplified a coordination of demands made by practical musicians and music theorists. First, the music itself must have sufficient technical interest to satisfy the performer and composer, and, second, the aural results must exemplify the proper theological and philosophical foundation to allow for appropriate metaphysical deductions. Sounds produced by the human voice or by musical instruments should be the realizations of an underlying system of symbolic ratios—an imperceptible harmonic *logos* which existed as a pattern in the mind of God. The musical composition would then exemplify and symbolize the laws of the divine universe.

This process produced a profound effect upon the development of the language of music during the Middle Ages. Polyphonic practice, for example, was subject to certain restrictions, for the choice of notes was governed by the classification of intervals as consonant and dissonant. Consonances were arranged in a hierarchy that reflected the divine numerical order, and music was composed in ways that emphasized these preferred intervals; the hallowed consonances—the octave, fourth, and fifth—were placed at all cadences and other important points. In this way the completed work remained within the philosophical and speculative framework of which music was a part; true polyphony had to be composed in accordance with philosophical and theological requirements so that it might function as a conventional symbolic code.

This preoccupation with speculative concerns was even more evident in the development of rhythm. Toward the end of the twelfth century, a system based upon the rhythmic theory presented by Augustine in *De musica* had replaced the even, unmeasured flow of earlier polyphony. Theoretical descriptions of the rhythmic modes, as this system was known, appeared in the thirteenth century, defining the basic principle of organization as a threefold unit of measure called a *perfectio*—a "perfection." Franco of Cologne, a theorist of the mid-thirteenth century, was the first to codify triple time as the basic meter. He described the *perfectio* in the following way:

> The perfect long is called first and principal, for in it all the others are included, to it also all the others are reducible. It is called perfect because it is measured by three "tempora," the ternary number being the most perfect number because it takes its name from the Holy Trinity, which is true and pure perfection.[11]

Franco was deeply influenced by medieval symbolism and theological doctrine, in which the number *three* was thought to be perfect; he had absorbed the Scholastic view that perfection was founded in the ternary principle, since God reaches perfection in the Trinity. This dogma was embodied in the musical *perfectio*, which was the equivalent of the dotted quarter note in modern musical notation. The other values, the quarter note and the eighth note, could be contained in the Holy Trinity—"true and perfect perfection." The result of the system, which formèd a conventional musical language known as the *Ars antiqua*, was that all medieval polyphony until the fourteenth century, insofar as it was in measured rhythm at all, was dominated by the ternary division of the "best."

The most eloquent spokesman for the principles embodied in the music of the *Ars antiqua* was the fourteenth-century music theorist, Jacques de Liège. In his monumental treatise, *Speculum musicae*, he drew upon ideas derived from Augustine, as well as Boethius, Isidore, and Cassiodorus. He was, in addition, profoundly influenced by medieval aesthetic theory, most notably the works of Saint Bonaventure.[12]

The *Speculum* demonstrates that Jacques had absorbed from the writings of Bonaventure the basic concepts concerning beauty and the principles of proportion shared by most medieval thinkers. Beauty consisted in symmetry or harmony of parts; it was an unfolding of the perfection of the object in terms of its form. This was to be understood in terms of proportion, for the object or the musical composition assumed a harmonious arrangement of parts according to the laws of number.

For Bonaventure this metaphysical construct was of primary importance, for he perceived the cognizance of beauty as a mystical experience. He believed that beautiful proportions produced delight in the soul through similitudes; in the pleasure of sense perception one could comprehend the "vestiges, representations, and . . . signs which were divinely given so that we can see God."[13] These spiritual sensations were mental perceptions which the soul experienced in the contemplation of truth; sweetness and harmony sent the soul to the image of God as to the fountain of all beauty.[14] According to Bonaventure, all knowledge came from God and must return to God; all modes of perception should conform to the uses of theology or revelation, the final end of which was salvation—union of the soul with God.

Advancing along the three paths of theoretical philosophy, the mind proceeded from the visible forms of visible things to the invisible causes of visible things and ascended finally to invisible substances and an understanding of their natures. Thus, by a progression through the stages of cogitation, meditation, and contemplation of the physical world the mind ascended to the creator, and to knowledge of the True.

Bonaventure emphasized how humans may contemplate God by ascending through the sensible realm, for he viewed "the physical universe and the soul as mirrors reflecting God and as rungs of a ladder leading to the Divine." The path he advocated led through seven different kinds of numbers by which, "as by the seven steps, we . . . ascend step by step from sensible things to the Maker of all so that God may be seen in all things."[15]

Calling upon the authority of Augustine,[16] Bonaventure distinguished the various kinds of numbers, which included concepts of ratio, harmony, proportion, and rhythm in addition to natural numbers. The first level consisted of *sounding numbers*, which existed in bodies, especially in sounds and voices. Next were the *encountered numbers*, ongoing numbers abstracted from sounding numbers and received in the senses; these were perceived rhythms existing in sense apprehension. *Expressive numbers* proceeded from the soul into the body and created rhythmic movements "as seen in gestures and dance." Next were *sensual numbers*, which were derived by "turning attention to the species received"; these became the pleasures caused by the rhythms. *Remembered numbers* consisted of melodies and rhythms which were retained in the memory and recalled at will. Most important were the *judicial numbers*, by which all the others were judged; to these highest numbers humans ascended step-by-step from the sounding numbers by means of the encountered, the sensual, and the remembered numbers. The judicial numbers necessarily transcended the mind since they were "infallible and beyond judgment"; these were the eternal verities by which we judge all matters concerning number.[17]

Bonaventure added a category to the divisions of Augustine, defining *artistic numbers* as those which were derived from judicial numbers; from these flowed the expressive numbers, which provided the patterns for the creation of numerous forms of artifacts.[18] These patterns consisted of spiritual impressions implanted by the judicial numbers in the mind of the artist or musician, who was then able to produce beautiful and well-proportioned objects.

All things must necessarily involve numbers, according to Bonaventure, since "beauty and pleasure do not exist without proportion, and since proportion exists primarily in numbers." In fact, "number is the foremost exemplar in the mind of the Creator, and in things, the foremost vestige leading to Wisdom." He believed that number "leads us most closely to God by means of these seven divisions; and it makes him known in all bodily and sensible things when we apprehend the numerical, delight in numerical proportions and judge irrefutably according to the laws of numerical proportion."[19]

Jacques de Liège believed that music might assist in this journey toward God. Since the first level in the mystical apprehension of the creator was located in the world of sensory impression, Jacques believed that *musica practica*, composed according to proper proportion, provided an audible "trace of God." It was here, through this musical "sign," that the mind could begin to contemplate the power, wisdom, and goodness of God. Initially, the music should be considered through rational reflection, then perceived in the light of faith, and finally realized as containing the presence of God within it. Thus, in contemplating the microcosm which was music, the mind was led to climb the ladder of created beings that went from the sensible, with which the spiritual soul was in contact, to the world of the spirit, which was free from all sensible limitation.

Audible music was a qualified entity, limited in time and space. But in thinking of music, the mind held the knowledge of a given being, and this thought was an image of the eternal Being who had left upon us the stamp of his work. Contemplating God through musical symbolism would lead to the consideration of the divine Being in the oneness of his essence and the plurality of his Persons—to contemplation of the divine Trinity.[20]

Augustine had provided a foundation for this concept when he advised, in book 1 of *DDC*,

> in this mortal life, wandering from God, if we wish to return to our native country where we can be blessed we should use this world and not enjoy it so that the "invisible things" of God "being understood by the things that are made" may be seen, that is, so that by means of corporeal and temporal things we may comprehend the eternal and spiritual.[21]

He explored this idea further in *De musica* when he discussed the role of music in the following way:

> the purpose of it is to lead young people of ability, and perhaps older people too, gradually, with Reason for our guide, from the things of sense

to God, in order that they may cling to Him who rules all and governs our intelligence, with no mediating nature between.[22]

Thus, Augustine had formulated concepts in *DDC* and *De musica* which became basic to medieval aesthetic theory. Drawing upon this conceptual framework, the fourteenth-century music theorist Jacques de Liège believed, as did Bonaventure, that artistic and musical symbolism contained both the intelligible power of God and the materials of humankind's redemption. Hence, Jacques emphasized that artists and musicians must labor with great care on their subjects and should perceive in their creations and in the material of their composition vestiges of a divinity that subsumed and supported the entire creative process. A work of art produced according to the "immutable rules of truth" would provide a symbolic vehicle through which the human spirit might draw near to the Divine Exemplar.

Notes

1. M. L. Colish, *The Mirror of Language: A Study in the Medieval Theory of Knowledge* (New Haven and London, 1968), viii.

2. Augustine *DDC* 2.1.1 (trans. Robertson, 34).

3. R. A. Markus, "St. Augustine on Signs," in R. A. Markus, ed., *Augustine: A Collection of Critical Essays* (New York, 1972), 74.

4. *DDC* 2.1.2 (trans. Robertson, 34).

5. *DDC* 2.2.3 (trans. Robertson, 34–35).

6. *DDC* 2.24.37.

7. *DDC* 2.25.38 (trans. Robertson, 61).

8. *DDC* 2.3.4 (trans. Robertson, 35–36).

9. B. D. Jackson, "The Theory of Signs in St. Augustine's *De doctrina christiana*," in R. A. Markus, ed., *Augustine: A Collection of Critical Essays* (New York, 1972), 112.

10. Augustine *De musica* 1.23.28 (trans. W. F. J. Knight [London, 1949]).

11. Franco of Cologne *Ars cantus mensurabilis* (trans. O. Strunk, in *Source Readings in Music History* [New York, 1950], 141).

12. Jacques de Liège is acknowledged to be the most important music theorist of the fourteenth century, and his *Speculum musicae* is recognized by musicologists to be the most complete and cogent summary of the theory and practice of music in the medieval world. For a more comprehensive treatment of the influence of medieval aesthetic theory in his work, see my article, "Jacques de Liège and the Bonaventuran Way to God," *Michigan Academician* 22 (1990): 77–86.

13. Bonaventure *The Soul's Journey into God* (trans. E. Cousins [New York, 1978], 76).

14. Bonaventure *De reductione artium ad theologiam* (trans. E. T. Healy [Saint Bonaventure, N.Y., 1955], 127).

15. Bonaventure *Journey* (trans. Cousins, 74).

16. Augustine *De musica* 6.5.16.

17. Bonaventure *Journey* (trans. Cousins, 75).

18. Bonaventure *Journey* (trans. Cousins, 75).

19. Bonaventure *Journey* (trans. Cousins, 75).

20. Jacques de Liège *Speculum musicae* (ed. R. Bragard, 7 vols. [Rome, 1955–1973], 7:60): "Dicendum quod non sunt incrependi illi qui cantus ex perfectis compositos in summam referunt Trinitatem. Unumquodque enim convenienter principium in illud reducitur a quo effective vel etiam exemplariter oritur, ut omne bonum in primum bonum quod verum in primam veritatem quae Deus est, omne ens in primum ens et omne esse in primum esse. Omnis enim multitudo procedit ab uno et omne esse a primo esse quod est esse Dei. Ab illo siquidem derivatur esse in aliis, his quidem clarius, his autem obscurius."

21. Augustine *DDC* 1.4.4 (trans. Robertson, 10).

22. Augustine *De musica* 6.1.1.

Plundering the Egyptians:
Petrarch and
Augustine's *De doctrina christiana*

CAROL E. QUILLEN

This paper explores how *De doctrina christiana*, particularly Augustine's views on scriptural obscurity, provides a key to understanding Petrarch's appropriation of Augustine's writings in the expression of his own humanist program. I focus particularly on how Petrarch uses the words of St. Augustine to assert an authoritative justification for the reading of pagan poetry and for his own poetic practice, a justification which Augustine would have repudiated.

Among the hundreds of letters contained in Petrarch's *Rerum familiarium libri* are two that especially attract students interested in the influence which Augustine's ideas about poetry exerted on Petrarch. One of these letters, addressed to Petrarch's brother Gerardo, deals with the relationship between poetry and theology.[1] Petrarch argues that poetry and theology are compatible, that the Bible itself is in some sense poetry about God. What is it but poetry, Petrarch asks, to call Christ sometimes a lion, sometimes a lamb, sometimes a worm? What are the parables in the Gospels if not nonliteral forms of expression, ways of speaking that defy normal usage and that we commonly call allegory? There are thousands of such examples in the Bible, proof, according to Petrarch, that this text owes much to poetic modes of speaking.[2] Petrarch goes on to state that the best interpreters of the New Testament—Jerome, Augustine, Ambrose—used poetry and rhythm in their writings.[3] "Do not, my brother," Petrarch warns, "shun that which you see pleased these men, who were themselves holy and beloved to Christ."[4]

The other letter of special interest is a response to a charge made against Petrarch. Giacomo Colonna had jokingly accused Petrarch of, among other things, feigning his professed admiration for Augustine.

Petrarch summarizes the charge in this way: "You say . . . that I, having embraced Augustine and his books with a kind of false friendship, have not really distanced myself from the poets and philosophers."[5] Petrarch responds to this accusation by subverting its premise. His friendship with Augustine was not incompatible with his respect for pagan writers. Why should I, he asks, tear myself from these authors when I see Augustine himself clinging (*inhaerere*) to them? "For unless this were so he never would have wrought the books of the *City of God*—not to mention his other works—from so much material taken from the poets and philosophers, never would he have embellished them with so many ornaments from the orators and historians."[6] Forsaking the poets and philosophers is, according to Petrarch, not the issue. Friends of Augustine need not abandon classical authors. This is one reason why Petrarch, unlike Giacomo Colonna, prefers Augustine to Jerome. Augustine had never suffered from Jerome's Ciceronian nightmare. He had never heard the eternal judge proclaim him not a Christian but a Ciceronian.[7] Unlike Jerome, Petrarch writes, Augustine used pagan texts without shame, and he gratefully acknowledged his special debt to the Platonists, in whose books he had discovered much of the Catholic faith, and to Cicero, whose *Hortensius* had converted him to the quest for truth. "No leader," Petrarch states, "should be despised who shows the way to salvation."[8]

And why, Petrarch asks, should Augustine not have recognized these debts to the studies of his youth? How, he writes, can either Plato or Cicero obstruct our pursuit of truth, when the school of one seems almost to teach the true faith and the writings of the other are signposts on the way to that faith?[9] Petrarch ends this part of his argument by reaffirming his devotion to Augustine: "But, to put an end to this playful trickery, Augustine himself knows whether or not I truly cherish him in my soul."[10]

In this argument, as in the one put forth in the letter to Gerardo, Petrarch uses Augustine's *example* in order to justify both reading pagan authors and his own poetic practice. "Quid autem inde divellerer, ubi ipsum Augustinum inherentem video?" Petrarch refers specifically to *De civitate dei* and the *Confessiones*. His position seems to be, if Augustine quoted these writers, then why shouldn't I do the same? If Augustine used rhythm and meter in his works, then why shouldn't I?

Yet, it is important to recognize that in neither *De civitate dei* nor the *Confessiones* does Augustine explicitly advocate the reading of pagan literature. That he quotes pagan authors should hardly surprise us. *De civitate dei*, for example, was written to play to a specific audience, men for whom a kind of paganism was a real alternative and whose expectations as readers assumed a certain fluency in the classical literary language that was the shared cultural capital of all late Roman elites. Augustine wrote with these expectations in mind. Furthermore, he could not have argued effectively against pagan religious culture and its adherents without referring to the texts in which it was embodied.

In the early fifth century, when Augustine finished *De civitate dei*, readers would not have understood this work as Petrarch later would, that is, as an *apologia* for pagan culture. In the early fifth century, it was, if anything, Christian intolerance and innovation that were on trial. From the first words of *De civitate dei* Augustine specifically defines his position against this cultural heritage. He undertakes to defend the "most glorious city of God," both as it exists in time and as it is in its abiding victory, against those who prefer their own gods to the founder of the more glorious and heavenly city.[11] The existence of a learned audience who did not accept the fundamental tenets of Christianity, who may have even blamed the intolerant policies of Christian emperors for the recent sack of Rome, determined not only the style but also the overall structure of the *City of God*. Augustine juxtaposes "your pride" to "our humility," "your warriors" to "our martyrs," "your literature" to "our discipline."[12]

If *De civitate dei* was written explicitly in opposition to the religio-literary culture of the late Roman elite, then how did Petrarch come to understand this same work as that culture's most eloquent defense and most compelling justification? A partial explanation surely lies in the different context in which Petrarch read Augustine's work. The literary language that had been the shared inheritance of Augustine's fifth-century audience was in the fourteenth century an exotic and occult treasure. Furthermore, the kind of literary paganism against which Augustine had argued was obviously not, in Petrarch's day, a real alternative.

Yet this explanation is hardly satisfactory in itself. I would like to suggest here that Petrarch's understanding of *De civitate dei* makes more sense if we imagine that he read this work in light of a particular interpretation of *DDC*.

Before turning to Petrarch's interpretation of *DDC*, however, let us recall the circumstances surrounding that work's composition. As Augustine wrote this treatise, he steered a course between extremes. On the one hand, he anticipated the criticisms of those who would dispense altogether with the teaching of interpretive precepts where Scripture was concerned. Although the experiences of some Christians clearly indicated that grace could be a sufficient teacher, we should not, advises Augustine, count on the operations of divine illumination alone. In other words, although the apostles did, at one time, when filled with the Holy Spirit, speak in the tongues of all races, we should not expect our children to learn Greek, Hebrew, and Latin in that fashion. We must not be so proud as to scorn the human skills and methods of teaching which God himself deigned to use in his communications with us.

On the other hand, Augustine discourages the would-be rhetors among his audience. Even when he took as his starting point the techniques of rhythm and meter that are described in classical treatises on rhetoric, he used these techniques to develop and to practice a rhetoric based upon completely different assumptions.[13] For example, in DDC, Augustine clearly begins his exploration of oratory with Cicero's distinctions among levels of style and his dictum that the level of style should suit the importance of the subject matter. Yet although Augustine ultimately incorporates a threefold categorization of style into his own explication of oratory, he first rejects this Ciceronian premise because for Christians, who understand all things in relation to salvation, "everything which we say matters."[14] Furthermore, the foundation of Christianity—the incarnation—derives its sublimity from its very inappropriateness, from its fusion of God and human being, omnipotence and humiliation, death and life. Ciceronian rhetorical theory cannot negotiate these contradictions, which pose very particular challenges to all Christian writers.[15] Hence when Augustine uses the idea of levels of style, he refers only to the purpose and audience of the author and not at all to subject matter.

Augustine also explicitly distances himself from the rhetorical tradition upon which he draws. At the beginning of the fourth book of DDC, before he begins to discuss oratory, he wards off "the expectation of readers who perhaps think that I will offer rhetorical precepts which I learned and taught in secular schools and I warn them not to expect these from me, not because they have no use, but if they have any, it must be learned separately, and not sought from me either in this or in any other work."[16] Similarly, as he interprets the Bible in his sermons, Augustine carefully distinguishes his use of rhetorical terms from their common, secular use. The following passage on allegory, taken from a sermon on Psalm 103, is given at some length because it invites comparison with Petrarch's words to his brother on theology and poetry.[17] Here Augustine carefully distinguishes the ecclesiastical meaning of the word *allegory* from its more customary theatrical connotations:

> Allegory is the word used when something signifies one thing in its literal words and another in its intellectual sense. Why is Christ called a lamb? Is he then a sheep? Does calling him a lion make him a beast? Is Peter hard because he is called a rock? When we use the word mountain to refer to

Christ do we mean that he is a mound of earth? And so the many words that sound one way but mean something else are called allegory. And whoever thinks that I'm talking about the theater here thinks that God told parables about the coliseum. Notice what the city does to our way of thinking because it is so full of spectacles and shows. I would speak more safely in the country. For there, men would never have heard or learned about allegory except from the Scriptures of God.[18]

Although the two passages share much, Petrarch points to a fundamental similarity between classical poetry and the Bible whereas Augustine wants to draw distinctions.

By steering such a course between the extremes of anti-cultural arrogance and hyper-refined vanity, Augustine establishes the terms upon which could be founded a uniquely Christian hermeneutic in which the arts would serve religious truth. In outlining these terms, Augustine borrows, to use Marrou's classic formulation, the techniques of classical culture but not its spirit.[19] Augustine's most famous, if often misunderstood, image for his act of appropriation comes, fittingly enough, from the Bible. Just as by divine injunction the Israelites took the gold and silver of their captors as they fled from Egypt, so too the Christians, as they separate themselves in spirit from the society of pagans, must carry with them whatever may be put in the service of God.[20]

In this way, Augustine incorporates some of the elements of his intellectual heritage into his outline of a different literary culture based on interpreting the Bible. So rich and complex was this text that alone it could provide the foundation for a rewarding and sophisticated intellectual life whose aim was the discovery of religious truth. Augustine imagined or, more accurately, took for granted that this process of discovery would be grounded in the liberal arts, especially grammar and rhetoric. God, after all, had chosen to reveal himself in language, through the Word. The techniques of analysis most appropriate to understanding the Bible were, therefore, as *DDC* makes clear, literary techniques, through which obscure or allegorical passages might be rendered comprehensible. Furthermore, Augustine believed that the obscurity and ambiguity of the Bible was divinely ordained. We humans delight in imagery. We take greater pleasure in learning through figures and tropes than we do through simple speech. And what we have gained through exertion we cherish all the more.[21]

That Augustine makes room for this kind of aesthetic and intellectual pleasure in his outline of a literary culture based on the Bible is at once highly significant and dangerously easy to distort. Let us be clear. While Augustine is quite willing to accept as legitimate, if problematic, the transient joys of textual analysis and interpretation, he rigorously subordinates them to the single lasting joy of eternal happiness and peace in God. Secondly, although Augustine acknowledges the excitement of reading, he focuses his attention on a single book. There is no room in his cultural vision for the pleasure of reading classical pagan texts as an end in itself.

Yet ironically, from Augustine's cultural program Petrarch fashioned a justification for reading precisely these pagan texts. "Quid autem inde divellerer, ubi ipsum Augustinum inherentem video?" he wrote to Giacomo Colonna. Petrarch's use of the verb *inhaerere* to describe Augustine's relationship to pagan authors is particularly telling. *Inhaerere* was not for Augustine an uncharged word. He used it in *DDC* to express what was for him a fundamental distinction between *uti* and *frui*, between the relationship of human beings to a creator and their relationship to created things. *Frui*, according to Augustine, means to cling to (*inhaerere*) something through love for its own sake. *Uti*, on the other hand, means to refer what we must use to the thing which we love wholeheartedly.[22] In other words, Augustine, ever attentive to the meaning of words, uses *inhaerere* to denote the uniquely binding love that humans ought to give to God alone. He repeats this use of the word in the *Confessiones*: "redite, prevaricatores, ad cor, et inhaerete illi, qui fecit vos."[23] Here Augustine specifically opposes this "clinging to God," a love that gives solace and rest because it endures forever, with the unpredictability of our attachment to mere transitory things. That Petrarch uses this word to denote Augustine's attachment to pagan poetry is emblematic of the gap that separates the two men.

How can we interpret the fact that Petrarch, an extremely self-conscious and careful reader, understood *De doctrina christiana*, and indeed Augustine's view of classical culture generally, not in terms of distance or critique but in terms of a compelling justification? And how, in the fourteenth century, did Augustine's works and words serve Petrarch's humanist cultural agenda? We can begin to answer these questions by recalling the intellectual milieu in which Petrarch lived and the specific challenges that he faced.[24]

Late medieval culture in Italy differed from that of other European regions partly because Italy was generally slow to assimilate French ideas at a time when Paris was the center of development in theology and philosophy as well as in the arts. Only in the mid-thirteenth century did Scholasticism and the Aristotelian philosophy on which it was based come to Italian universities, where the study of law dominated other pursuits. Furthermore, Aristotelian philosophy entered the universities like the one in Bologna in close connection with the teaching not of theology but of medicine, at a time when medicine was emerging as a speculative, theoretical discipline. At both Padua and Bologna, medicine represented the culmination of the curriculum in the liberal arts, which included metaphysics, natural science, logic, rhetoric, and grammar.[25] Thus doctors both had completed courses in the "lesser" arts and were the primary students and teachers of philosophy. They were also Petrarch's most formidable intellectual opponents.

The training which these doctors had received helps to account for Petrarch's interchangeable use of the labels *doctor, dialectician, scholastic,* and *follower of Aristotle.* Such men shared at least a background in natural science and metaphysics, methods of analysis, and standards of proof that were at odds with Petrarch's commitment to poetry and to the classical literary tradition but that were equally sophisticated and certainly well respected. In order, then, for Petrarch to put forth his own cultural vision, he needed to find an authority that would allow him to buck the assumptions held by the most prominent intellectuals of his age. Augustine's works provided that authority.

Let us now consider how *DDC* could have served to legitimate not Augustine's outline of a Christian literary culture but Petrarch's humanistic one as he formulated it in the face of viable fourteenth-century alternatives. First, Augustine takes for granted the discursive nature of God's revelation to humans. He assumed that the methods of analysis and discovery appropriate to any true philosopher were derived from grammar and rhetoric. This starting assumption was not shared by Petrarch's intellectual opponents, and it enabled him to formulate both his denigration of syllogistic logic and an alternative conception of the philosophic quest that was grounded in literary analysis and not in Aristotelian logic.

More significantly, Petrarch noted Augustine's explanation for obscurity in the Bible, his assertion that such obscurity was divinely ordained for our aid and pleasure. Indeed, Petrarch at times almost echoed Augustine's own arguments, stating that difficulty in interpretation excites the mind in a beneficial way.

Yet Petrarch goes much farther than merely echoing Augustine's own arguments. Consider Petrarch's *Invective contra medicum,* which contains his most sustained and thorough justification of poetry. Here Petrarch moves from citing Augustine's discussions of the difficulty involved in reading Scripture to a discussion of the analogous difficulties of reading poetry, by stating, "If these things are rightly said of Scripture, which has been set forth for everyone, how much more appropriately are they said of those things [poetry] which is aimed at the very few?"[26] This analogy dignifies secular literary pursuits both through an assertion of their difficulty and through the association of poetry and Scripture. Petrarch uses Augustine's words to initiate and to authorize a justification for poetry that will underlie other attempts by later humanists to legitimate their skills and their enterprise.[27]

Yet that justification undermines Augustine's own arguments. Although Augustine took for granted the discursive nature of God's revelation to human beings, and himself relied upon classical discussions of meter, rhythm, and figures of speech, he used these discussions in *De doctrina christiana* in order to develop a rhetoric based upon different assumptions. He explicitly set himself apart from the tradition on which he drew by insisting upon the distinction between his definitions of rhetorical terms and their secular use. Petrarch, on the other hand, emphasizes the similarities between poetry and the Bible in order to ennoble poetry in the face of Scholasticism and its emphasis on logic rather than on rhetoric in reading and interpretation. And, by asserting the difficulty of reading poetry, he even suggests that poetry could serve for learned people a purpose similar to that served for everyone by the Bible. This suggestion Augustine surely would have rejected.

In the *Invective contra medicum* Petrarch uses Augustine's authority in order to suggest that poetry might, at least for the learned few, serve a function similar to the Bible. In the *Secretum*, he goes even further, creating in the persona of the interlocutor "Augustinus" an image of Augustine that could authorize the textual practices valued by Petrarch and characteristic of humanism.

Written in the late 1340s, the *Secretum* is a dialogue between two interlocutors, "Franciscus" and "Augustinus," in which "Augustinus" offers spiritual counsel to "Franciscus," who is struggling to live virtuously. The dialogue, which is divided into three books representing three different conversations, is overseen by the figure of Truth. As the two interlocutors discuss the right way to live and how to surmount spiritual malaise, both rely upon frequent references to classical authors. "Franciscus" is clearly based on Petrarch himself and "Augustinus" upon the historical Augustine, one of Petrarch's favorite authors.

Although "Augustinus" is clearly based upon Augustine, scholars have long wondered at the contrast between the character in Petrarch's dialogue and the historical bishop of Hippo. Most of this scholarship has focused on the voluntarism of "Augustinus." How could Augustine, the Doctor of Grace, inform an interlocutor who emphasizes instead, and in the words of Virgil, Seneca, and Cicero, each human being's freedom to choose?

This dissonance between the Augustine recognized by scholars as historical and Petrarch's "Augustinus" strikes modern readers of the

Secretum almost immediately. Near the beginning of book 1, for example, "Augustinus" states as a necessary conclusion, "just as a man who through profound and concentrated meditation has recognized that he is unhappy desires not to be unhappy, and he who has begun to desire this will pursue his desire, so he who has pursued it will be able to accomplish it."[28] A little later in the dialogue "Augustinus" asserts this voluntarism even more clearly: "whoever desires to put off his unhappiness, provided that he desires this truly and fully, will not be thwarted in this desire."[29] Even the account which "Augustinus" gives of his conversion fails to mention the role of grace:

> Et tamen hec inter idem ille qui fueram mansi, donec alta tandem meditatio omnem miseriam meam ante oculos congessit. Itaque postquam plene volui, ilicet et potui, miraque et felicissima celeritate transformatus sum in alterum Augustinum, cuius historie seriem, ni fallor, ex *Confessionibus* meis nosti.

> And nonetheless with all of this I remained the man I had been, until finally profound meditation heaped before my eyes all my unhappiness. And so after I willed completely, immediately I was able to do it, and with wonderful and fortunate speed I was transformed into another Augustinus, whose history you know, unless I am mistaken, from my *Confessions*.[30]

Gone from this account are all suggestions of divine grace instilled through the words of Paul. Conversion itself has become an act of will.

Our knowledge of Petrarch's complex reading practices and interpretive habits warns against the naive presumption that in the *Secretum* he simply "got Augustine wrong." Indeed, as Victoria Kahn has shown, our narrow concentration upon the "anti-Augustinian" voluntarism of "Augustinus" has encouraged us to read the *Secretum* almost exclusively in ideological terms, as the site of an ideological confrontation whose opposing and irreconcilable positions are expressed by the two interlocutors: "Franciscus" on one side and "Augustinus" on the other.[31] Although within this framework scholars have proposed various readings of the dialogue, many have understood "Franciscus" as speaking for a commitment to "the world," secular literature, or personal experience and "Augustinus" as speaking for religious withdrawal and the authority of tradition.[32] Even those scholars who find that "Franciscus" and "Augustinus" ultimately agree have highlighted the ideological dimensions of the dialogue.[33] Thus Elena Razzoli called the *Secretum* a confession, and Carlo Calcaterra saw the dialogue as indicative of a deep religious crisis which Petrarch underwent in the early 1340s, a crisis reflected as well in his other writings of the period, particularly the *Psalmi penitentiales*.[34] This way of reading the *Secretum*, regardless of whether one takes "Franciscus" or "Augustinus" as the "victor" in the dialogue, posits a Petrarch perennially torn by a conflict between Christianity and the *saeculum*, between religious withdrawal and a nascent humanist spirit committed to individual experience in the world.

More recent readings of the *Secretum* have taken as a starting point not ideological conflict within the dialogue but its structure as a text. David Marsh, for example, finds in the *Secretum* the beginnings of a revival of the free inquiry of the Ciceronian dialogue, a genre that the "historical" Augustine had condemned. "The spirit of Ciceronian dialogue," Marsh writes, "was revived by the Italian humanists in a conscious effort to return to the ideal freedoms of Roman discussion and to break out of the confines of medieval thought created, at least in part, by the Augustinian condemnation of Academic argument. Petrarch's *Secretum* reasserts the methodological freedom of Ciceronian eclecticism through the words of his interlocutor Augustinus."[35] Marsh here suggests that Petrarch uses "Augustinus" to undermine discursive structures—categories of analysis, a vocabulary, techniques of argument—that were historically authorized or even initiated by Augustine's works.

Similarly, Victoria Kahn highlights the "intertextual dimension" of the *Secretum* by defining as its primary concern not the religio-ethical problem of "Franciscus' " way of life but rather "the problem of defining the will itself as a faculty of interpretation."[36] Augustine, according to Kahn, represents for Petrarch the possibility of both a kind of interpretation and a kind of coherent and exemplary narration[37]—one that invites imitation—enabled by his conversion. Had the conflict within Augustine's will not been resolved, he would not have been able to tell his story in the *Confessiones* because he would not have understood what his memories, his past, meant. Right interpretation is, in other words, a function of the disposition of the will. As Kahn writes, "The moral problem is an interpretive one, for the will to conversion is at the same time a will to a certain kind of interpretation."[38] From this perspective, the *Secretum* defines reading itself as a "problematic activity"[39] by challenging the viability of the practices of identification and imitation invited by exemplary narratives like the *Confessiones*.[40]

The work of Marsh, Kahn, Freccero, and others has thus highlighted the interpretive and linguistic problematic dramatized in the *Secretum* while downplaying the ethical and religious questions that had preoccupied earlier scholarship. These scholars read the *Secretum* not as Petrarch's confessions but as a reading of, or a response to, the *Confessiones* of St. Augustine. I would like to suggest further that the response to Augustine's work given in the *Secretum,* a response informed by a reading of *DDC,* creates in turn an image of Augustine that could authorize the textual practices valued by Petrarch and characteristic of humanism, an Augustine for whom the reading of poetry can bring redemption.

Consider this passage, taken from the first book of the dialogue. Here, during the course of a discussion of what keeps "Franciscus" from singlemindedly pursuing and attaining virtue, "Augustinus" describes the process through which the soul, whose origin lies in heaven, degenerates from its pristine and noble state "ex contagio corporis huius,"[41] out of the polluting contact of the body. Furthermore, "Augustinus" states, so corrupted is the soul that it no longer remembers its true origin and maker. The interlocutor recalls a passage from Virgil's *Aeneid* which captures these sentiments:

> Nempe passiones ex corporea commistione subortas oblivionemque nature melioris, divinitus videtur attigisse Virgilius, ubi ait:
>> Igneus est illis vigor et celestis origo
>> seminibus, quantum non noxia corpora tardant
>> terrenique hebetant artus, moribundaque membra.
>> Hinc metuunt cupiuntque dolent gaudentque, neque auras
>> respiciunt, clause tenebris et carcere ceco.

Certainly it seems that Virgil, divinely inspired, alluded to the repeated onslaught of the passions and the oblivion of our better nature when he said:

> Fiery energy is in these seeds, their source is heavenly;
> but they are dulled by harmful bodies, blunted
> by their own earthly limbs, their mortal members.
> Because of these, they fear and long, and sorrow
> and joy, they do not see the light of heaven.[42]

"Augustinus" then leads "Franciscus" to interpret this passage as describing the four-part passion of the soul, an interpretation that is confirmed, again according to "Augustinus," by "that saying of the apostle: 'The body, because it is corrupt, irritates the soul, and earthly habitation depresses its ability to function.' "[43]

This passage in the *Secretum* is especially fascinating because in it "Augustinus" subverts the interpretation of exactly the same Virgilian lines that is given in book 14 of *De civitate dei.* Here Augustine uses the quotation from Virgil in order to dramatize the fundamental differences between the point of view of the poet and that of followers of the Christian religion.

Quamvis enim Vergilius Platonicam videatur luculentis versibus explicare sententiam dicens:

    Igneus est illis vigor et caelestis origo

    Seminibus, quantum non noxia corpora tardant

    Terrenique hebetant artus moribundaque membra,

omnesque illas notissimas quattuor animi perturbationes, cupiditatem ti-morem, laetitiam tristitiam, quasi origines omnium peccatorum atque vi-tiorum volens intelligi ex corpore accidere subiungat et dicat:

    Hinc metuunt cupiuntque, dolent gaudentque, nec auras

    Suspiciunt, clausae tenebris et carcere caeco:

tamen aliter se habet fides nostra.

For although Virgil seems to explain in splendid poetry Platonic doctrine when he says,

    Fiery energy is in these seeds, their source is heavenly;

    but they are dulled by harmful bodies, blunted

    by their own earthly limbs, their mortal members,

and, wanting the four best-known disturbances of the soul—desire, fear, joy, and sadness, that is the sources of all sin and vice—to be understood to arise out of the body, he adds,

    Because of these, they fear and long, and sorrow

    and joy, they do not see the light of heaven;

nonetheless our faith considers these things differently.[44]

Augustine argues that according to the Christian religion the body is *not* the source of the corruption of the soul, for neither the flesh nor anything else made by God is by nature corrupt. Rather, sin renders the whole of the human person subject to corruption: "for flesh did not make the soul sinful, but a sinful soul made the flesh corruptible."[45] Virgil's lines, which implicate the very nature of the body, are thus at odds with Christianity. This is a very different reading from that offered in the *Secretum*. Where Augustine draws distinctions, "Augustinus" discerns similarities, in effect inverting the interpretation given in *De civitate dei*.

The "Augustinus" of Petrarch's dialogue goes on to describe further the corrupting influence exerted upon the soul by the body. Images of visible things, he states, admitted one at a time through the bodily senses, press together in the innermost regions of the soul, they weigh the soul down and derange it because it cannot dispel or contain so many things that are alien to it. This plague of fantasmata hurts the soul and prevents it from practicing the pure meditation that alone can lead it to the one true source of light.[46]

After "Augustinus" has offered these reflections, the following exchange between the interlocutors occurs:

Fr.: Huius quidem pestis, cum sepe alias, tum in libro *De vera religione* cui nichil constat esse repugnantius, preclarissime meministi. In quem librum nuper incidi, a philosophorum et poetarum lectione digrediens, itaque cupidissime perlegi: haud aliter quam qui videndi studio peregrinatur a patria, ubi ignotum famose cuiuspiam urbis limen ingreditur, nova captus locorum dulcedine passimque subsistens, obvia queque circumspicit.

Aug.: Atqui licet aliter sonantibus verbis secundum catholice veritatis preceptorem decuit, reperies libri illius magna ex parte philosophicam precipueque platonicam ac socraticam fuisse doctrinam. Et nequid tibi subtraham, scito me, ut opus illud inciperem, unum maxime Ciceronis tui verbum induxisse. Affuit Deus incepto, ut ex paucis seminibus messis opima consurgeret. Sed ad propositum revertamur.

Fr.: Certainly you brilliantly represented this plague both in other works and in the book *On True Religion*, to which nothing is more repugnant than this very plague. Recently, having strayed from reading the poets and philosophers, I encountered that book, and eagerly I read it through, like someone who, driven by zeal for exploring wanders from his own country, and when he enters the unknown border of some famous city, enthralled by the novel sweetness of places and stopping here and there, he stares at everything he meets.

Aug.: But for the most part you will find that, although it is expressed in other words as befits a teacher of Catholic truth, the teaching in that book was philosophical and especially Platonic and Socratic. And, lest I keep anything from you, know that one particular saying of your Cicero especially led me to begin that work. God was present at the beginning, so that out of a mere few seeds there arose a rich harvest. But let us return to our subject.[47]

This too is a remarkable passage. "Franciscus" first describes his encounter with *De vera religione* as that of a foreigner exploring the exotic sights of a strange land. Having left his own territory, the study of poets and philosophers, he delights in the novel sweetness of Augustine's alien text.[48] Yet "Augustinus," rather than reinforcing the sense of otherness imparted by *De vera religione*, instead undermines it by suggesting that the differences between this text and the writings of the poets and philosophers already familiar to "Franciscus" are differences in words not in doctrine. "Augustinus" goes on to disclose, "nequid tibi subtraham," that *De vera religione* was inspired by nothing other than a passage from "Franciscus'" own Cicero. Which passage? "Franciscus" begs to know, before they continue the conversation. "Augustinus" replies:

> Cicero siquidem in quodam loco, iam tunc errores temporum perosus, sic ait: "Nichil animo videre poterant, ad oculos omnia referebant; magni autem est ingenii revocare mentem a sensibus et cogitationem a consuetudine abducere." Hec ille. Ego autem hoc velut fundamentum nactus, desuper id quod tibi placuisse dicis opus extruxi.
>
> *Fr.:* Teneo locum: in *Tusculano* est: te autem hoc Ciceronis dicto et illic et alibi in operibus tuis delectari solitum animadverti; nec immerito; est enim ex eorum genere, quibus cum veritate permixtus lepos ac maiestas inest. Tu vero iantandem, ut videtur, ad propositum redi.

> Indeed in a certain place Cicero, even then detesting the errors of the times said this: "They were able to see nothing with the soul, but referred all things to the eyes; for it belongs to a great intellect to recall the mind from the senses and to lead thought away from the customary." So said Cicero. I, then, having come upon this foundation, built on it the work which you say has pleased you.
>
> *Fr.:* I know the passage: it is in the *Tusculan Disputations*. Moreover I have noticed that here and there in your works you delight in this saying of Cicero, and not without cause, for it is one of those sayings in which lies charm and majesty mixed with truth. But finally now, as seems proper, we must return to the matter at hand.[49]

De vera religione not only contains for the most part the doctrine of the poets and philosophers but also, as "Augustinus" confides to "Franciscus," has as its very basis a quotation from the *Tusculan Disputations*.

These passages from the first book of the *Secretum* go much further than simply asserting an affinity between Augustine's works and those of the pagan philosophers and poets dear to Petrarch. Through the words of "Augustinus," Petrarch has created an intellectual genealogy for *De vera religione* and for Augustine in which Cicero figures as a primary forebear, and from which the Bible and self-consciously Christian writings are excluded. Petrarch thus establishes for himself and for his own successors a Pater Augustinus who can authorize as redemptive both the texts and the interpretive practices of humanism.

If book 1 of the *Secretum* constructs an "Augustinus" who authorizes the redemptive power of poetry, the rest of the dialogue outlines the reading habits and interpretive techniques that will best tap that power. Underlying the dialogue is the assumption that reading can cure spiritual unhappiness. Throughout, passages from pagan literature provide the language through which the conversation is conducted, the language in which "Augustinus" both probes the soul of "Franciscus" and offers his cure. These literary passages thus function in the *Secretum* as quotations from the Bible function in Augustine's *Confessiones*. Petrarch has used the words of his classical heros, of Virgil, Horace, and Cicero, in the way in which, in the *Confessiones*, the historical Augustine had used the word of his God.

Thus in the *Secretum* and the other works of Petrarch discussed here, Augustine's authority serves to legitimate Petrarch's humanist project. By inventing an Augustine who not only sanctioned but insisted upon the use of classical literature in the human search for spiritual health, Petrarch bequeathed to his successors a powerful authorizing voice for what would become a formidable challenge to the educational status quo and to existing literary standards. This humanist vision was certainly not advocated by Augustine, either in *DDC* or anywhere else. Yet Petrarch's creative appropriation of the words and arguments of *DDC* testify, more than any stricter interpretation ever could, to the complexity and abiding significance of Augustine's work. And these, it seems to me, are exactly the qualities which make *De doctrina christiana* a truly classic text.

Notes

1. Francesco Petrarca *Familiarium rerum libri* 10.4 (ed. V. Rossi and U. Bosco [Florence, 1933–1942]). I refer to these letters hereafter as *Fam.*, followed by book and letter number plus, for passages within letters, the sectional divisions supplied by Rossi and Bosco.

2. *Fam.* 10.4.1–2: "theologie quidem minime adversa poetica est. Miraris? parum abest quin dicam theologiam poeticam esse de Deo: Cristum modo leonem modo agnum modo vermem dici, quid nisi poeticum est? mille talia in Scripturis Sacris invenies que persequi longum est. Quid vero aliud parabole Salvatoris in Evangelio sonant, nisi sermonem a sensibus alienum sive, ut uno verbo exprimam, alieniloquium, quam allegoriam usitatiori vocabulo nuncupamus? Atqui ex huiusce sermonis genere poetica omnis intexta est." Unless otherwise noted, all translations in this essay are my own.

3. *Fam.* 10.4.8: "Novi autem Testamenti duces, Ambrosium Augustinum Ieronimum, carminibus ac rithmis usos ostendere non operosus labor est."

4. *Fam.* 10.4.8: "Noli itaque, frater, horrere quod Cristo amicissimis ac sanctissimis viris placuisse cognoscis."

5. *Fam.* 2.9.8: "Dicis me, non modo vulgus insulsum, sed celum ipsum fictionibus tentare: itaque Augustinum et eius libros simulata quadam benivolentia complexum, re autem vera a poetis et philosophis non avelli."

6. *Fam.* 2.9.8: "Quid inde divellerer, ubi ipsum Augustinum inherentem video? quod nisi ita esset, nunquam libros *De civitate dei*, ut reliqua sileam,

tanta philosophorum et poetarum calce fundaret, nunquam tantis oratorum ac historicorum coloribus exornaret."

7. *Fam.* 2.9.9: "Nunquam enim in somniis ad tribunal eterni Iudicis tractus accesserat Augustinus meus, sicut Ieronimus tuus; nunquam exprobari sibi ciceronianum nomen audierat." For Jerome's description of his nightmare, see his *Epistula* 22, addressed to Eustochium.

8. *Fam.* 2.9.11–12: "Nemo dux spernendus est qui viam salutis ostendit."

9. *Fam.* 2.9.12: "Quid ergo studio veritatis obesse potest vel Plato vel Cicero, quorum alterius scola fidem veracem non modo non impugnat sed docet et predicat, alterius libri recti ad illam itineris duces sunt?"

10. *Fam.* 2.9.14: "Ut vero iantandem huic lascive calumnie finis fiat, vere ne an falso Augustinum animo complectar, ipse novit."

11. Augustine *De civitate dei* 1.praef.

12. See P. Brown, *Augustine of Hippo* (Berkeley, 1967), 299–312.

13. This is clear from *De doctrina christiana;* and see E. Auerbach, *Literary Language and Its Public in Late Latin Antiquity and the Middle Ages,* trans. R. Mannheim (London, 1965), ch. 1, "Sermo humilis."

14. *DDC* 4.18.35: "omnia sunt magna, quae dicimus." Here I follow Auerbach, *Literary Language,* 35–37.

15. I am grateful to Werner Kelber, whose lecture, "Christianity and the Victimization of the Jews: Metaphysics and Marginality in the Fourth Gospel," delivered at the Houston Colloquium in Judaic Studies, 13 September 1990, helped me to think about this problem.

16. *DDC* 4.1.2: "Primo itaque exspectationem legentium, qui forte me putant rhetorica daturum esse praecepta, quae in scholis saecularibus et didici et docui, ista praelocutione prohibeo atque, ut a me non exspectentur, admoneo, non quod nihil habeant utilitatis, sed si quid habent, seorsum discendum est, si cui fortassis bono viro etiam haec vacat discere, non autem a me vel in hoc opere vel in aliquo alio requirendum."

17. See above, note 2.

18. Augustine *Enarrationes in psalmos* 103.1.13. The whole passage reads as follows: "Ergo venti, animae in allegoria non absurde accipiuntur. Videte autem ne putetis nominata allegoria pantomimi aliquid me dixisse. Nam quaedam verba, quoniam verba sunt, et ex lingua procedunt, communia nobis sunt etiam cum rebus ludicris et non honestis; tamen locum suum habent verba ista in ecclesia, et locum suum in scena. Non enim ego dixi quod apostolus non dixit, cum de duobus filiis Abrahae diceret: *Quae sunt,* inquit, *in allegoria.* Allegoria dicitur, cum aliquid aliud videtur sonare in verbis, et aliud in intellectu significare. Quomodo dicitur agnus Christus: numquid pecus? Leo Christus: numquid bestia? Petra Christus: numquid duritia? Mons Christus: numquid tumor terrae? Et sic multa aliud videntur sonare, aliud significare; et vocatur allegoria. Nam qui putat me de theatro dixisse allegoriam, putat et Dominum de amphytheatro dixisse parabolam. Videtis quid faciat civitas ubi abundat spectacula: in agro securius loquerer; quid sit enim allegoria, non ibi forte didicissent homines, nisi in scripturis Dei. Ergo quod dicimus allegoriam figuram esse, sacramentum figuratum allegoria est."

19. H. I. Marrou, *Saint Augustin et la fin de la culture antique* (Paris, 1949).

20. *DDC* 2.40.60: "Philosophi autem qui vocantur, si qua forte vera et fidei nostrae accomodata dixerunt, maxime Platonici, non solum formidanda non sunt, sed ab eis etiam tamquam ab iniustis possessoribus in usum nostrum vindicanda. Sicut enim Aegyptii non tantum idola habebant et onera gravia quae populus Israhel detestaretur et fugeret, sed etiam vasa atque ornamenta de auro et de argento et vestem, quae ille populus exiens de Aegypto sibi potius tamquam ad usum meliorem clanculo vindicavit, non auctoritate propria, sed praecepto dei ipsis Aegyptiis nescienter commodantibus ea, quibus non bene utebantur." Although many take this image as indicative of Augustine's view toward pagan culture generally, he is here speaking much more specifically about his philosophical, and particularly the Platonic, heritage.

21. *DDC* 2.4.

22. *DDC* 1.4.4: "Frui est enim amore inhaerere alicui rei propter se ipsam. Uti autem, quod in usum venerit, ad id, quod amas obtinendum referre, si tamen amandum est."

23. Augustine *Confessiones* 4.12.

24. Aspects of this argument are addressed in a different context in my essay, "A Tradition Invented: Petrarch, Augustine, and the Language of Humanism," *Journal of the History of Ideas* 52:2 (1992): 179–207.

25. On this milieu, see P. O. Kristeller, "Humanism and Scholasticism in the Italian Renaissance," in M. Mooney, ed., *Renaissance Thought and Its Sources* (New York, 1979), 85–105; N. Siraisi, *Arts and Sciences at Padua: The Studium of Padua before 1350* (Toronto, 1973), ch. 5; A. Sorbelli, *Storia della Università de Bologna* (Bologna, 1944); H. Rashdall, *The Universities of the Middle Ages,* ed. F. M. Powicke and A. B. Emden, 3 vols. (Oxford, 1936) 1:233–53.

26. Francesco Petrarca *Invective contra medicum* 3.70 (ed. P. G. Ricci [Rome, 1950]): "Que, si de scripturis illis recte dicuntur, que sunt omnibus proposite, quanto rectius de illis que paucissimis?"

27. For example, see Coluccio Salutati's letter to Giovanni da Samminiato, in *Epistolario di Coluccio Salutati,* letter 23 (ed. F. Novati, 4 vols. [Rome, 1891–1905], 4:170–204).

28. Francesco Petrarca *De secreto conflictu curarum mearum* (hereafter *Secretum*) 1 (ed. E. Carrara, in *Prose* [Milan, 1955], 28): "sicut qui se miserum alta et fixa meditatione cognoverit cupiat esse non miser, et qui id optare ceperit sectetur, sic et qui id sectatus fuerit, possit etiam adipisci."

29. *Secretum* 1 (ed. Carrara, 30): "qui miseriam suam cupit exuere, modo id vere pleneque cupiat, nequit a tali desiderio frustrari."

30. *Secretum* 1 (ed. Carrara, 40).

31. See the perceptive comments of V. Kahn, "The Figure of the Reader in Petrarch's *Secretum,*" *PMLA* 100 (1985): 154–66, reprinted, without notes, in H. Bloom, ed., *Petrarch* (New York, 1989), 139–58. I am much indebted to this article.

32. See the brief survey of some more recent, but representative, scholarly literature in O. Giuliani, *Allegoria retorica e poetica nel Secretum del Petrarca* (Bologna, 1977), 9–29.

33. Kahn, "Figure of the Reader," 156.

34. E. Razzoli, *Agostinismo e religiosità del Petrarca* (Milan, 1937), 12; C. Calcaterrra, "Sant'Agostino nelle opere di Dante e del Petrarca," in *Nella selva del Petrarca* (Bologna, 1942), 247–360, 291 ff. See also the discussion of H. Baron, *Petrarch's "Secretum": Its Making and Its Meaning* (Cambridge, 1985), 215–23. Baron takes issue here with the impressive work of F. Rico, *Vida u obre de Petrarca I: Lectura del "Secretum"* (Chapel Hill, N.C., 1974).

35. D. Marsh, *The Quattrocento Dialogue* (Cambridge, 1980), 9. A little later in this work, Marsh seems to invoke a more traditional reading of the dialogue, when he writes (16): "Petrarch's *Secretum* marks the beginning of the revival of classical dialogue by breaking with the dogmatism of the medieval dialogue and by asserting the Ciceronian notion of free discussion. The *Secretum* presents a dramatic exchange between Petrarch's literary self, 'Franciscus,' and his depiction of Augustine, 'Augustinus,' in a symbolic confrontation between the author's awakening modernity and the Church Father's condemnation of classical dialogue."

36. Kahn, "Figure of the Reader," 155.

37. Kahn, "Figure of the Reader," 156.

38. Kahn, "Figure of the Reader," 164. Kahn (156) thus finds it especially significant that in the dialogue "Franciscus' " love for Laura "is glossed as a will to interpretation" when "Augustinus" remarks (*Secretum* 3 [ed. Carrara, 142]), "verumque est, cum in aliis tum in hac precipue passione, quod unus quisque suarum rerum est benignus interpres."

39. Kahn, "Figure of the Reader," 164.

40. On the readership constituted by the text of the *Confessiones*, see ch. 2. See also J. Freccero, "The Fig Tree and the Laurel: Petrarch's Poetics," *Diacritics* 5 (1975): 34–40, reprinted, without notes, in H. Bloom, ed., *Petrarch* (New York, 1989), 43–55. Freccero points out (37) that in the *Secretum* "Franciscus" acknowledges the fig tree under which Augustine was converted "as an example for all men," whereas "Augustinus" grants that the laurel, "the symbol of poetic supremacy," belongs to "Franciscus" alone. Freccero sees this distinction as indicative of the differences between Augustine's use of allegorical signs that refer to truths beyond themselves and Petrarch's autoreflexive poetics in which language is the only reality.

41. *Secretum* 1 (ed. Carrara, 64).

42. *Secretum* 1 (ed. Carrara, 64); *Aeneid* 6.730–34 (trans. A. Mandelbaum [Toronto, 1971], 156). On the Virgilian passage, see M. Murrin, *The Allegorical Epic: Essays in Its Rise and Decline* (Chicago, 1980), 27–50. According to Murrin (29), this is "the sole passage of direct philosophy" in the *Aeneid*, and aspects of it were recognized as Platonic by commentators, including Augustine, from Servius to Landino. On Landino and the Renaissance reception of the *Aeneid*, see C. Kallendorf, "Cristoforo Landino's Virgil and the Humanist Critical Tradition," *Renaissance Quarterly* 36 (1983): 519–46. On allegory generally, see M. Murrin, *The Veil of Allegory: Some Notes toward a Theory of Allegorical Rhetoric in the English Renaissance* (Chicago, 1980); and M. Quilligan, *The Language of Allegory: Defining the Genre* (Ithaca, 1979).

43. *Secretum* 1 (ed. Carrara, 64): "illud apostolicum: 'Corpus quod corrumpitur, aggravat animam, et deprimit terrena inhabitatio sensum multa cogitantem.' " "Augustinus" here incorrectly identifies this biblical passage which is really from the Book of Wisdom 9:15. He does this, as Carrara points out in his notes to the text of the *Secretum,* because he is recalling a passage from *De civitate dei* 14.3, in which Augustine quotes both from Paul and this line from the Book of Wisdom.

44. *De civitate dei* 14.3. *Aeneid,* trans. Mandelbaum, 156.

45. *De civitate dei* 14.3: "nec caro corruptibilis animam peccatricem, sed anima peccatrix fecit esse corruptibilem carnem."

46. *Secretum* 1 (ed. Carrara, 66).

47. *Secretum* 1 (ed. Carrara, 66).

48. See Kahn, "Figure of the Reader," 159, for a different reading of this passage: "It is characteristic of Petrarch to describe his encounter with an authoritative precursor as an encounter with an alien other, but his use of the term 'peregrinatio' here, as well as 'captus locorum dulcedine,' suggests that his reading of *De vera religione,* like his reading of the *Confessiones* and . . . of his own *Secretum,* fails to have the moral effect that 'Augustinus' associates with right reading." See also B. L. Ullman, "Petrarch's Favorite Books," in *Studies in the Italian Renaissance* (Rome, 1955), 117–37. Ullman here discusses the famous list, made by Petrarch, of several books. The heading for the list reads: "Libri mei Peculiares. ad reliquos n(on) tra(n)sfuga sed explorator tra(n)sire soleo" ("Favorite Books," 122). Ullman offers this translation: "My specially prized books. To the others I usually resort not as a deserter but as a scout" ("Favorite Books," 118). Petrarch's remark here is, again as Ullman notes, an allusion to Seneca *Epistula* 1.2.5: "Soleo enim et in aliena castra transire, non tamquam transfuga, sed tamquam explorator." Clearly this language invites comparison with that used in the *Secretum.*

49. *Secretum* 1 (ed. Carrara, 66).

The *De doctrina christiana* and Renaissance Rhetoric

JOHN MONFASANI

I have to start with a confession. I accepted the invitation to contribute to this volume not because I had a special theory about the *De doctrina christiana* in the Renaissance but, on the contrary, because I did not. Despite the references one encounters in the secondary literature to the importance of the *DDC*, I have never found it to be of any great relevance when reading Renaissance texts. So I decided to see what, if anything, I had missed.

As a matter of convention, one may apply the term *Renaissance* to fourteenth- and fifteenth-century Italy and to all of Europe from the late fifteenth to the early seventeenth century. But how does one gauge the influence of the *DDC* on rhetoric in the period? After all, the few details of rhetoric which Augustine provided in book 4 were readily available in the classical manuals,[1] and, in the context of the Renaissance passion for the recovery of classical rhetoric, his advocacy of the discipline would seem to be bringing coals to Newcastle.

Perhaps the best issue with which to begin is the broader question of Augustine's influence in the Renaissance.[2] Certainly he was a best-selling author. The *Gesamtkatalog der Wiegendrucke* reports 187 editions of his writings in the first forty-five years of printing.[3] For the sixteenth century, the *Index Aureliensis* lists 487 editions of Augustine, including thirteen massive *opera omnia*.[4] Augustine was easily the most printed patristic author and, after Aristotle and Cicero,[5] perhaps the most printed of all ancient authors. As for the *DDC*, printers unquestionably saw a market for it. It was issued seven times before 1501[6] and at least seventeen more times in the sixteenth century, and these figures do not take into account its inclusion in the thirteen early modern *opera omnia* of Augustine.[7] Furthermore, in the 1460s, at the dawn of printing, John Mentelin at Strasbourg and Johann Fust and Peter Shöffer at Mainz published book 4 of the *DDC* separately three times in quick succession.[8] As James J. Murphy has remarked to me, book 4 of the *DDC* was the first work of Augustine to have been printed. These first German printers obviously thought it would sell well among German clerics, and, apparently, it did, if we can judge by the quick reprints.

The fresh cultural force of humanism would also seem to have enthusiastically embraced St. Augustine. In the fourteenth century, Francesco Petrarch creatively incorporated both the texts and the persona of St. Augustine into his own writings.[9] One could argue that Petrarch's well-known predilection for finding friends among the Augustinian friars reflected in large measure a shared admiration for the sainted bishop of Hippo.[10] The first great northern humanist and, indeed, the greatest of the sixteenth-century humanists, Erasmus of Rotterdam, edited an important *opera omnia* of Augustine in 1528–1529.[11] Furthermore, according to the widely accepted view of Charles Béné, not only did Erasmus take Augustine as his main spiritual and cultural guide, but he did so precisely from that moment in his youth when he read the *DDC* for the first time.[12] According to Béné, the influence of the *DDC* can be traced through many of Erasmus's writings.[13]

Nor was Erasmus the only leading sixteenth-century humanist to edit Augustine. The most illustrious of the Spanish humanists, Juan Luis Vives, published a major annotated edition of the *City of God*, which he dedicated to King Henry VIII of England. Vives's text went through numerous printings and was eventually translated into English and French.[14]

If we move to philosophy, we find that the most original philosopher of the early Renaissance, Nicholas of Cusa, drew inspiration from Augustine[15] and that Marsilio Ficino, the founder of Florentine Platonism and the translator of Plato and Plotinus, studied Augustine closely and extracted from him some of his most characteristic doctrines.[16]

In religion, Augustine's authority grew with the Reformation. Beginning with Martin Luther, Protestants found in St. Augustine a powerful patristic warrant for their doctrines of grace and free will.[17] Rising to the challenge, Catholic theologians, such as Girolamo Seripando in the first half of the sixteenth century[18] and Michael Baius and Cornelius Jansen in the second half, strove to bring the Church into accord with what they believed to be authentic Augustinian doctrine.[19]

Yet, as impressive as this evidence is, it is of unequal and sometimes deceptive value. We must not forget that Augustine was a canonized *auctor*, an authority worth citing in support of a view even if he did not inspire it or actually agree with it. Forgeries and pseudepigrapha are two forms of tribute posterity pays to authority. In this sense, the Renaissance paid Augustine a very large tribute. Of the previously mentioned 187 incunabula of his writings, 116 of them, or 62 percent, were not authentic works of Augustine.[20] The most widely printed Augustine in the fifteenth century was not the historical Augustine but the Augustine posterity created to serve its own interests and needs.[21]

In respect to the *DDC*, it was printed separately only once in the fifteenth century, being part of a collection of Augustinian opuscula all other times. Even the separate printing of book 4 ceased after the 1460s as the market for it evaporated and never reappeared again. Interest in the complete *DDC* picked up in the sixteenth century since we can count twelve separate printings. But even here we have to be careful, inasmuch as there were no separate printings after 1556. If not for the *opera omnia*, there would have been no edition of the *DDC* for almost the whole second half of the sixteenth century.

Augustine's influence in Renaissance (i.e., pre-Cartesian) philosophy is relatively slight after Ficino.[22] Of course, no one denies the continued importance of Augustine in religious thought. Yet, by the same token, no one has ever proved that a reading of Augustine inspired Martin Luther's doctrine of salvation by faith alone[23] or Ulrich Zwingli's sacramentarianism[24] or John Calvin's church organization.[25] Rather, having decided on these core positions, the founders of Protestantism judiciously used Augustine when and where it suited them.[26] For Protestantism, Augustine was not so much a creative force as a fount of authority to be exploited after pivotal doctrines had been determined.

Similarly, despite Charles Béné's thesis to the contrary, Erasmus intellectually owed little to Augustine. As Jacques Chomarat has recently shown, Erasmus cited Augustine primarily as a historical source and as a way of shielding himself from scholastic critics.[27] Indeed, even Béné had to admit that Erasmus could be quite critical of Augustine.[28]

Enthusiasm for Augustine could also be selective. Juan Luis Vives seems to have had little use for Augustine other than as a historical source.[29] Likewise, Petrarch focused on those texts of Augustine rich in pyschological and historical lore; Augustine's more dogmatic writings, however, such as the *De trinitate* and the anti-Pelagian and anti-Donatist texts, though known to Petrarch, exercised little apparent influence on him.[30] Indeed, he so misconstrued Augustine's mature position on free will that in his *Secretum* he portrayed the African doctor as a vigorous proponent of the capacity of human beings to turn away from sin by dint of their own willpower.[31]

What is more significant is that Italian humanists after Petrarch generally ignored Augustine. Apart from Maffeo Vegio,[32] none of the major Quattrocento humanists evinced any special enthusiasm for him or his writings.[33]

A fortiori, Augustine's *DDC* caused no special stir among Italian humanists. Even Petrarch cited it only twice.[34] The *DDC* simply had little to satisfy the secular interests of Italian humanism.[35] In the most important and largest *Rhetoric* of the Quattrocento, George of Trebizond never mentioned it.[36] Lorenzo Valla, in his *Dialectica*, where he talked about signs, language, and rhetoric, cited it only in passing or in criticism.[37] Guarino of Verona did refer to it in his commentary on the *Rhetorica ad herennium*,[38] but he was the exception that proves the rule since, as far as I know, no secular Quattrocento rhetoric, as distinct from a commentary, cited the *DDC* as useful to its purpose.

Even when the teachers of rhetoric were religious, Augustine remained a non-factor. The Jesuits were the single most important group of teachers of classical rhetoric in the sixteenth and seventeenth centuries. The modern textbook they most commonly used was Cyprian Soarez's *De arte rhetorica*.[39] I could find in Soarez's manual no reference to, or use of, Augustine. On the other side of the religious divide, Philip Melanchthon established the basic form of humanistic education among Protestants.[40] The result was the same: Augustine played no explicit role in Melanchthon's *Rhetoric*.[41]

One might explain this negligence on the grounds that these Renaissance authors all agreed with Hagendahl in reading Augustine's work strictly as advice for Christian preachers and not, as Marrou would have it, as a program of Christian culture.[42] But then how does one explain the fact that when in 1478 the Italian Franciscan Lorenzo Guglielmo Traversagni, while resident in England, published the first classicizing homiletics of the Renaissance, the *Margarita eloquentiae castigatae*, or *Nova rhetorica*, he too made no use of the *DDC* beyond citing it as one of Augustine's many eloquent writings?[43] Traversagni did away with the intricate system of themes and divisions which characterized the medieval *artes praedicandi*.[44] Instead, he applied to the sermon the rules of classical demonstrative oratory, i.e., the oratory of praise and blame. But except for the obvious points that classical rhetoric could be exploited for the benefit of homiletics and that classical precepts could be illustrated from Christian sources, there are no significant points of contact between Traversagni's manual and the *DDC*.[45] Given the growing cult of classicism, it was inevitable that with or without the encouragement of the *DDC*, classicizing homiletics would have appeared.

At the very least, the *DDC* should have offered a convenient patristic sanction; but Traversagni did not even cite it for that purpose.

Very early on, Northern humanists showed an interest in homiletics. But when they began to produce classicizing manuals in the first half of the sixteenth century, they too ignored Augustine. Johann Reuchlin was one of the founders of Christian humanism in the North. In 1504 he published the first homiletics of the movement, the *Liber congestorum de arte praedicandi*.[46] In it, Reuchlin neither mentioned nor, as far as I can tell, used the *DDC*. Erasmus published his massive *Ecclesiastes, aut De ratione concionandi* in 1535. He did mention Augustine, but merely as a historical figure and not as someone with valuable advice for preachers.[47]

The Reformation did not change this state of affairs. None of the four separate homiletics written by Philip Melanchthon nor the homiletics compiled from Melanchthon's teaching by Veit Deitrich ever mention Augustine, let alone show signs of his direct influence.[48] The same disregard for Augustine shows up in *De formandis sacris concionibus* of the Lutheran theologian Johann Hoech.[49]

Augustine fared better in the Catholic camp, but not consistently so. For instance, Luca Baglioni, O.F.M., in his *L'arte del predicare* of 1562, referred to Augustine mainly to rebuke him for departing from Cicero;[50] and, later in the century, the Thomist Lodovico Carbone published a very classicizing homiletics which had little use for Augustine.[51] But the first classicizing homiletics of the Catholic Reform, Alfonso Zorrilla's *De sacris concionibus recte formandis formula* of 1543, took a different tack. Zorilla plagiarized shamelessly from the recent Lutheran homiletics, as John W. O'Malley has proved.[52] But in at least one crucial respect Zorilla innovated upon his Lutheran sources: he added a chapter *De officio oratoris* ("On the Duty of the Orator"), much of which he gave over to quoting and paraphrasing Augustine's treatment of the classical *officia oratoris* in book 4 of the *DDC*.[53] How this reflects other developments we will see shortly.

After the Council of Trent and its decree on preaching in 1563, the Catholic Reform unequivocally called forth a tradition of homiletics which drew upon the *DDC*. As Marc Fumaroli has pointed out,[54] three members of St. Charles Borromeo's circle at Milan, namely, Agostino Valiero in his *De ecclesiastica rhetorica*,[55] Giovanni Botero in his *De praedicatione verbi*,[56] and Francesco Panigarola in his gargantuan *Il predicatore*,[57] cited Augustine's *DDC*.[58] Valiero's and Panigarola's works enjoyed some success (Botero's was never reprinted), but even more popular were the homiletics of two Spanish authors who wrote with an eye on St. Augustine: the *De modo concionandi* of Diego de

Estella, O.F.M., who dedicated the second edition of his work to Borromeo,[59] and the *Ecclesiasticae rhetoricae* of Luis de Granada, O.P., who corresponded with Borromeo.[60] Granada's work was the most overtly Augustinian of all the Catholic Reform homiletics. He quoted generously from the *DDC*, and, what is especially interesting, as we shall see shortly, he explicitly relied on Augustine in his chapters on the three *officia oratoris*, i.e., on the obligation of the orator to teach, please, and move his audience.[61] His compatriot Diego de Estella also had separate chapters on the *officia oratoris*.[62]

If we were to end our survey here, we would have to discount the *DDC* as a creative force on Renaissance rhetoric apart from its influence on some Catholic Reform homiletics. However, Granada's extensive use of Augustine for the *officia oratoris* is a clue to a much wider and more fundamental influence.

Why did Granada cite Augustine instead of Cicero? Even Augustine himself cited Cicero as the source of this rhetorical doctrine.[63] Quintilian also mentions the *officia oratoris*.[64] It was Augustine, however, who first ordered them in a way which privileged teaching.[65] He was also the first to make them a coherent centerpiece of rhetorical theory.[66] Quintilian had mentioned them only in passing and did not base his rhetorical instruction on them as fundamental first principles. And Cicero, even in the *Orator*, where the *officia oratoris* loom more importantly than anywhere else in his writings, did not organize his rhetorical instruction around them or make them the dominant theme of the discussion.[67] Significantly, both in the *De oratore* and in the *Orator*, Cicero attributed the doctrine of the *officia oratoris* to M. Antonius, the man whom he characterized as having scant respect for rhetorical system building.[68] Furthermore, Cicero was not consistent in describing the *officia oratoris*.[69] He sometimes substituted proof (*probare*) for teaching (*docere*). He never arranged the *officia* in hierarchical order but, rather, treated them, in effect, as all equally important for good oratory. He even vacillated on which obligation, moving or teaching, should be called "of necessity."[70]

The focus of Augustine's book, on the other hand, as its title states, was precisely teaching, *doctrina*.[71] In the chapters immediately preceding the introduction of the *officia oratoris*, Augustine expounded at length on the necessity of teaching clearly and correctly.[72] Apropos of the *officia oratoris*, though Augustine impressed upon the reader the importance of all three *officia*, he unequivocally made teaching the one universal obligation of the preacher. It alone could stand alone.[73] And when he quoted Cicero, he quoted the one and only Ciceronian passage which lent itself to his hierarchical interpretation of the *officia oratoris*, namely,

Orator 69, where, in describing a rising crescendo of achievement, Cicero called proof (*probare*, not *docere*) a matter of necessity, pleasing a matter of agreeableness, and moving a matter of success. When he appropriated this passage, Augustine altered the quotation to suit his purposes, replacing *probare* with *docere* as that which was "a matter of necessity."[74] Implicitly, Augustine had reduced pleasing and moving to the status of useful attributes.[75] They were secondary in the sense that the mere proclamation of the truth could, and did, at times gain the conviction of the audience. Moreover, in all cases, the preacher had to teach, if he was to preach the truth and not merely entertain.[76]

As far as I can tell, no rhetorician exploited Augustine's reworking of the *officia oratoris* until the Renaissance. The *officia oratoris* do not appear in the manuals of late antique lesser Latin rhetors[77] or in the medieval *artes praedicandi*.[78] In the Renaissance, neither George of Trebizond's *Rhetoricorum libri V* nor the lesser Quattrocento rhetorics that followed after it made any significant use of the *officia oratoris*.[79]

This changed with Lorenzo Valla. In his *Dialectica*, written in the 1440s, Valla attempted a revolutionary reordering of the linguistic arts. He argued that all logic was merely a subdivision of rhetoric because the logician had only to teach while the orator had also to please and to move in addition to teaching.[80] His inspiration for this scheme was perhaps an *obiter dictum* of Quintilian, his favorite author.[81] However, as we have seen,[82] Valla certainly knew Augustine's *DDC*. In so using the *officia oratoris*, Valla stood Augustine on his head: he accepted Augustine's strongly hierarchical formulation of the *officia* in order to denigrate teaching in comparison with moving and pleasing.

The Dutch humanist Rudolph Agricola reacted against Valla's revolutionary proposal and restored the primacy of teaching in one of the most influential books of the Renaissance, the *De inventione dialectica*, which he completed in 1480.[83] Once printed in 1515, the *De inventione dialectica* transformed Renaissance culture almost immediately. Hithertofore, although at the grammar-school level humanists could and did replace medieval Latin with classical Latin, they really had no effective substitute for the logic which dominated the curriculum after grammar. Agricola provided a new vision and a new text to effect this transformation.

Like Valla, Agricola identified the three *officia oratoris* with the whole realm of discourse. But unlike Valla, he privileged the first *officium*, teaching, as the highest and only universal obligation of a speaker.[84] He then went on to identify teaching with logic. Logic he divided into invention and judgment. Leaving judgment aside as something minor, he proceeded to make topical invention the core of his system of probative discourse. Since topical invention was the essence of rhetorical argumentation, Agricola had given humanists the means for taking over logic and, therefore, for monopolizing general education.[85]

Agricola's ideas penetrated Italy only slowly and to a limited extent. But in his native north he was a smash success. We can count more than fifty editions in the forty years after 1515.[86] Epitomes and commentaries followed hard upon this success. Agricola's two-part logic provided the means by which humanists could take over instruction in logic in much of northern Europe.

Agricola never mentioned the *DDC* anywhere in the *De inventione dialectica*. But the two works share two distinctive characteristics which suggest that consciously or unconsciously Agricola was influenced by Augustine.

The first characteristic, probably coincidental, has to do with the stark bipolarity of Agricola's system, which divides all logic into invention and judgment. Cicero made this unusual division at the start of his *Topica* and hinted at it in the *Orator*;[87] and Boethius repeated Cicero's dichotomy at the beginning of his *De topicis differentiis*. These classical authorities are sufficient to explain Agricola's dictum. However, at the beginning of the *DDC* and again at the start of book 4 Augustine posits a fundamental division in Christian erudition between the finding and the imparting of what is to be understood, i.e., between the *modus inveniendi intelligenda* and the *modus proferendi intelligenda*. It is possible, but not demonstrable, that when thinking about logic as the cognitive basis of learning and discourse, Agricola assimilated Augustine's bipolar scheme for the Christian teacher.

Second, and much more decisive, is how Agricola handled the *officia oratoris*. Central to his vision was the notion that teaching (*docere*) is the fundamental obligation of all discourse while pleasing (*delectare*) and moving (*flectare*) are secondary. Consequently, the first and frequently the only obligation of a speaker is to teach. Agricola followed Valla in equating logic with teaching[88] but opposed him by privileging teaching as the supreme function of an orator. Rudolph Agricola had no precursor in his hierarchical ordering of the *officia oratoris* except Augustine. Augustine would have protested against how Agricola sharply separated teaching from pleasing and moving. But, I would contend, Agricola's formulation drew out a logic implicit in Augustine's treatment of the *officia oratoris*.

In the light of his own experience, Agricola understood oratory primarily in terms of academic and religious discourse. He lacked an appreciation for the political oratory which was an essential part of the historic experience of the Italian republican tradition.[89] Thus, whereas Italy's secular humanists ignored Augustine's homiletics, Agricola would have found its stress on teaching as totally applicable to his own experience and therefore suitable as a basis for a general theory of discourse.

If what I have argued is correct, then, in the first half of the sixteenth century the peculiar mania for topical invention as the basis of discourse and teaching reflected the influence of the *DDC* once removed. One might also argue that in the second half of the century the even more peculiar mania for a universal teaching method created by Peter Ramus's reworking of Agricola reflected the same Augustinian influence twice removed.

But rather than attempting to trace this increasingly tenuous line of influence, I would like to call attention to another Renaissance innovation in rhetorical doctrine which stems from Agricola's reading of the *DDC*, namely, the addition of a *genus didacticum* to the three classical *genera causarum* of judicial, political, and epideictic oratory. As far as I know, the *genus didacticum* made its first appearance in the history of rhetoric four years after the first printing of the *De inventione dialectica*, when, in 1519, Philip Melanchthon published his *Rhetoric*. In this first edition Melanchthon did not make teaching a specific oratorical genus but assigned it to epideictic oratory, listing among its forms the *oratio ad docendum* and the *artificium docendi*.[90] The second edition of his *Rhetoric* appeared in 1521, and it plainly described the *genus didacticum* as the fourth kind of oratory.[91] Not surprisingly, the *genus didacticum* soon became a trademark of Melanchthon's homiletical manuals as well as Lutheran homiletics in general.[92] Melanchthon's *genus didacticum* also made an appearance in the Catholic Reform homiletics of Luis de Grenada.[93] The innovation never caught on, however, outside of homiletics. One reason for this failure probably lay in the fact that Peter Ramus's famous method of teaching reduced all discourse to a sort of *genus didacticum* and therefore made Melanchthon's innovation redundant.

To end by way of summary, the only segment of Renaissance rhetoric for which I would confidently assert the palpable direct influence of the *DDC* is Catholic Reform homiletics. I think one can also make a plausible case that Augustine's discussion of the *officia oratoris* in the *DDC* influenced how Lorenzo Valla and Rudolph Agricola thought about rhetoric and logic. If this is so, then at least indirectly, the *DDC* exercised quite a large influence on the new rhetoric of the Renaissance.[94]

Notes

1. At *DDC* 4.1.2 (ed. Martin, *CCSL* 32:116–17), Augustine specifically explained that his intention was not to expound the *praecepta rhetorica*. He directed the reader to the standard manuals for such detail.

2. In general, see P. O. Kristeller, "Augustine and the Early Renaissance," in *Studies in Renaissance Thought and Letters* (Rome, 1956), 355–72.

3. *Gesamtkatalog der Wiegendrucke,* 8 vols. to date (Leipzig, 1925–), nos. 2862–3048.

4. *Index Aureliensis: Catalogus librorum sedecimo saeculo impressorum,* part 1, vol. 2 (Baden-Baden, 1966), nos. 110.67–110.553.

5. For Aristotle, see *Gesamtkatalog der Wiegendrucke,* nos. 2334–2498; and F. E. Cranz, *A Bibliography of Aristotle Editions 1501–1600,* 2nd ed., rev. C. B. Schmitt (Baden-Baden, 1984). For Cicero, see *Gesamtkatalog der Wiegendrucke,* nos. 6707–7041; and *Index Aureliensis* 8 (Baden-Baden, 1989), nos. 137.204–140.070.

6. *Gesamtkatalog der Wiegendrucke,* nos. 2862–66 and 2868, as part of Augustine's opuscules; no. 2902, separately.

7. The *opera omnia* listed in the *Index Aureliensis,* are nos. 110.079, 175, 201, 256, 258, 335, 339, 359, 402, 426, 443, 489–91 (common printing among three Venetian publishers); 499–500 (common printing between two Lyons publishers). As part of Augustine's opuscules: 110.73, 79, 166, 292, 299 (I sampled two collections of opuscules [Paris, 1521; and Venice, 1545] and found that they contained the *DDC*). Separately: 113, 126, 149, 170, 185, 212, 221, 238, 255, 259, 317, 341.

8. *Gesamtkatalog der Wiegendrucke,* nos. 2871–73.

9. See Kristeller, "Augustine," 361–63; P. De Nolhac, *Pétrarque et l'humanisme,* 2nd ed., 2 vols. (Paris, 1907), 2:191–202; E. Luciani, *Les "Confessions" de saint Augustin dans les lettres de Pétrarque* (Paris, 1962); P. P. Gerosa, *Umanesimo cristiano del Petrarca: Influenza agostiniana, attinenze medievali* (Turin, 1966); and P. Courcelle, *Les "Confessions" de saint Augustin dans la tradition littéraire,* 2nd ed. (Paris, 1968), ch. 5.

10. See U. Mariani, *Il Petrarca e gli agostiniani* (Rome, 1959); A. M. Voci, *Petrarca e la vita religiosa: Il mito umanista della vita eremitica* (Rome, 1983), 81–87.

11. A less complete *opera omnia* appeared at Hagenau in 1521, before Erasmus's edition of Basel, 1528–1529. On this last edition, see Kristeller, "Augustine," 366–67; and J. Chomarat, *Grammaire et rhétorique chez Erasme,* 2 vols. (Paris, 1981), 1:454.

12. C. Béné, *Erasme et saint Augustin* (Geneva, 1969), especially 62–67, 183–86.

13. Ibid., passim; see especially the synoptic tables of borrowings on 433–48.

14. Kristeller, "Augustine," 366.

15. See F. E. Cranz, "The Transmutation of Platonism in the Development of Nicolaus Cusanus and of Martin Luther," in *Nicolò Cusano agli inizi del mondo moderno: Atti del Congresso internazionale in occasione del V centenario della morte di Nicolò Cusano, Bressanone, 6–10 settembre 1964* (Florence, 1970), 73–102, especially 81–83, 90–91, 94, 96–97.

16. Kristeller, "Augustine," 368–71.

17. For the importance of Augustine in shaping Luther's thought, see G. Rupp, *The Righteousness of God* (London, 1953), 92, 155–56, 185–86.

18. See H. Jedin, *Girolamo Seripando,* 2 vols. (Würzburg, 1937).

19. On Baius, see X. Le Bachelet, "2. Baius Michel," in *Dictionnaire de théologie catholique* 2 (Paris, 1910), 38–111. For more recent literature on Jansenism, see A. Sedgwick, *Jansenism in Seventeenth-Century France: Voices from the Wilderness* (Charlottesville, Va., 1977).

20. See *Gesamtkatalog der Wiegendrucke,* nos. 2933–3048, in addition to the pseudonymous writings included in nos. 2862–68, 2915.

21. The proportion between authentic and apocryphal texts after the fifteenth century is not easily determined because in listing sixteenth-century editions the *Index Aureliensis* does not distinguish between authentic and pseudonymous writings.

22. See Kristeller, "Augustine," 371. Philosophical interest in Augustine took an up-turn in the seventeenth century, in part because of French Jansenism. For the question of Augustine's influence on Descartes, see E. Gilson, *Etudes sur le role de la pensée médiévale dans la formation du système cartésien,* 2nd ed. (Paris, 1951), 191–201, 289–94; and N. Abercrombie, *Saint Augustine and French Classical Thought* (Oxford, 1938), 57–90. For influence on Pascal, see Abercrombie, *Saint Augustine,* 91–117. For influence on Malebranche, see H. Gouhier, *La philosophie de Malebranche et son expérience religieuse,* 2nd ed. (Paris, 1948), 279–311 and *ad indicem*; and B. K. Rome, *The Philosophy of Malebranche* (Chicago, 1963), 55, 133–43, 206–8, 240–41, and 266–67.

23. On imputation, see Rupp, *Righteousness of God,* 174. On Luther's approach to *caritas,* see Anders Nygren, *Agape and Eros,* trans. P. S. Watson (New York, 1953), 638–41, 692, 709–16.

24. But he would happily cite Augustine where he found him useful in arguing against Luther on a point of eucharistic theology. See G. R. Potter, *Zwingli* (Cambridge, 1976), 325; but cf. 83 for a rejection of Augustine's ecclesiology.

25. See F. Wendel, *Calvin: The Origins and Development of His Religious Thought,* trans. P. Mairet (New York, 1963), 124–25, and passim, for general reliance on Augustine. Calvin's non-episcopal church organization is, of course, quite alien to Augustine.

26. E.g., see P. Fraenkel, *Testimonia Patrum: The Function of the Patristic Argument in the Theology of Philip Melanchthon* (Geneva, 1961), 30–31, 93–96, 192–93, 299–303, 327.

27. See Chomarat, *Grammaire et rhétorique,* 1:167–79; see also 1:424–25, 542–43, 555, 566–67.

28. See Béné, *Erasme,* 88–93; and the passages cited by Chomarat, *Grammaire et rhétorique,* 1:177–78. See also Kristeller, "Augustine," 367.

29. Kristeller, "Augustine," 366, especially note 50.

30. Cf. De Nolhac, *Pétrarque,* 2:204–5; Gerosa, *Umanesimo cristiano,* 166–74, tries to identify all the Augustinian texts that Petrarch might have read, but he cannot show that the doctrinal works played a signficant role in Petrarch's thought apart from supplying bits of historical and bibliographical information.

31. See G. A. Levi, "Pensiero classico e pensiero cristiano nel *Secretum* e nelle *Familiari* del Petrarca," *Atene e Roma,* series 2, no. 1 (1933): 63–82, at

68; K. Heitmann, "L'insegnamento agostiniano nel *Secretum* del Petrarca," *Studi petrarcheschi* 3 (1961): 187–93; and C. Trinkaus, *In Our Image and Likeness: Humanity and Divinity in Italian Humanist Thought,* 2 vols. (Chicago, 1970), 1:7. However, F. Rico, *Vida u obra de Petrarca,* vol. 1: *Lectura del "Secretum"* (Padua, 1974), 70–71, argues that Petrarch's Stoic reading of Augustine is defensible on the basis of selective passages from the *Confessiones, De libero arbitrio,* and *De spiritu et littera.*

32. See C. Testore, "Vegio, Maffeo," *Enciclopedia Cattolica* 12 (Vatican City, 1954), cols. 1162–64; D. Webb, "Eloquence and Education: A Humanist Approach to Hagiography," *Journal of Ecclesiastical History* 31 (1980): 19–38, at 28 ff; and for the most recent treatment, C. Kallendorf, *In Praise of Aeneas: Virgil and Epideictic Rhetoric in the Early Italian Renaissance* (Hanover, N.H., and London, 1989), 100–128, 202–6.

33. In general, see Kristeller, "Augustine," 362. For Salutati, see R. Witt, *Hercules at the Crossroads: The Life, Works, and Thought of Coluccio Salutati* (Durham, N.C., 1983), 296. For Leonardo Bruni, see *The Humanism of Leonardo Bruni: Selected Texts* (Binghamton, N.Y., 1987), trans. G. Griffiths, J. Hankins, and D. Thompson. For Poggio Bracciolini, see E. Walser, *Poggius Florentinus* (Leipzig, 1914), 78–79, 130–32, 362 (Poggio read Augustine while living in England, cited him as an authority, and owned a collection of his writings). For Ambrogio Traversari, see C. L. Stinger, *Humanism and the Church Fathers: Ambrogio Traversari (1386–1439) and Christian Antiquity in the Italian Renaissance* (Albany, N.Y., 1977), 114–15. For Guarino da Verona, see R. Sabbadini, *La scuola e gli studi di Guarino Guarini* (Catania, 1896), 67, 139, 142 (Guarino once gave a lecture series on the *De civitate dei*). For George of Trebizond, see my *George of Trebizond: A Biography and a Study of His Rhetoric and Logic* (Leiden, 1976), 180; and my *Collectanea Trapezuntiana: Texts, Documents, and Bibliography of George of Trebizond* (Binghamton, N.Y., 1984), 577–92, where Augustine is cited mainly to be contradicted. For Lorenzo Valla, see note 37, below.

34. Gerosa, *Umanesimo cristiano,* 168, note 61.

35. For instance, Aurelio Brandolini's *De ratione scribendi libri tres* is unique among Quattrocento rhetorical manuals for even discussing homiletics (see p. 7 of the Frankfurt, 1568, ed.).

36. Cf. my *George of Trebizond,* ch. 9.

37. See *Laurentii Valle Repastinatio Dialectice et Philosophie,* ed. G. Zippel, 2 vols. (Padua, 1982), in the index, 2:620–21. I would not endorse all of Zippel's citations, but the reference to the *DDC* at p. 93.6 is sound. Valla had mixed reactions to Augustine. On the one hand, according to M. Fois (*Il pensiero cristiano di Lorenzo Valla nel quadro storico-culturale del suo ambiente* [Rome, 1969]), Augustine inspired much of Valla's moral thought in the *De vero bono;* but even Fois had to admit that Valla owed much to Lactantius on this count, that he criticized Augustine in other works concerning various points of Scripture, theology, and history, and that he preferred Jerome to Augustine. Moreover, in the *De vero bono,* Valla never saw fit to mention Augustine except once in

passing at the very start. S. I. Camporeale, *Lorenzo Valla: Umanesimo e teologia* (Florence, 1972), points out more of Valla's criticisms of Augustine.

38. I consulted the ed. of Venice, 1483: Cicero *De inventione* and (Ps.-Cicero) *Rhetorica ad herennium* (= Hain-Copinger 5078; *Gesamtkatalog der Wiegendrucke* 6736/7); see fol. A5r.

39. This work went through 207 editions between 1562 and the eighteenth century. See L. J. Flynn, "The *De arte rhetorica* of Cyprian Soarez," *Quarterly Journal of Speech* 42 (1956): 367–74; and "Sources and Influence of Soarez' *De arte rhetorica*," *Quarterly Journal of Speech* 43 (1957): 257–65.

40. See K. Hartfelder, *Philipp Melanchthon als Praeceptor Germaniae* (Berlin, 1889); and P. Petersen, *Geschichte der aristotelischen Philosophie im protestantischen Deutschland* (Leipzig, 1921), 19–108.

41. To be read in Philip Melanchthon, *Opera omnia* 13, ed. K. G. Bretschneider (Halle, 1846), 413–50.

42. See H. Hagendahl, *Augustine and the Latin Classics*, 2 vols. (Göteborg, 1967), 2:565–69; H. I. Marrou, *Saint Augustin et la fin de la culture antique*, 4th ed. (Paris, 1958), 380–85. See in general G. A. Press, "Subject and Structure of Augustine's *DDC*," *Augustinian Studies* 11 (1980): 99–124.

43. See Lorenzo Guglielmo Traversagni, *Margarita eloquentiae castigatae*, ed. G. Farris (Savona, 1978), 32. This omission certainly was not due to any lack of admiration for Augustine. Traversagni gave a course at Cambridge on the *De civitate dei*. See Giovanni Farris, *Umanesimo e religione in Lorenzo Guglielmo Traversagni (1425–1505)* (Milan, 1972), 77–82; and J. J. Murphy, "The Double Revolution of the First Rhetorical Textbook Published in England: The *Margarita eloquentiae* of Gulielmus Traversagnus (1479)," *Texte: Revue de critique et de théorie littéraire* 8–9 (1989–1990): 367–76.

44. See T. M. Charland, *Artes praedicandi: Contribution à l'histoire de la rhétorique au moyen âge* (Paris-Ottawa, 1936); and H. Caplan, *Of Eloquence: Studies in Ancient and Medieval Rhetoric*, ed. A. King and H. North (Ithaca, N.Y., 1970), 40–78 and 134–69.

45. For a contrary view, see Murphy, "Double Revolution," 371.

46. I consulted the London, 1570, ed.

47. See *Ecclesiastae sive De ratione concionandi* 1, in Desiderius Erasmus, *Opera Omnia*, ed. J. LeClerc, 10 vols. (Leiden, 1703–1706; reprint Hildesheim, 1962), 5:801, where Erasmus notes that Bishop Valerius of Hippo allowed Augustine while still a presbyter to preach even when Valerius presided at mass. For an analysis of the *Ecclesiastae*, see Chomarat, *Grammaire et rhétorique*, 2:1059–71, who has no need to cite Augustine anywhere.

48. Melanchthon's four homiletics are to be read in *Supplementa Melanchthoniana: Philipp Melanchthons Schriften zur praktischen Theologie, Teil II: Homiletische Schriften*, ed. P. Drews and F. Cohrs (Leipzig, 1929). Cf. U. Schnell, *Die homiletische Theorie Philipp Melanchthons* (Berlin and Hamburg, 1968). I consulted Veit Dietrich's *Ratio brevis sacrarum tractandarum concionum* in the London, 1570, ed. cited in note 46, above.

49. I consulted this work in the London, 1570, ed. cited in note 46, above.

50. See fols. 13v–15r of the Venice, 1562, ed.; cf. also Marc Fumaroli, *L'âge de l'eloquence: Rhétorique et "res literaria" de la Renaissance au seuil de l'époque classique* (Geneva, 1980), 136.

51. I consulted at Columbia University the rare 1595, Venice, ed. of his *Divinus orator vel De rhetorica divina libri septem.* Carbone quoted the DDC only amid other authorities at the start (pp. 5–6).

52. I consulted the 1543, Rome, ed. See J. W. O'Malley, "Lutheranism in Rome 1542–1543—The Treatise by Alfonso Zorilla," *Thought* 54 (1979): 262–73; reprinted in his *Rome and the Renaissance: Studies in Culture and Religion* (London, 1981), no. 10.

53. Fols. 30v–31r of the 1543 ed.

54. Fumaroli, *L'âge de l'eloquence,* 142–43.

55. I consulted the ed. of Verona, 1732. For the *DDC,* see book 1, ch. 4 *ad finem* (p. 4); book 2, ch. 1 (p. 45); and book 3, ch. 52 (p. 229).

56. The rare *editio unica* is Paris, 1585. I consulted the copy Stamp. Barber. Y. IX. 6. of the Biblioteca Apostolica Vaticana. For Augustine, see especially fols. 44v–45r, 89r, and 91r. The general thrust of Botero's exemplification of sacred eloquence smacks of the *DDC.*

57. I used the ed. of Venice, 1609, where the *DDC* is cited amid other Christian sources. See pp. 27–29, 48, 55–56; note especially p. 45, where Panigarola takes from the beginning of book 4 of the *DDC* Augustine's distinction between "modum inveniendi quae intelligenda" and "modum proferendi quae intellecta sunt."

58. On Borromeo and the preaching of the Catholic Reform, see J. W. O'Malley, "Saint Charles Borromeo and the *Praecipuum Episcoporum Munus*: His Place in the History of Preaching," in J. M. Headley and J. B. Tomaro, ed., *San Carlo Borromeo: Catholic Reform and Ecclesiastical Politics in the Second Half of the Sixteenth Century* (Washington, D.C., 1988), 139–57. Borromeo himself made no explicit use of Augustine in his *Instructiones praedicationis verbi dei,* which I consulted in the *Acta ecclesiae Mediolanensis* (Milan, 1583), fols. 212v–221v.

59. I consulted the ed. of Verona, 1732. For the *DDC,* see ch. 2 *ad initium* (p. 10) and ch. 25 (p. 58).

60. I consulted the Spanish version in *Biblioteca de autores españoles* 11 (Madrid, 1863). For his relationship with Borromeo, see O'Malley, "Saint Charles Borromeo," 147.

61. See book 5, ch. 17–18.

62. See ch. 23, 26–27; but he does not clearly indicate the Augustinian inspiration for these chapters. See also the brief remarks of Valiero, *De ecclesiastica rhetorica,* at the start of book 1.

63. See A. E. Douglas, "A Ciceronian Contribution to Rhetorical Theory," *Eranos* 55 (1957): 18–26, 23 ff; T. Sullivan, *S. Aurelii Augustini Hipponiensis episcopii De doctrina christiana liber quartus: A Commentary, with a Revised*

Text, Introduction, and Translation (Washington, D.C., 1930), 9–10; and my "Lorenzo Valla and Rudolph Agricola," *Journal of the History of Philosophy* 28 (1990): 181–99, at 184–85 for citations.

64. See my "Lorenzo Valla and Rudolph Agricola," 185, note 19.

65. Sullivan, *Commentary*, 103.3, cites Cicero's *De oratore* 2.310 and *Brutus* 89 as anticipations of Augustine's "twofold division" of the *officia oratoris*. She is right about the twofold division but wrong about the *officia oratoris*. Augustine contrasted the *officium* of teaching with the *officia* of moving and pleasing. Cicero, on the other hand, contrasted teaching and persuasion. Cicero's point in *De oratore* 2.310 was that when teaching, one may make a show of one's didactic technique, but when persuading, one ought to conceal one's artifice. Similarly, in *Brutus* 89, Cicero contrasted logic and disputation, which aimed at teaching, and oratory, which aimed at persuasion.

66. See DDC 4.12.26–17.34; Sullivan, *Commentary*, 9–10, 54, 102–3, 176–77, 180; J. B. Eskridge, *The Influence of Cicero upon Augustine in the Development of His Oratorical Theory for the Training of the Ecclesiastical Orator* (Menasha, Wis., 1912), 16–17; and M. Testard, *Saint Augustin et Cicéron* (Paris, 1958), 190–92, 217, and 268–69. Not as useful is L. D. McNew, "The Relation of Cicero's Rhetoric to Augustine," *Research Studies of the State College of Washington* 25 (1957): 5–13.

67. The only discussion is *Orator* 69. In treating rhetorical doctrine, Cicero was more concerned with the three styles of oratory than with the three duties of the orator. I would agree with George Kennedy (*The Art of Rhetoric in the Roman World* [Princeton, 1972], 207) that with the *De oratore* the three duties of the orator "become the central concept of Cicero's rhetorical theory"; but *de facto* the theory of the three duties of the orator did not force Cicero to change how he organized his exposition of rhetoric.

68. See *De oratore* 2.121, 128, 310; *Orator* 69 ("auctore Antonio").

69. The late Renaissance scholar Lodovico Carbone remarked on his hero's vacillations in his *De officio oratoris libri V* (Venice, 1596), 31–32.

70. In *De optimo genere oratorum* 3 he says, "docere debitum est, delectare honorarium, permovere necessarium"; whereas in *Orator* 69 he states, "probare necessitatis est, delectare suavitatis, flectere victoriae."

71. On the issue of *doctrina*, see Press, "Subject and Structure."

72. DDC 4.10–11.

73. See DDC 4.12.27: "Horum trium, quod primo loco positum est, hoc est docendi necessitas, in rebus est constituta, quas dicimus, reliqua duo, in modo quo dicimus." 4.12.28: "Si autem adhuc nesciunt, prius utique docendi sunt quam movendi. Et fortasse rebus ipsis cognitis, ita movebuntur ut eos non opus sit maioribus eloquentiae viribus iam moveri. . . . Et ideo flectere necessitatis non est quia non semper opus est si tantum docenti vel etiam delectanti consentit auditor. . . . Sed neque delectare necessitatis est. Quandoquidem cum dicendo vera monstrantur, quod ad officium docendi pertinet, non eloquio agitur neque hoc adtenditur ut vel ipsa vel ipsum delectet eloquium, sed per se ipsa, quoniam vera sunt, manifestata delectant." I have altered Martin's punctuation (*CCSL* 32:135–36).

74. *DDC* 4.12.27. Cf. Testard, *Saint Augustin et Cicéron,* 268–69.

75. This is different from the Stoic position which reduced the duty of the orator to teaching alone; cf. Quintilian *Institutionis oratoriae* 5.proem.1.

76. See note 67, above; and Augustine's comments in *DDC* 14.30–31.

77. See the texts (including Ps.-Augustine's *Rhetorica*) in C. Halm, ed., *Rhetores Latini Minores* (Leipzig, 1863).

78. Cf. the discussion and texts in Charland, *Artes Praedicandi.* Medieval commentaries on the *Auctor ad Herennium* and Cicero's *De inventione* may constitute the exception to the rule. That is why I restrict my remarks to manuals. On the commentary literature, see J. O. Ward, "From Antiquity to the Renaissance: Glosses and Commentaries on Cicero's *Rhetorica,*" in J. J. Murphy, ed., *Medieval Eloquence* (Berkeley, 1978), 25–67; and "Renaissance Commentators on Ciceronian Rhetoric," in J. J. Murphy, ed., *Renaissance Eloquence* (Berkeley, 1983), 126–73.

79. In my *George of Trebizond,* 269, I spoke of the *officia oratoris,* where I should have spoken of the *partes rhetoricae.*

80. See my "Lorenzo Valla and Rudolph Agricola," at 183–85.

81. Cf. *Institutio oratoria* 10:1.78: "His aetate Lysias maior, subtilis atque elegans et quo nihil, si oratori satis sit docere, quaeras perfectius."

82. See note 37, above.

83. For primary and secondary bibliography on him, see F. Akkerman and A. J. Vanderjagt, eds., *Rodolphus Agricola Phrisius, 1444–1485: Proceedings of the International Conference at the University of Groningen, 28–30 October 1985* (Leiden, 1988). See also P. Mack, *Renaissance Argument: Valla and Agricola in the Traditions of Rhetoric and Dialectic* (Leiden, 1993).

84. See my "Lorenzo Valla and Rudolph Agricola," 183–84.

85. See P. Mack, "Rudolph Agricola's Topics," in Akkerman and Vanderjagt, ed., *Rodolphus Agricola Phrisius,* 257–69. On topics in the medieval tradition, see E. Stump, "Topics: Their Development and Absorption into Consequences," in N. Kreztmann, A. Kenny, J. Pinborg, and E. Stump, eds., *The Cambridge History of Later Medieval Philosophy* (Cambridge, 1982), 271–99.

86. See W. J. Ong, *Ramus and Talon Inventory* (Cambridge, Mass., 1958), pp. 534–58. See also Mack, *Renaissance Argument,* 257–302.

87. Cf. *Orator* 43: "Nam et invenire et iudicare, quid dicas, magna illa quidem sunt et tamquam animi instar in corpore, sed propria magis prudentiae quam eloquentiae."

88. This identification would have been natural to Agricola in any case because of his training in the medieval university curriculum, where the theme of *logica docens* was common, especially in the Franciscan tradition of Bonaventure and Scotus, with which Agricola was philosophically sympathetic. See C. Prantl, *Geschichte der Logik in Abendland,* 4 vols. (Leipzig, 1855–1870), 3:204–5; and my "Lorenzo Valla and Rudolph Agricola," 185 and 190–91.

89. Even when he came to Italy, he stayed in Pavia, which was the university town of the duchy of Milan, and in Ferrara, which was the site not only of another university but also of a princely court.

90. See his *De rhetorica libri tres* (Cologne, 1519), fol. A6r–v. He also spoke of *didacticon* when dealing with judicial oratory (fol. F6r).

91. I consulted the ed. of Cologne, 1523. He maintained this innovation in the third and last edition of the *Rhetoric;* see his *Opera* 13:423–29, for a discussion *de genere didascalico.* See also Schnell, *Die homiletische Theorie Philipp Melanchthons,* 42–44.

92. See my discussion of the homiletics of Melanchthon, Dietrich, and Hoech in "Humanism and Rhetoric," in A. Rabil, Jr., ed., *Renaissance Humanism: Foundations, Forms, and Legacy,* 3 vols. (Philadelphia, 1988), 3:171–235, at 206–7 (and 201 for the *Praecepta rhetoricae inventionis* of the Lutheran scholar David Chytraeus). For Melanchthon alone, see Schnell, *Die homiletische Theorie Philipp Melanchthons;* and Drew and Cohrs, *Philipp Melanchthons Schriften zur praktischen Theologie,* for Melanchthon's four homiletic treatises written between 1529 to 1552, all of which inculcate the *genus didacticum* in one form or another and make teaching a prime responsibility of the preacher.

93. See book 4, ch. 6 of Granada's *Ecclesiasticae rhetoricae.*

94. I note here that in his innovative *De ratione dicendi* of 1532 (in his *Opera omnia,* 7 vols. in 8 [Valencia, 1782–1790], 2:143–237), Juan Luis Vives included different chapters *de docendo, de persuadendo,* and *de movendis affectibus* (book 2, ch. 11–13; see also the end of ch. 10). I suspect the direct influence of Augustine here, but, given the late date of the work, one can only guess the relevant weight of the possible influences.

2000. 10. 30   34.50